# THE POLITICAL PUNDITS

# RECENT TITLES FROM THE PRAEGER SERIES IN POLITICAL COMMUNICATION
Robert E. Denton, Jr., General Editor

# THE POLITICAL PUNDITS

## DAN NIMMO
## JAMES E. COMBS

*Praeger Series in Political Communication*

New York
Westport, Connecticut
London

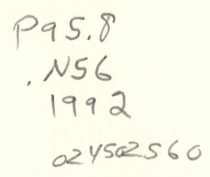

**Library of Congress Cataloging-in-Publication Data**

Nimmo, Dan D.
  The political pundits / Dan Nimmo, James E. Combs.
      p.     cm. — (Praeger series in political communication)
  Includes bibliographical references and index.
  ISBN 0–275–93541–8 (alk. paper).—ISBN 0–275–93545–0 (pbk. :
alk. paper)
  1. Mass media—Political aspects.  2. Communication in politics.
3. Mass media criticism.     I. Combs, James E.  II. Title.
III. Series.
  P95.8.N56     1992
  302.23—dc20       91–34491

British Library Cataloguing in Publication Data is available.

Library of Congress Catalog Card Number: 91–34491
ISBN: 0–275–93541–8
       0–275–93545–0 (pbk.)

First published in 1992

Praeger Publishers, One Madison Avenue, New York, NY 10010
An imprint of Greenwood Publishing Group, Inc.

Printed in the United States of America

The paper used in this book complies with the
Permanent Paper Standard issued by the National
Information Standards Organization (Z39.48–1984).

10 9 8 7 6 5 4 3 2 1

To
Waldo Lydecker:
Priest, Bard, Sage, Oracle, and
most of all, *Activist* Pundit—
but not much of a Healer.

# Contents

# About the Series

Those of us from the discipline of communication studies have long believed that communication is prior to all other fields of inquiry. In several other forums I have argued that the essence of politics is "talk" or human interaction.[1] Such interaction may be formal or informal, verbal or nonverbal, public or private but it is always persuasive, forcing us consciously or subconsciously to interpret, to evaluate, and to act. Communication is the vehicle for human action.

From this perspective, it is not surprising that Aristotle recognized the natural kinship of politics and communication in his writings *Politics* and *Rhetoric*. In the former, he establishes that humans are "political beings [who] alone of the animals [are] furnished with the faculty of language."[2] And in the latter, he begins his systematic analysis of discourse by proclaiming that "rhetorical study, in its strict sense, is concerned with the modes of persuasion."[3] Thus, it was recognized over twenty-three hundred years ago that politics and communication go hand in hand because they are essential parts of human nature.

Back in 1981, Dan Nimmo and Keith Sanders proclaimed that political communication was an emerging field.[4] Although its origin, as noted, dates back centuries, a "self-consciously cross-disciplinary" focus began in the late 1950s. Thousands of books and articles later, colleges and universities offer a variety of graduate and undergraduate coursework in the area in such diverse departments as communication, mass communication, journalism, political science, and sociology.[5] In Nimmo and Sanders's early assessment, the "key areas of inquiry" included rhetorical analysis, propaganda analysis, attitude change studies, voting studies, government and the news media, functional and systems analyses, technological changes, media technologies, campaign techniques, and research techniques.[6] In a survey of the state of the field in 1983, the same authors and Lynda Kaid found additional, more specific areas of concern such as the presidency, political polls, public opinion, debates, and advertising to name a few.[7] Since the first study, they also noted a shift away from the rather strict behavioral approach.

Today, Dan Nimmo and David Swanson assert that "political communication has developed some identity as a more or less distinct domain of scholarly work."[8] The scope and concerns of the area have further expanded to include critical theories and cultural studies. While there is no precise definition, method, or disciplinary home of the area of inquiry, its primary domain is the role, processes, and effects of communication within the context of politics broadly defined.

In 1985, the editors of *Political Communication Yearbook: 1984* noted that "more things are happening in the study, teaching, and practice of political communication than can be captured within the space limitations of the relatively few publications available."[9] In addition, they argued that the backgrounds of "those involved in the field [are] so varied and pluralist in outlook and approach, . . . it [is] a mistake to adhere slavishly to any set format in shaping the content."[10] And more recently, Swanson and Nimmo called for "ways of overcoming the unhappy consequences of fragmentation within a framework that respects, encourages, and benefits from diverse scholarly commitments, agendas, and approaches."[11]

In agreement with these assessments of the area and with gentle encouragement, Praeger established in 1988 the series entitled "Praeger Series in Political Communication." The series is open to all qualitative and quantitative methodologies as well as contemporary and historical studies. The key to characterizing the studies in the series is the focus on communication variables or activities within a political context or dimension. Scholars from the disciplines of communication, history, political science, and sociology have participated in the series.

I am, without shame or modesty, a fan of the series. The joy of serving as its editor is in participating in the dialogue of the field of political communication and in reading the contributors' works. I invite you to join me.

                                                        Robert E. Denton, Jr.

## NOTES

1.  See Robert E. Denton, Jr., *The Symbolic Dimensions of the American Presidency* (Prospect Heights, IL: Waveland Press, 1982); Robert E. Denton, Jr., and Gary Woodward, *Political Communication in America* (New York: Praeger, 1985; 2nd ed., 1990); Robert E. Denton, Jr., and Dan Hahn, *Presidential Communication* (New

York: Praeger, 1986); and Robert E. Denton, Jr., *The Primetime Presidency of Ronald Reagan* (New York: Praeger, 1988).

2. Aristotle, *The Politics of Aristotle*, trans. Ernest Barker (New York: Oxford University Press, 1970), p. 5.

3. Aristotle, *Rhetoric*, trans. Rhys Roberts (New York: Modern Library, 1954), p. 22.

4. Dan Nimmo and Keith Sanders, "Introduction: The Emergence of Political Communication as a Field," in *Handbook of Political Communication*, Dan Nimmo and Keith Sanders, eds. (Beverly Hills, CA: Sage, 1981), pp. 11–36.

5. Ibid., p. 15.

6. Ibid., pp. 17–27.

7. Keith Sanders, Lynda Kaid, and Dan Nimmo, eds. *Political Communication Yearbook: 1984* (Carbondale, IL: Southern Illinois University, 1985), pp. 283–308.

8. Dan Nimmo and David Swanson, "The Field of Political Communication: Beyond the Voter Persuasion Paradigm," in *New Directions in Political Communication*, David Swanson and Dan Nimmo, eds. (Beverly Hills, CA: Sage, 1990), p. 8.

9. Sanders, Kaid, and Nimmo, *Political Communication Yearbook*; p. xiv.

10. Ibid., p. xiv.

11. Nimmo and Swanson, "The Field of Political Communication;" p. 11.

# Foreword

Historically, the mass media were heralded as the ultimate instruments of democracy. Print, radio, and TV were destined to unite, educate, and, as a result, improve the actions and decisions of the polity. As sources of timely public information, they provide the greatest potential for understanding ourselves, our society, and even the world.

However, there is growing sentiment among scholars and political observers that the mass media have not made us more informed in our electoral choices or more democratic in terms of electoral participation. As a nation we seem to be less informed, less concerned, and certainly less involved in politics. Many blame the practice of news journalism. The very form and content of contemporary news is like feeding the nation "Twinkies," which are delicious but have no nutritional value.

The problem, according to Neil Postman (1985), is not that the media present us with entertaining matter but that all subject matter is presented as entertaining (p. 87). The result is pure spectacle. Murray Edelman (1988) argued that:

The spectacle constituted by news reporting continuously constructs and reconstructs social problems, crises, enemies, and leaders and so creates a succession of threats and reassurances. These constructed problems and personalities furnish the content of political journalism and the data for historical and analytic political studies. They also play a central role in winning support and opposition for political causes and policies. (p. 1)

The spectacle of politics is no longer reserved for elections. It is now a daily, or, better yet for most Americans, a nightly event. The "players" are no longer only politicians but also the news reporters, anchors, and pundits. It is now nearly impossible to distinguish between political talk and political action. For Murray Edelman (1988), "The construction of a spectacle and everyday political action are the same thing, though the pretence that they are separate helps legitimize official actions" (p. 125).

Political talk about politics has become more important than the reporting of political facts. Richard Brookhiser, in writing about the 1984 presidential campaign, argued that journalists are too preoccupied with the "nuts and bolts": with the strategies and numbers of campaigns rather than the words, themes, and ideas of an election. By focusing on the inside story, journalists assume the tasks of defining, explaining, and interpreting the contest (in Will, 1988, pp. 15–16). All the political discussions, according to Edelman (1988), "now become devices for creating disparate assumptions and beliefs about the social and political world rather than factual statements" (p. 10). As a result, "the political entities that are most influential upon public consciousness and action, then, are fetishes: creations of observers that then dominate and mystify their creators" (p. 11).

The press has become so process-oriented that, according to Larry Sabato (1991), the media today are like sharks in a feeding frenzy. The new standard of "attack jounalism" has transformed American politics. The press has become so obsessed with the reporting and discussion of gossip and personal news that it "prefers to employ titillation rather than scrutiny; as a result, its political coverage produces trivialization rather than enlightenment" (p. 6). Because of the competitive nature of news organizations, the twenty-four-hour delivery of news, and the celebrity status of journalists, there is a growing appetite for personalized news, opinions, and insight.

The expanded role of the press and the increase in "political talk" have led to an expanded cast of characters. Anchors, reporters, and correspondents could not provide all the "objective" commentary and sound bites that were necessary. Thus enters the pundit, "one who gives opinions in an authoritative manner." Dan Nimmo and James Combs have once again, in a perceptive and entertaining way, identified a new trend in American politics. As politics become even more of a spectator sport, they examine the growing role and impact of punditocracy upon democratic citizenship.

"Talk may be cheap," but punditry is big business. As a group, pundits are a new source of political power and influence. They have become a new obstacle between leaders and the public. Pundits have transformed public debate from what politicians say about issues to what pundits say politicians should say about issues. They have gone from dispensing wisdom to witticism, from criticism often to cynicism.

Nimmo and Combs effectively demonstrate that punditry has become the "fifth estate" of American politics. Through their exploration, we understand the importance and potential dangers of punditocracy.

There are several important contributions that this book makes to the study of political communication. First, it serves as another case study and example of mediated politics in the United States. Pundits further mediate the realities of our already mediated politics of elections and the public debate of issues and policies. We are still discovering, after nearly half a century of television, the impact of various media on the practice of politics. Second, the study contributes to our theoretical knowledge of the role and function of contemporary public opinion formation and leadership in America. The process by which "private opinions" become social issues and public policy is of great importance to the study of American politics. Finally, this study provides insight into the ever evolving and changing nature of American democracy. Has the practice of punditry replaced public debate? Have pundits become the "gladiators" of democracy? As citizens, we are becoming reduced to the roles of spectators, cheerleaders, and "couch potatoes" of the political process.

Finally, I have a confession. I am a pundit, albeit a very minor one. My "babble" shows up in the *Washington Post* and other regional newspapers from time to time. I also serve as a political analyst for a local television station, providing commentary, interview remarks, and election night analyses. It is often a frustrating experience. I must tell "what it means" in fifteen seconds or less. I do not have time to think, but only to react. Sometimes I have the sneaking suspicion that the reporters are seeking a sound bite that supports a preconceived slant of a story.

Of course, it is nice when people comment on what you say, even if they do not like or agree with it. I thought I was contributing to public debate and providing a context for political events, statements, or behavior, but after reading *The Political Pundits*, I am more than a little worried. This book should be mandatory reading for all journalists and pundits, great or small.

Robert E. Denton, Jr.

## REFERENCES

Edelman, Murray. (1988). *Constructing the Political Spectacle*. Chicago: University of Chicago Press.
Postman, Neil. (1985). *Amusing Ourselves to Death*. New York: Penguin Books.
Sabato, Larry. (1991). *Feeding Frenzy: How Attack Journalism Has Transformed American Politics*. New York: Free Press.
Will, George. (1988). *The New Season*. New York: Simon and Schuster.

# Preface

This book is about an ancient practice whose traditions are chronicled in the Holy Bible, countless sacred and secular texts, volumes of history, works of fiction, and philosophical tomes. It is a practice whose currency and vitality fill today's newspapers, newsmagazines, radio programs, and television productions. It has carried several labels: prophesy, revelation, gossip, fortune telling, reporting, interpretation, analysis, and opinion leadership are but a few. It consists of commenting on events, reports of events, and the people who make them. We call that activity *punditry*.

Since our principal interests lie in politics and communication in and about politics, this book, therefore, surveys political punditry. In the pages that follow we explore the character of political punditry: its traditions, current practices, imperatives, and consequences for democratic government. Along the way we consider various types of pundits and look closely at specific pundits from the distant past, recent past, and present. Our sources for this study are diverse. They include, for example, the published views of noted pundits of the past and the present. Moreover, we have recorded and analyzed for thematic content video and radio talk shows featuring punditry. We have also analyzed the thematic content of the major publications of media watchdog organizations and the TV programming of key media critics. Finally, we have interviewed both media critics and syndicated columnists regarding their respective political roles.

There was a time that required the active, reflective, democratic citizen to ponder the political question, "What's happening?" and then respond by either accepting things as they were or trying to change them. Nowadays, however, as the intricacies, subtleties, and complexities of political life—not to mention the sheer magnitude and pervasiveness of political happenings—have expanded, few citizens have the time or the inclination for asking what is occurring politically. The questions now are, "Who knows what's happening?" and "What might those who know counsel citizens to do?" In response to the question of who knows, there is now a political class of pundits, a cadre of purported political knowledgeables who appear and reappear in, but seemingly never disappear from, all manner of forums and venues of public political discussion. We close our discussion by pondering whether the interests of democratic citizenship are well or ill served by this burgeoning, but relatively unexamined, punditocracy.

# Introduction: From Delphi to Democracy, the Sources of Punditry

Imagine a traveler from a foreign land visiting in the Washington, D.C., area over a weekend. On Monday the stranger has scheduled a meeting in the nation's capital. That seems far away. Today is a cold, damp, rainy day that makes sightseeing out of the question. There is no point in trying to get a football match on TV: What the visitor knows as football, Americans call "soccer," and they do not telecast it anyway. Reading a Harlequin romance novel would certainly have no appeal. Consequently, since Washington is one of the great political centers of the world, our friend sets out to find what is happening in the politics of the capital and the nation. Moreover, having been cooped up in a DC-10 airplane for hours, the traveler is curious about what has happened across the world.

There are, of course, the lead stories in the newspapers. A flick of the remote control produces a TV headline news service. However, our traveler is a "news junkie" with an insatiable curiosity and an appetite for information that goes beyond the surface of events. What is the story behind the news? Who knows what is *really* happening? Who is knowledgeable to *interpret* the news? "Inquiring minds," say the ads, may turn to the *National Inquirer*, but tabloids are scarcely the answer. The visitor wants sources of news that not only tell what is happening but, moreover, *why* it is happening and why it is happening *now*.

As the traveler watches, reads, and listens, it becomes apparent that there is more interpretation of the news than appeared at first. For example, a network news anchor reports news as fact: This, that, and the other is happening. For major events, however, the anchor turns to someone who gives a brief interpretation: This is happening because of

X, Y, and Z but not A, B, and C; it is happening now because D, E, and F preceded it, bringing about the event; we can expect G, H, and I to come from what is happening but not J, K, and L. "Take my word for it," the analyst seems to say. The anchor thanks the analyst and smiles at the camera, satisfied that the audience has received a quick and accurate insight into what is happening.

However, there is much more. There are "public affairs" shows that do nothing but provide talk about the news and what it means. On TV and radio throughout the weekend, little knots of reporters, politicians, and representatives of interest groups—even movie stars and starlets—solemnly discuss and debate what is occurring and why. The discussion sometimes grows confusing, for the participants disagree not only about why something is happening but even about the fundamental facts of the event. Adding to what is now becoming a surfeit of interpretive news are the editorial and opinion ("op-ed") pages of the newspapers. Moreover, should that not be enough, one can turn to newsmagazines and journals of opinion, finding diverse and often contradictory ideological, partisan, and idiosyncratic views, some of which seem to make sense and some that do not.

After all this exposure to news interpretation, the visitor leaves Washington after Monday's meeting, reflecting that Americans certainly are an opinionated lot, or at least that their press includes a great deal of talk about the news, an abundance of virtually instant reflection on and remastication of the events of the day. At least for the politically attentive Americans there seems to be no dearth of experts, analysts, and opinion makers who are eager to offer their particular, and often peculiar, slants on politics for everyone's edification. Aboard the jumbo jet the traveler wonders: Was all that interpretation, analysis, and opinion really edifying or was it just a babble (or "Babel") of voices competing for people's attention?

## TOWERS OF BABEL

One of the enduring and instructive myths from the ancient Near East is the story of the Tower of Babel. When the early civilizations began to appear in the Fertile Crescent, they made two key advances for civilized peoples: First, they developed a sense of the significance of time, and second, they introduced writing and literacy. The first advance provided a perception of history and society. These early cultures—the Sumerians, for instance—experienced time as a dynamic linking of past, present, and future. Sensing that they existed in time and space as a people, they created dynasties, customs, and laws governing their conduct. Their oral tradition of communicating these conventions imparted and preserved a political identity, what political scientists now call a *political culture.*

Second, the development of writing and records added a new dimension to communication. Now, rules of property, marriage, power, and other conduct could be recorded over time. Literacy demanded people who could keep records, master writing, and articulate ideas in ways beyond those associated purely with the oral tradition. A class of people emerged who were adept at the skills of literacy. This class, which was comprised of priests, scribes, prophets, and "learned men" (as contrasted with the "wise men" of earlier times) were what we now designate as intellectuals, earning their living by the mastery of the new technique of communication. As kings ruled by skill at building coalitions and soldiers by winning battles, the masters of talking and telling, writing and recording, reading and interpreting, became powerful in their own right. Soon both kings and soldiers called on this learned class to perform a wide variety of political tasks, not the least of which was to justify kingly rule and soldierly conquest.

Thereby arose a new source of power, the power of political intelligence. That power rested in control over the resources of discourse and a claim to be the only valid authority to interpret that discourse. Such intelligence might not command the allegiance of allies or win battles by force of arms, but it seemingly could work wonders. The masters of intelligence built reputations for knowing what others could not, for possessing abilities denied ordinary people, and for understanding things neither known nor seen by the unlearned.

As city-states and empires proliferated in the cradle of civilization, virtually all of them had a class of discourse experts located at the power centers of these new, powerful societies. Often they were part of a priestly class that controlled access to the sacred truths associated with the temple religion that supported power, such as the ziggurat of Babylon. Sometimes they were scribes or advisers who lived in palaces of the powerful. In Israel, they appeared in a different form—as itinerants, such as the prophets of the Old Testament, who acted as independent critics of the powerful. Nevertheless, in all cases their value to society was in their grasp of what language meant. This could range from nothing more than their ability to read official scrolls and tablets to such claims as an exclusive insight into the divine will of God or the gods. In Egypt Joseph became a power at the court of Pharaoh because of his reputed ability to interpret dreams, long before the time of Sigmund Freud.

The Holy Bible's Book of Genesis (11:1–9), in the tale of the Tower of Babel, aptly suggests, in apocryphal if not historical fashion, the burgeoning variety of voices spawned by the new intelligentsia. The imperial city-states of the ancient Near East heretofore had offered their peoples the advantages of civilization, not the least being security from attack. However, these same city-states provoked in their inhabitants aspirations for greatness that went well beyond mere efforts to be secure. The chief articulators of this "call to greatness" were the newly emergent literate apologists for power. The legend of the tower tells of humanity's power to do evil, which springs from the corruption of pride that rests on the power of language.

Once, "the whole earth had one language and few words," begins the legend. Like all the early civilizations that emerged in the Fertile Crescent, people found reasons to "come, . . . build a city." Armed with the self-confidence that the power of a unified language gave them, apparently they wished to build in Babylon "a tower with its top in the heavens" so as to "make a name for [themselves]." The literate civilization no longer would exist for security alone but also for fame. Such fame would rest on a people unified by "one language and few words," one that would not "be scattered abroad upon the face of the whole earth," or so the literati agreed.

However, the god Yahweh knew that any unity of language and power, as symbolized by the Tower of Babel, was a force for evil, a corruption based on pride that would make the likelihood of sin in the world greater than ever: "This is only the beginning of what they will do; and nothing that they propose to do will now be impossible for them." To prevent the spread of evil, Yahweh simply "confused" their language "that they may not understand one another's speech." Yahweh scattered people in a multiplicity of languages and cultures. The dream of the Tower of Babel was abandoned. Consequently, according to legend, we have been babbling ever since Babel, speaking in many different languages and using many words. Augmenting the proliferation of babble since Babel has been the emergence of pundits, specialists seeking to understand—or exploit—the eternal confusion.

## FROM BABEL TO PUNDITRY

The myth of the Tower of Babel is one of humankind's oldest, and most insightful, stories. Whether literal or metaphorical, it reminds us that systems of power—from the city-states of old to the nation-states of the twentieth century and the European Community of the twenty-first—rest not only on representative institutions, large-scale bureaucracies, and technological/armed might, but also on symbols. To these objects of social discourse we accord meaning and purpose. Through symbols, both linguistic and iconic, we acquire a vocabulary of motives. We learn how to respond to rhetorical appeals that mobilize and manipulate symbols as goads to action or inaction. Symbols, or everyday Towers of Babel, are a source of both clarity and confusion: clarity through providing the means of legitimizing power, cloaking it as authority that we should obey, and confusion if the symbols that cloak the power fail to keep abreast of always-changing and perhaps unmanageable circumstances, thus challenging the dictum that authority should be obeyed (Burke, 1969a, 1969b).

### Babble as Grounds for Authority

Early in the twentieth century, the German sociologist Max Weber formulated a classic typology of the sources, or grounds, for authority (Weber, 1947). After surveying a vast array of historical types of power, he formulated a threefold distinction. First, authorities may be grounded in a claim to traditions; rulers should be obeyed, for it is their divine right or heritage, or because custom demands it. The pope of the Roman Catholic Church and the ruling houses of Saudi Arabia, for instance, exemplify authority grounded in tradition. Second are those who base their assertion of authority in legal-rational standards. They claim to rule from contractual documents (such as the Constitution of the United States), agreed upon administrative procedures (e.g., as rules for election and/or appointment to office), or rational expertise (as in naming an eminent scientist or physician to a governing position). Third, there is the claim to rule on the basis of one's own authority, which Weber called charismatic authority. Charismatic authorities may build on tradition (as did Jesus of Nazareth) or exploit legal-rational institutions (as did Adolf Hitler); they assert, however, something more. In other words, they themselves are authorities in their very beings and can thus command followership and/or obedience.

Of course, things are not quite so neat as Weber's ideal types of authority make them. A country like the United States has political traditions, which a new president must respect. The presidency is also a legal-rational institution, and hence, a president must act in accordance with procedures of a rule-guided bureaucracy. Finally, the president may be charismatic, deriving power from the ardor and devotion of a popular following responding to unseen, hard-to-grasp intangibles that are attributed not to tradition or the office but to the person who holds it.

Weber's schema is useful to a point. Does it, however, help our perplexed foreign visitor who devotes a weekend harkening to the babble of voices emanating from the public affairs media? The visitor does not perceive the people who speak and write about politics as possessing authority because they are traditional patriarchs, nor do they necessarily occupy legal positions or possess rational expertise that renders them authoritative. Few could be said to be charismatic and to be watched, listened to, or read because of special, intangible personal power. What

claim to authority do these babblers about politics and public affairs
make that might strike the fancy of a foreign traveler, or, for that matter,
millions of Americans who watch, hear, and read towering quantities
of such babble in a given day? Why does the public take the babblers
seriously?

### The Babble of Punditry and the Punditry of Babble

The media babblers encountered by our traveler from a distant land
comprise a loosely defined collection of communicators whom we call
*pundits*. The phrase "political punditry" identifies a contemporary phenomenon, namely, the proliferation and power of discourse through the
mass media. As William Safire has pointed out it is a term with an
interesting etymology (1978, p. 580). The word came into English usage
at least by the early nineteenth century, and was derived from the ancient
Indian language Sanskrit *pandita* for "scholar, learned man," and
adapted to Hindi as *pandit*, an honorific title first applied to a Brahman
with a profound knowledge of Sanskrit, Hindu law, and ancient wisdom. It survives in modern India to honor a learned person or teacher
who is not only an authority but also a revered political figure.

When *pundit* entered English usage, the implication of one who commanded deference because of learned authority was soon complemented
by reference to one who gives opinions in an authoritative manner. As
Safire noted, the word then came to be used in mocking the pretensions
of those who nag politicians through public and widely circulated observations (p. 580). He cited this 1921 *New York Times* editorial regarding
the writing style of President Warren G. Harding, a style the newspaper
admired: "[He] is not writing for the superfine weigher of verbs and
adjectives, but for men and women who see in his expressions their
own ideas, and are truly happy to meet them. . . . [It] is a good style, let
the pundits rage about it as they will" (p. 580). More recently, presidents
and presidential aspirants have been equally critical of pundits. Stump-
ing for Republican candidates in Tyler, Texas, on November 5, 1990,
President George Bush said, "The cynics, these Washington pundits
that we see on those tiring shows all the time— . . . I don't know if you're
like me, maybe you've enjoyed these things. But I can only take so much
self-flagellation . . . Don't tell me what's wrong about this country, show
me what's right about it" (Associated Press, 1990). Moreover, Jesse Jackson, responding to press criticism, said derisively, "The seven million
votes I got [in 1988] didn't come from no *pundits*" (Safire, 1990, p. 10).

Undaunted by criticism, however, pundits have survived and pros-
pered. Numerous political observers—journalists, retired politicians, ex-
bureaucrats, entertainers, teachers, and so on—now make punditry a
profession, or at least a craft, and perhaps an industry, and insist that

they and their opinions be taken more seriously than any others. The way is prepared for wars between pundits who send their armies of opinions into battle with each other. Moreover, individual pundits have sought to monopolize the domain of political discourse by making their personal opinions heeded by those who debate opinions in the first place. Political debate today often rages not over issues, or even what politicians say about issues, but about what pundits say politicians *should* say about issues.

A pundit, wrote Safire, "is an expert on nothing but an authority on everything, a harmless nudge" (1990, p. 12). Not everyone thinks pundits are so harmless, however. In fact, when Safire claimed that punditry should be "self-denigrating" and should never forget to poke fun at its "pretensions of sagacity" (p. 12), he is admitting that the pundit can be more than just a "harmless nudge" and should call to account pretenses at sagacity, no matter who makes them. In any event, as pundit after pundit sought political influence by voicing views from media "towers of babble" and became famous, they, like the learned of Babel, became subjects of criticism and ridicule as well as notoriety. The profession of public *punditry* came under derisive attack, such as those launched by George Bush and Jesse Jackson. Detractors now label pundits in derogatory language: as mandarins, panjandrums, cognoscenti, savants, swamis, soothsayers, seers, magicians, sages, wise men, shamans, prophets, oracles, illuminati, know-it-alls, and so forth. Critics charge that political pundits make special, and unjustified, claims to knowledge. There have been several notable attacks on punditry in recent presidential administrations. Former president Dwight Eisenhower received roaring applause at the 1964 Republican convention when he mentioned "sensation-seeking columnists and commentators (Safire, 1978, p. 580)." Similarly, Vice President Spiro Agnew derided the "nattering nabobs of negativism" (Safire, 1978, p. 580) during Richard Nixon's presidency.

Since the term *pundit* and the role have associations with older forms of wisdom, the pundit invites us to take what he or she says seriously; nonetheless, since punditry often has a pretentious quality, the role also invites mockery and contempt. Contemporary American pundits serve both political functions: they are targets of both respect and scorn. Thus, a pundit—William Safire himself is a good example (Shapiro, 1990)—is an important participant in governing as an "opinion molder," or, more derisively, an "opinion-monger," who arouses conversation and controversy among the political strata.

In the pages that follow we seek neither to acclaim nor to denigrate but rather to understand political punditry in contemporary America. The pundits that babble from the towers may be nudges but they are not harmless. As being heirs to an ancient label for sagacity and wisdom suggests, what pundits do is not novel. However, in an important sense, by practicing their craft through the far-reaching channels of mass circulation newspapers, newsmagazines, influential opinion journals, television, cable TV, satellite TV, and radio, they go far beyond the pundits of any earlier era, for now they have the capacity to reach mass audiences that Yahweh "scattered abroad upon the face of the whole earth." Whether one thinks them pretentious and wrong-headed or courageous and right-thinking, they now constitute a source of opinion-formation and opinion-articulation, agenda-setting and agenda-evaluation, so vast as to make the United States a *punditocracy* (Alterman, 1988): a nation where the mediation of opinion by important and highly visible media figures is paramount. Assertions like those of Alterman (and many others whom we shall encounter in the pages that follow) warrant that we inquire into how pervasive punditry is, what role it plays in politics, and the ways in which it is practiced.

## THE HERITAGE OF PUNDITS' AUTHORITY

Before turning to the character of punditry in contemporary politics, let us put our examination in a broader context than developed thus far. Consider the world after the Tower of Babel when there was no longer "one language and few words." The civilizations that emerged in the Near East and the Mediterranean differed markedly from one another. However, all shared one aspiration: to establish and perpetuate a legitimate form of authority that could command obedience. Obedience to authority would require more than political acumen on the part of rulers and more than the force of arms. Authority would make an epistemic claim: to be the sole representative of a kind of special knowledge.

A traditional authority lays claim to the authoritative sources of tradition; those who know the special knowledge of sacred traditions possess the right to rule. The ruling myth, or legitimating story, resided in a holy book, in priestly accounts of the origins of the state, or in legends of the mighty acts of the reigning dynasty. In any case, there was a form of special knowledge that justified the rule of those who governed in the past and who could do so in the future. Tradition was the source of the mystic cloak of power. If tradition says that rule of a city was founded by the goddess Athena, or that a tribal code was given by God to Moses and kept in the Ark of the Covenant in the holy of holies, who can argue otherwise?

Legal-rational sources of authority may, of course, draw on ruling instruments that are steeped in tradition. The Constitution of the United States is rich in tradition as well as legal and rational procedures. At the heart of such legal-rational sources, however, are the sacred rules and procedures, or, more accurately, the special knowledge of them, which is possessed only by those who can interpret their meaning—courts, judges, lawyers, and legal scholars are examples. Like traditional forms of knowledge, rationality is ultimately couched in mystery, a combination of technique and mystique. Like nation-states founded on tribal tradition, those citing legal-rational sources of authority construct a myth of the state identifying who possessed the special knowledge that justified who are the rulers and who are the subjects (Cassirer, 1955).

The third of Weber's three sources of authority is the charismatic. Here special knowledge is not that of tradition or of law but of the itinerant. The claim is, in part, derived from a unique and personal epistemic authority. For example, Jesus asserted, "Ye have heard that it hath been said by them of old time . . . But I say unto you . . . " (Matthew 6: 33–34). However, that is not the only form of itinerant knowledge. In societies driven by charismatic authority, people or groups make claims to special knowledge that are in some measure independent of the city- or nation-state's traditions or laws. In those societies we find that punditry flourishes.

Weber did not explore the varieties of itinerant, charismatic authority that are the ancient sources of modern punditry. Here we explore three types: the oracular knowledge exemplified by the Greek oracle at Delphi, the prophetic knowledge professed by the prophets of ancient Israel, and the sophistic knowledge asserted by the itinerant philosophers of Greece during its decline in influence.

The city-states of ancient Greece rested in part, but not solely, on traditional authority. Independent of tradition was an itinerant authority based in the mythology surrounding the temple dedicated to Apollo at the sacred site of Delphi, on the slopes of Mount Parnassus. Delphi became the spiritual capital of the Greek world owing to the reputation for sagacity of the priests who practiced divination there. The priests claimed to interpret the utterances of the god Apollo—certainly special knowledge if there ever was. The oracular knowledge emanated from Apollo through vapors that came from a cleft in the ground, which was believed to be the sacred center of the universe. The vapors induced ecstasy in the female priest, who was called the *Prophetes*. The priestess spoke in tongues that were deemed to be the voice of Apollo. The priests of Delphi interpreted the *Prophetes'* murmurings, usually in obscure and enigmatic ways.

Cryptic or not, priestly interpretations had a reputation for authenticity. Apollo was the God of Truth, and whatever the priestess at Delphi said was certain to happen. For instance, the Delphic Oracle allegedly predicted accurately that Oedipus would kill his father and marry his mother, a fate Oedipus tried to escape but could not. Even though the prophecies and prescriptions of the oracle were often mundane and even foolish, their packaging in a mystification of language and ritual made them no less appealing than is the claim, made in TV ads, that a lotion made from "pearl drops" will make a woman younger "without a face lift." The commonplace virtues enshrined in the temple ("Know thyself," "Nothing in excess") and the puzzling predictions of the priests added to, rather than detracted from, the oracular reputation for being divine. Skepticism of Delphi oracularism did not flourish until Greece's self-destruction in the Peloponnesian War. Prior to that event, the Delphic Oracle remained an insight to special knowledge which was consulted by the politically powerful every bit as much as by common members of the populace.

Another example of itinerant authority in ancient times consists of the prophets of Israel. The Hebrew legacy of prophecy included a motley array of the holy; diviners, fanatics, recluses living in the desert, doomsayers, and trance-speakers were but a few. Among the most notable prophets were Samuel, Amos, Jeremiah, Isaiah, and John the Baptist. They were radical critics of power and wealth who decried the hypocrisies of their age. Both rulers and the populace, however, bestowed on them special status because of their intimate relationship with the god Yahweh. Their influence was enormous in selecting and undoing rulers, spurring religious and political reform, and reminding Israel of its covenant and destiny. The power of the prophets derived not from holding ruling positions, from armies, or from wealth, but from the power of a special knowledge and a special relationship with the divine.

Finally, the heritage of modern punditry is traceable to a class of itinerant, professional philosophers called the Sophists. The Sophistic movement claimed that wisdom could be taught. The Sophist was a "wisdom expert," albeit in a far different sense of wisdom than that envisioned by Socrates. The word *sophistes* connotes someone who practices a profession of wisdom. Sophists taught ambitious young men a pragmatic humanism, an ancient version of the contemporary success ethic. Rather than virtue as an inherent value, the Sophists taught "know-how" or "knack"; namely, the techniques of what works in politics and life to achieve success. Socrates undertook a search for wisdom, but the Sophists taught skill and facility; Socrates emphasized dialectical reasoning, but the Sophists taught oratorical glibness. For Sophists, the science of logical argumentation yielded to the art of emotional persuasion. Special knowledge was neither oracular nor prophetic, but rather was technical. We explore the full ramifications of that view in Chapter Four.

Here, then, were the ancient beginnings of the idea that a professional class set apart by virtue of a claim to special knowledge could exercise political influence. Oracles, prophets, and sophists were eager to share their insights, but only in ritual formats of their own choosing. Their special knowledge was instructed knowledge in two senses. First, they

became political instructors in sharing their knowledge. Second, people
believed that the knowledge of oracles, prophets, and sophists was itself
instructed by sources unreachable and unfathomable by ordinary mortals without the ancient pundits' assistance.

## FROM ITINERANT INSTRUCTOR TO MEDIA PUNDIT

Since ancient times, various groups and individuals have laid claim
to being special because they possess superior and instructed knowledge. The history of religions such as Christianity, Islam, and Hinduism
provides numerous examples of claims to oracular, prophetic, or sophistic knowledge. Catholic churchmen or Islamic mullahs, Protestant
clergy or Buddhist holy men, TV evangelists or writers of inspirational
and apocalyptic tracts—all have kept alive the tradition of sacral knowledge mediated by the learned who master mysteries. Our topic, however, is not religion but politics, not the sacred but what many citizens
would call the profane. Who are the learned authorities who claim to
have mastered the mysteries of politics? By what media do they instruct
us in their special knowledge? We address the second question first, for
its answer does much to inform us how we might identify politics'
learned authorities.

### Pundits as Media Authorities

The modern contemporary pundits who are familiar fixtures of the
political scene are, we contend, direct descendants of the pundits of
ancient times. Like their ancient counterparts, modern pundits require
a public forum. Ancient oracles, prophets, and sophists were not only
given a chance to speak, they also had a popular forum, be it the temple
of the oracle at Delphi, the palace steps of ancient Israel, or the agora
(marketplace) at Athens. The United States has, to be sure, its versions
of the temple, palace, and marketplace: the church, capitol steps, and
shopping mall. However, if the nation's pundits appeared in these forums and only in these forums, people would scarcely take note of their
instructions. If ancient punditry evolved out of the history of religion,
modern punditry emerged out of the history of journalism, and especially news reporting via the mass media.

In the late eighteenth century, Edmund Burke observed that the press,
which had spread widely through the developing technology of printing,
had become a political institution. Referring to the "three estates" of
government described by French philosopher Baron de Montesquieu—
the executive, legislative, and judicial, Burke added that the press was
a "fourth estate" (Burns, 1977, p. 176). By the twentieth century journalism had become the principal means of *mediating*, that is, standing

between people and the world and reporting to them what they could not see or experience themselves. Through newspapers, teletype, radio, newsmagazines, movie newsreels, television, and computer networks, the news instructed people in what they could not learn for themselves (Bennett, 1988; Entman, 1989; Nimmo and Combs, 1990).

As with any form of communication, the news, and the news media, did not consist of disembodied information. It was, after all, communicated by *someone*. Moreover, it was not simply information, for by itself, news was often no more understandable than the muttering of the *Prophetes* of Mount Parnassus. Journalists not only reported the news, they often interpreted it. Those who did so gradually took on a new and privileged status within the craft of journalism. They attained the stature of media authorities, public figures who were featured, praised, and celebrated—by their news organizations and then by their audiences—for knowing what the news really meant and for revealing their special knowledge to audiences. Here were twentieth-century oracles, prophets, and sophists with a public forum of hundreds of thousands, even millions.

Being featured in newspapers, on radio and TV, or via other mass media did not, of course, guarantee a status as a media authority. Being in the public eye through the means of mass communication provided a credential, a license to instruct. There was no guarantee that audiences would pay heed. A reputation for *media* authority was not the same as one for media *authority*. The latter depended on the credence accorded media figures in the performance of the pundit role. In large measure, one's credentials as a media authority depended on the plausibility of one's utterances. From Delphi to *Doonesbury*, the pundit's reputation as a media authority has depended not on the truth and/or accuracy of what she or he instructs as special knowledge but on *credibility*. Moreover, as with the ancients, building a reputation for credibility requires a mastery less of special, revealed knowledge than of the discursive rituals appropriate to the specific public forum provided by a specific medium.

For example, one of the oldest and most cherished public forums for punditry in the history of print journalism is the column. (We explore the columnist's punditry in greater detail in Chapters One and Two). A glance through major newspapers offers a host of columnists writing about virtually everything: music, hunting and fishing, baseball, cars, food and drink, and, most certainly, politics. Virtually every newspaper has an opinion-editorial page with both regular and invited columnists, some local and some syndicated. It is the op-ed columnists who devoted themselves to political and social questions. The op-ed column is a stylistic dramatization not only of the subject or issue at hand, but also of the pundit's rightful status to speak on it authoritatively.

A typical column has a definite rhetorical style designed to dramatize the authoritative opinion of the pundit. In some measure, the pundit's stylistic power determines how well readers receive the column; it can enhance or detract from the columnist's reputation for timely credibility. Like a sonnet, the column has an expected and ritually drawn structure (oftentimes, statement of the problem, discussion of legitimate alternatives, argumentative defense of one choice and attack of others, conclusion, and recommendation). To the degree that readers of columns have come to expect columns to adhere to standardized formats and rituals, whether one is persuaded by a columnist's point of view may well depend not on what was written, but how. In this sense the column is a triumph of sophistic technique and style over what a Socrates might have deemed substance and reason.

## Categories of Punditry: Venerable and Fashionable

The columnist illustrates our general answer to the question we posed earlier, namely, "Through what media do learned authorities instruct us in their special knowledge?" The answer is the mass media, a forum of media authorities. Moreover, the columnist as pundit suggests one, but only one, answer to the question we also posed earlier, namely, "Who are the learned authorities that claim to have mastered the mysteries of politics?" There are, in fact, so many specific pundits (columnists, self-styled experts, news "analysts," and so forth) that it will assist us if we categorize pundits as a means of simplifying the discussion that follows in this book.

To that end we begin by considering a category of punditry that may, on first blush, appear to apply to pundits in the ancient era of oracles, prophets, and sophists, yet have no relevance to the present. However, as we shall see in Part One of this book, "Traditions of Political Punditry," this category of venerable pundits includes those who still ply their craft today.

### The Venerable Pundits: Priests, Bards, and Oracles

Even though contemporary pundits are creatures of modern media and circumstances, they fulfill a very old need. In that sense, pundits are heirs of the ancient oracles, prophets, and sophists more than they might think. Like their primordial counterparts, they play a definite and functional social role or, perhaps more accurately, different social roles. Thomas M. Lessl (1989) has analyzed two distinct venerable social roles dating back to the ancients: the priest and the bard. Both roles are of contemporary relevance in discussing political pundits.

The priest's rhetoric, says Lessl, originates within a "certain elite substratum of society and represents a reality that the audience can only superficially hope to approach." The origins of priestly utterances reside "outside of ordinary human experience as revelations of spirit or nature." Priestly communication is vertical. In other words; it is "descending from above," filled with mystery, and "empowered with extra-human authority" (p. 183). In everyday parlance, the priest talks down to people. The priest knows what ordinary people do not and cannot know.

The bard, by contrast, is a voice that speaks for a popular rather than an elite culture, what Lessl labels a *hegemonic* culture. The bard identifies with the "commonsense experience already integral" to the audience's identity. Bardic communication is lateral: It extends across "well traveled highways" of a culture familiar to us; "it speaks to the profane dimension of human experience" (p. 185). Bards are like us; they tell us stories about ourselves. That the bard is like us to the degree of coming from a popular rather than an elite culture does not, however, make the bard any less a pundit than the priest. What the bard does that is pundit-like is to exercise a skill, talent, or technique that not all of us have, namely, rendering the profane dramatic through storytelling. Thus, "when bards talk, it is our own voice that we hear, the faint murmuring of a collective consciousness amplified in the poetic and often recognizable as myth" (p. 184). As we shall see often in this book, a flair for the dramatic and the poetic is key to the pundit's role.

The priestly voice, suggests Lessl, mediates elite knowledge, or *gnosis*, exercising power through the use of the "esoteric code" of a "secret and protected language." Such discourse involves dual, and often conflicting, purposes: It gives rise to "intermittent moments of transparency and opacity, communication which strives at one turn to convey . . . truth in the idiom of the people and at another to veil understanding in cryptic tongues." While bardic rhetoric is "reflexive" so that audiences see or hear "a culture speaking about itself to itself," reminding the folk "of *who they are*," priests speak in an "extensive" voice, using "the speech of one culture to another," reminding people of *"what they might become*," and interpreting "all experience in terms of the specialized priestly subculture" (p. 188).

It is possible to extend Lessl's argument. Not only do priestly and bardic roles exist in religious, scientific, and aesthetic cultures (the foci of Lessl's analysis), they also do so in political cultures. Moreover, not only do political cultures have their venerable priestly and bardic pundits, there is also a proliferation of political oracles. A priest is the voice of transcendent identity (saying, in effect, "Identify with the values and ideas of my elite subculture if you wish to achieve knowledge"), a bard is the voice of popular identity ("Identify with the people if you wish to achieve knowledge"), and the oracle is the voice of temporal, passing, short-lived identity ("Identify with the meaning of the times and of

history if you wish to possess knowledge"). The priest offers elite forensic wisdom and the bard, popular folk wisdom; the oracle holds out
a dynamic wisdom associated with grasping the essence of time and
change. "What they might become" (the priestly message) and "who
they are" (the bardic message) encounters "what is becoming," the
oracle's interpretation of all experience in the relationship of past, present, and future.

Let us underscore the distinction between priests, bards, and oracles
more fully. A priest plays a catholic role, expressing the defined viewpoint of an elite subculture by generating a mythology, an ideology, or
propaganda. The priest offers elitist views as authoritative and universal
(and, therefore, catholic); all humankind can identify with such universal
principles. A priestly hierarchy claims to possess a science (in the sense
of a true and universally applicable body of knowledge and a method
of acquiring that knowledge) that all humankind should adhere and
submit to for their salvation and enlightenment. A bard plays a Homeric
role, expressing the popular stories of cultural identity of a group, nation,
or perhaps all humankind. The bardic mythos is populist, and in some
sense, anti-elite, grounding true experience in folktales that are the common possession of the many rather than the few. Everything from epic
to fairy tale makes up the Homeric legacy celebrated by bards. It may
or may not coincide with the interests and perspective of an elite, but
its function is in its popular articulation.

When a priestly or bardic pundit acquires a reputation for being wise,
learned, and correct over an extended time, he or she achieves the status
of a sage. Today we accord sage status to respected scientists, journalists,
and academicians, and even to organizations such as the National
Weather Service, the National Bureau of Economic Research, and the
Brookings Institution. Although the instruments of analysis of the contemporary oracle-sage are more modern and scientific than those of
Delphi, their function is the same. To sustain the reputation of sage,
pundits must be perceived as profound, visionary, learned, serious, and
disinterested. Political pundits in particular seek to display virtues that
the Romans called *gravitas* (having an air of grave concern with things
and an ability to measure their gravity) and *civitas* (a selfless concern for
public matters and civic improvement). In Chapter Three we examine
the role of the political pundit as a sagacious person.

Finally, the oracle at Delphi was the most well-known and established
of those who guarded and interpreted the mysteries of time. There were,
however, other oracles that followed, and the venerable oracular tradition persists today. They possess sage status with their *gravitas* and
*civitas*, but they add to that serious claims of knowing the future. Soothsayers of Rome, for example, were not itinerant priests or bards but
oracles. Rulers consulted them to learn the whims of fortune. "Beware

the Ides of March," the soothsayer warned Julius Caesar. Caesar did not pay heed and paid the price with his life. In contemporary America, whoever claims a prophetic special knowledge, advising the rulers and the ruled with an air of authority, continues the venerable oracular tradition. They may be economists (predicting bull or bear markets), weather forecasters (now called "staff meteorologists" on local TV and radio), fortune-tellers, or bookmakers. The political columnist touts the success or failure of a presidency and the political pollster predicts what the outcome would be "if the election were held today." We encounter in Chapters Three and Four several examples of pundits acting as latter-day political oracles.

Oracles, of course, enact a Delphic role stemming not from their possession of a universal science or articulation of a cultural story but from their abilities at prescience. An oracle does not voice a universal truth or a cultural story; rather she or he attempts to presage the unknowns of time through prediction (or sometimes retrodiction, namely; understanding the past) as either a cautionary warning of future possibilities to be avoided or a foreshadowing of future necessities that will come to pass regardless. More often than not, the Delphic prediction can be a self-fulfilling prophecy that comes true precisely because it was predicted. (Think of the economic forecaster who predicts that the value of shares in Oracle, Inc., will plunge; stockholders hear the prediction, sell to avoid a loss, glut the market with shares, and thus ensure that the prediction of a plunge is on the mark.)

Each of these venerable priestly, bardic, and sagely oracular approaches to punditry, of course, dates back several centuries. Moreover, as we shall describe in Part One, pundits practice each approach in contemporary America. The ancient priests of the ziggurats were the forerunners of priestly groups, but so too were the philosophical groups of Greece, such as the Pythagoreans, the Platonic and Aristotelian scholars, and the Sophists. They pioneered the art of itinerant priestliness with a reputation for special knowledge. Like the priestly pundits of modern times that we shall discuss in Chapter One, those of yore moved in elite circles and espoused esoteric doctrines. They held no public offices yet acted as advisers to rulers who were desirous of learning the secrets and mysteries of governance. In that respect they were the earliest of the pundits to specialize in campaign and policy analysis and whom we shall consider in Chapter Four.

The prophets of ancient Israel performed in bardic fashion. Although they possessed priestly attributes as well, such as their claim to special access to the deity, their true power was in their assertion of speaking for Israel against elites who had lost touch with both divine and popular will. They were unofficial critics of power, holding no portfolios of government yet taken seriously by governors. Jeremiah, Isaiah, and others became powerful as itinerant and holy bards who defended the special cultural identity of Israel against elite malfeasance. Like many subsequent bards, religious or secular, they spoke for the populist notion that *vox populi vox Dei* (the voice of the people is the voice of god). The bardic pundits whom we analyze in Chapter Two (and many of the talk show personalities whom we consider in Chapter Five) share a similar view, namely, that virtue resides in the folk wisdom of the "man [or woman] in the street."

### The Trendy Pundits: Thinkers, Talkers, and Critics

The modern pundit, by and large, seeks an answer not to the journalist's question of what's happening? but rather to the question of *who knows* what's happening? News is the first-order palpable response to the widespread interest in what is going on; newsworthy punditry is a second-order, "abstracted" response to the query of who knows what is occurring. In contemporary political punditry, the search for an answer to "Who knows?" frequently involves the venerable priestly, bardic, and oracular approaches of old. There are, however, fashionable, trendy, and timely variations on these ancient practices, variations that add their own particular nuances of punditry.

In current politics, punditry has become a popular art form. Punditry proliferates, in part, because editors of newspapers and newsmagazines, radio executives, and TV producers think it sells. Consider our national newsweeklies. *Newsweek* features a "Conventional Wisdom Watch," and *Time*, a "Talking Heads Sweepstakes." Both glean and report the current inside opinions created by in-house pundits—a version of Hollywood and the fashion world's views on "who's hot and who's not." That punditry can be merchandised is, however, not the only reason why it proliferates. With the arrival of cable, and then satellite, television punditry shifted from a cottage industry of the occasional priest, bard, or oracle to the growth industry of media personalities, which includes thinkers, analysts, and experts, talk show hosts, guests, and callers, and a vast array of media critics. We explore these fashionable types of punditry in detail in Part Two, "Current Trends in Political Punditry." Here is a brief preview of such trends.

As TV channels increased across the spectrum with the spread of cable and satellite facilities, the demand for programs to air increased. Old movies, reruns of "The Andy Griffith Show" and "Leave It to Beaver," tractor pulls, and around-the-clock sermons could not satisfy the demand forever. There is, however, the old adage that "talk is cheap." Producers discovered that with punditry in fashion, it could be programmed, aired, and marketed with relatively little expense. Today there is virtually an inexhaustible supply of public forums available for punditry on television. One network, the Cable Satellite Public Affairs Network (C-SPAN), when not airing congressional proceedings, provides almost wall-to-wall punditry. Cable News Network (CNN), Consumer News and Business Channel (CNBC), Financial News Network (FNN) all added to the glut of media punditry. Punditry has not been limited to politics. Thus, FNN has a regular roundup of oracular predictions about the future of the stock market called "Guru Review"; ESPN (Entertainment Sports Programming Network) and Sportsvision program groups of sports pundits discussing current events in the sports world; The Nashville Network (TNN) features "good old boys" sitting around talking authoritatively about hunting and fishing; and, during the professional football season, viewers can find on the USA network the punditry of professional gamblers, selling their services and advising on "The Line" of a given game.

What qualifies people to participate in such roundtable discussions and forums, to be interviewed, to opine, to pontificate, and to prognosticate at such length? Usually it is a reputation for expertise in some political area, such as campaigns and elections, domestic policy, foreign policy, the environment, or drugs abuse. In short, they must possess special knowledge; they must know what other people do not and cannot know. "Should TV news conduct political polls?" Interested viewers could have watched C-SPAN for 90 minutes on October 20, 1989, and learned the special knowledge and insights on this problem of Jeff Alderman, director of polling for ABC News; Ken Bode, director of the Center for Contemporary Media; Douglas Davis, art and media critic for the *New York Times*; Robert Hannaford, a professor of philosophy; and Everett Ladd, a political scientist and director of the Center for Public Opinion Research. Similarly, you may pick almost any other leading question during any given week throughout the year. C-SPAN (which should be an acronym for the "Cable Satellite Pundits' Authority Network") will round up a band of thinkers, scholars, experts, specialists, and analysts to probe, ponder, and pontificate. In Chapter Four, we ourselves probe and ponder the role of pundits who parade as thinkers, experts, and technicians.

A professional journalist, columnist, and pundit, Christopher Hitchens (1987), offered insights into the workings of another set of fashionable punditry. We speak of the pundits who appear as hosts, guests, and callers on "talk" radio and TV. Hitchens dubbed the genre "conversational television." Afficianados of such talk shows find them lively, insightful, and enlightening, characterized by spontaneous outpourings of wit, wisdom, and special knowledge, but Hitchens suggested that this is not the case. He called them "audio-visual chewing gum" which is "so arranged as to act as an echo chamber for politicians and a tiny repertory of pundits" (p. 75).

Moreover, Hitchens said of talk shows, "they are fixed. Rigged" (p.

75). For example, the White House brings pressure on TV networks to tone down hostile or probing questioning on interview programs by refusing to allow administration figures to appear with certain reporters. As a result "the questioning is anodyne and sycophantic, a form of helpful prompting" (p. 76). Political talk shows consisting of exchanges between reporters, Hitchens charged, were rehearsed not only to let reporters predetermine what they were going to say, but also to prevent some things from being said at all. For example, when nationally syndicated columnist George Will of "This Week with David Brinkley" (see Chapter Five) was ridiculed by cartoonist and pundit Gary Trudeau in *Doonesbury*, Will forbade fellow pundit Sam Donaldson from making any reference to the cartoon during a rehearsal run-through; on the air, no *Brinkley* panelist spoke of the cartoon. Concluded Hitchens, "The entire media culture of Washington [has] been conditioned for soft lobs, first-name exchanges, and a jostle for the eye of [White House media controllers]." We explore the world of talking punditry in detail in Chapter Five.

Until his death in 1963, A. J. Liebling was a sensitive and acute observer of the workings of journalism and the press. He was sometimes caustic, sometimes humorous, and always conscious of threats to press freedom and performance no matter where those threats might originate. One such threat, he thought, came from the disturbing tendency to drop the label "journalism" and speak instead of "communication." Communication, Liebling wrote (1961) meant "simply getting any idea across"; communication *"has no intrinsic relation to truth"* (emphasis added). Communication, he continued, "is neutral. It can be a peddler's tool, or the weapon of a political knave, or the medium of a new religion." He went on, " 'Journalism' has a reference to what happens day by day, but 'communication' can deal just as well with what has not happened, what the communicator wants to happen, or what he wants the dupe on the other end to think." To illustrate the facile nature of "communication" he wrote this mock exchange:

Q—What do you do for a living?
A—I am a communicator.
Q—What do you communicate? Scarlet fever? Apprehension? (p. 36)

Since Liebling's time another type of punditry has become fashionable. Its practitioners set themselves up to look at what is communicated—on TV and radio and in newspapers; by reporters, journalists, politicians, and, notably, by other pundits. Is it true? Is it accurate? Is it entertaining? Is it science? Is it art? These are the questions they ask and try to answer. As we shall see in a detailed discussion in Chapter Six, these media pundits have several designations and are variously labeled TV reviewers, TV critics, and entertainment reviewers. We will speak of them as media critics. Critics keep abreast of the coverage of politics in all the principal media. There are various types of critics, each performing a specialized brand of media criticism. Politicians, reporters, and pundits sometimes laud the critics, but more frequently, they heap criticism on the critics themselves. Their role in politics and in punditry is increasingly important, and controversial. Whether they communicate anything other than "apprehension" remains to be seen.

## THE FIFTH ESTATE: PUNDITRY ON PUNDITRY?

We have said that media punditry has become a growth industry. That is certainly the case in politics. The various media organizations draw on a corps of people who claim expertise, special knowledge, and the opportunity to demonstrate their authority in public forums. It is the conviction of this book that punditry now constitutes a fifth estate alongside Montesquieu's three and Burke's fourth. Punditry is a knowledge industry that has grown into a political force demanding recognition, understanding, and reckoning. In endeavoring to do so here, we realize that we too are making a claim, namely, to possess knowledge and the right to speak about punditry. Are we thereby pundits of pundits? We leave that to readers to decide after considering what we have to say.

Our major purpose is a form of demystification. We are not bent on exposing media pundits as frauds, although fraudulence we will, on occasion, find, nor do we charge that pundits are foolish or stupid, although we will find instances of such. Nor, too, are we particularly interested in personal profiles that praise or blame particular pundits, although profiles there will be that point to praiseworthy and questionable pundit performances. Rather, our task is to clarify a mystery: Why the pundits? What is it about the contemporary American political condition that magnifies the role of media pundit? Do media authorities constitute a punditocracy? If so, what are the consequences of the existence of a fifth estate for democracy?

These are not merely academic questions. Opinion leadership has long been a subject of interest to social scientists. It is also of no small interest to anyone wishing to know who holds power and who holds power by making their, and our, ideas clear or, perhaps, obscure. If the rise of punditocracy augurs fundamental changes in how we are governed and how we govern ourselves, then it certainly deserves close scrutiny. Thus we must address one of the oldest of questions; Who knows? And a more recent one, *Who knows* who knows?

# PART I

# TRADITIONS OF POLITICAL PUNDITRY

*Chapter One*

# The Priestly Caste: Speaking of, with, and for Political Elites

At least since the early sixteenth century, when Niccolò Machiavelli (1979) emphasized the differences between the "few" and the "many," social scientists have studied in detail the separation and relationship between elites and the mass of humanity. Elites exercise power through access to institutions, acting in institutional roles, ruling, and/or exercising influence over the decisions and reputations of rulers. Thus, "elites are people who occupy power roles in society" (Dye, 1990, p. 4). Power is not restricted merely to persons who occupy positions of formally designated institutional authority. There are also informal roles that number people among the politically elite—a "fat cat" campaign contributor seeking a hearing or favor from a senator; an ad hoc group of "wise men" who meet with a president at a time of crisis; and a journalist cultivated by politicians because of a reputation for influencing public opinion are but three typical examples.

Influence over mass opinions can take many forms. A populist politician rises in the esteem of members of elites if he or she has the "support" of, or understands "the pulse" of "the public." Organized propaganda campaigns by interest groups acquire reputations among elites and masses alike for almost "magical" powers if political observers attribute shifts in public sentiment to them. Certainly a major, and often decisive, form of power is to claim to see and say what is happening in the context of elite circles of power, to shape whom elites take seriously and whom they do not. Who makes such claims, purporting to know what is happening among elites? Who thereby has power over elite opinion? If elite opinion is, as political scholars since Machiavelli have insisted, preponderantly important, then those who influence powerful elites are themselves considered powerful.

Harkening back to the ideas of sociologist Max Weber (1947), power involves the chance that one's will is asserted and accepted in a community setting despite resistance or indifference to that will. Given Weber's view of power, the means that are necessary and proper to maximizing power chances are key to exercising power at all. Among those means are strategies of influence and persuasion that command the attention of, and make an impression on, elites. Such strategies guide elites in formal and informal positions of governing authority. They are key elements in forming networks of political communication within and across elite groups.

Elites talk to one another about what is occurring; they have a stake in knowing what is going on. Because of their formal and informal positions of influence, members of political elites are "insiders." However, there is no assurance that they are necessarily more knowledgeable or wiser than anyone else about what is happening. In the wake of unfolding and puzzling events, elites, too, seek out people with a reputation for special knowledge about what is going on; in other words, elites turn to those "who know." Since members of political elites cannot know everything, they count on persons who specialize in doing so, or at least have a reputation for doing so. They seek out pundits.

One venerable pundit that speaks to, of, with, and for elites is the priest, whom we introduced in the preceding chapter. Modern American pundits are obviously not priests in the traditional sense of occupying a role in a formal priestly caste connected with a church or temple. However, they do perform priestly functions that render the priestly metaphor appropriate. A priestly pundit is one whose reputation, however achieved or deserved, yields stature among political elites. The priest, although occupying no formal or informal position of authority within the elite circle, still moves within it. The priest has access to elite members and is at ease among them. The priest not only speaks to them and with them, but has permission to speak of and for them to those outside elite circles. Moreover, members of political elites trust the priests' word for what is happening within and outside the elite circle. In sum, the priest mediates political knowledge among insiders (elites) and between insiders and outsiders (the populace mass).

This obviously highly privileged, and highly prized, role of the priestly pundit yields a political caste, a priesthood not of "believers" but of possessors of special knowledge. It is a priesthood that guards closely its reputation for knowing "what's really happening"; its right to speak to, with, of, and for political insiders; and its "by invitation only" membership in the caste. There is no school for this priesthood, no specified credentials, no vows, and no solemn rituals of initiation. The one qualification for membership appears to be acceptance by elder priests of the acolyte as "one of us." Such acceptance hinges chiefly on the capacity of the new Brahman members to exhibit (as in exhibitionist) mastery of the style, language, and confidence of the priesthood.

In this chapter we explore the tradition of the priestly pundit in American politics. We look first at the general style and manner of the priestly pundit. We turn then to some specific priests in the tradition of American punditry: noted columnist Walter Lippmann, radio commentator H. V. Kaltenborn, and the "conscience" of CBS News, Edward R. Murrow. As news values have changed during the television era, so too has the priestly style and language. We look at a member of the priesthood who contributed considerably to stylistic change, Eric Sevareid, and to what the changes have wrought.

## THE PRIESTLY MUSE

Priestly pundits are members of an establishment. They are also establishmentarian. We employ *establishment* here in its strict dictionary sense, namely, a group that tacitly controls a given activity, usually in a manner to preserve that control. Any political elite comprises a loose collectivity of one or more political establishments. For instance, active and retired military officers constitute a military establishment. President Dwight Eisenhower, upon leaving office in 1961, warned of the dangers of the United States being subverted by a "military-industrial complex," a defense establishment.

The priestly establishment is a loose collectivity of journalists, analysts, policy experts, and other specialists who voice their special knowledge in public forums. Be they reporters, feature writers, or columnists; TV correspondents, anchors, or commentators; specialists in law, taxes, the environment, energy, military affairs, or foreign affairs, professing is their profession. They may not know one another but they often do. What unites them is their privileged status as widely recognized, famous public figures whose opinions should be taken seriously. The activity they tacitly control is that of interpreting what is occurring for political elites and nonelites. In so doing, they seek to preserve control over their own reputations for being among those "who know."

Priestly pundits are establishmentarians in the sense that they rub elbows and speak to, with, of, and for established elites in political, economic, military, and other corridors of power. Consider some noted newspaper journalist of priestly status: Tom Wicker of the *New York Times*, David Broder of the *Washington Post*, or Al Hunt of the *Wall Street Journal*. Priests profess to insiders and the interested that, in effect, "this is where the action is, where the important people relate, where big stakes are commonplace." Were a priest to level with us, the Brahman might confide:

I may authoritatively speak of elites because I have access to them, and therefore know of whom and of what I speak. I not only speak of them, I also speak *to* them. I can speak of a "senior official" because I spoke to that official. I am a highly placed and reliable source because I speak to "highly placed and reliable sources." For the benefit of those without access to the inner circles of temples and palaces, I will tell you what the people who matter are thinking and doing or should be thinking and doing.

If called upon, and I often am, I can—but only if *I* choose—be a spokesperson for the official line, touting an elite policy or politician, or supporting the regime against its detractors. Or, as is also my wont, I may attack particular politicians and policies. Don't get me wrong, however. I support the established way of doing things, whether I agree or disagree in print. The establishment is, after all, what provides me with my status as priest. I have a vested interest in its perpetuation and will not undermine it. I will not pull back the curtain on the wizard and reveal him to be a mere mortal. Instead, I cloak my support or criticism of elites I *know* in the mysteries of power that I also *know*. Thereby I serve Established Innocence.

The term *muse* derives from the nine sister goddesses of Greek mythology who presided over forms of expression: songs and poetry and the arts and sciences. More generally, the term applies to a "guiding genius," someone who muses or reflects and ponders on important matters. A priestly pundit muses on politics and instructs the opinions of the informed elites and the ignorant masses. The musings of the political priest are mini-sermons that define the political situation for the benefit of the powers that be. Moreover, being in the service of those powers—and in the service of the priestly establishment—makes the musement of the priestly pundit distinct.

The musement of the priest is not the "pure play" of "Musement" of which philosopher Charles Sanders Peirce wrote (1958, p. 360). Peirce's Musement involved "a lively exercise of one's powers" with "no rules, except this very law of liberty," wherein the mind scans "universes of experience" (ideas, brute action, and signs) for "some connection" (quoted in Seboek and Eco, 1983, p. 26). Priestly punditry is not an exercise in free inquiry. Pundits direct their musings at and for those who rule and, hence, cannot simply cast them as "pure play" lest they not be taken seriously. Priestly punditry is scarcely a form of *a*musement, since it is about the supposedly serious business of advising serious elites on weighty matters. Even the musing of a priestly pundit such as syndicated columnist, talk show host, and publisher William F. Buckley, Jr. (though peppered with humor, wit, and satire), speaks to serious elite concerns (see Chapter Five).

The musement of the priestly pundit is actually a form of *be*musement. That is, at one and the same time it is engrossed in deep, serious thought and cast in language that confuses, even stupefies. Pundit musing is a reflection on and articulation of the language of elite rule. That language is, to use psychologist William Stephenson's (1967) distinction, one of work rather than play. Work is serious activity, not undertaken for its own sake but to achieve an end; in other words, one works for a wage. Play is nonserious, to be enjoyed for its own sake and then, perhaps, forgotten. Work is interested rather than disinterested, always constrained by elaborate communication rules rather than the "law of liberty."

Priestly musing is not dreamy speculation; rather, it is formulated with a political logic applied to the elite conduct of affairs of state. In typical manifestations, such as columnists' musing on the op-ed page of major newspapers, priestly pundits frame their thoughts in Machiavellian language as if they were advising a king. The esoteric code they articulate is a political language of words and images that give metaphorical support to the conduct of rule even as it may criticize the conduct of those who do rule. As Lessl (1989), noted, the rhetoric of the priest descends "from above as an epiphanic Word, filled with mystery and empowered with extra-human authority" (p. 185). Even though in their role as pundits political priests are manipulators of political symbols in public commentaries on politics, they are also the guardians of political symbols, for by extolling how things should "really be done" under the constitutional arrangement that is "the American way," they ultimately defend the mystery surrounding governance and, thereby, the hierarchy of power that the mystery underpins. Thus does musing become bemusing.

In classical rhetorical terms, political priests are the guardians of Logos, the expression of political reason in the words they use to explain, yet shroud, the established political and priestly order in impenetrable mystery. Political priests perform in didactic and persuasive ways: They both instruct the few about the wisdom of right action and teach the many about the wisdom of the correctly instructed few. (We shall see in Chapter Two that bards, in contrast to priests, are bearers of pathos, appealing to popular emotions rather than elite reason, while oracles and sages, as we note in Chapter Three, concentrate on ethos, attempting to glean the character of unfolding events leading to a predictable future.)

Priestly pundits thus conduct institutionalized rituals of reasonable discourse, exploiting elite tongues and tones that wrap events in a rhetorical aura of bemusement. Priestly musing demonstrates mastery of both the esoteric, obscure code that shrouds the mystery of power, and of the ability to translate that unspeakable knowledge into an exoteric,

popular code comprehensible to political "junkies" who are attentive to
public affairs media featuring priestly sermonettes. The pundit of priestly
robes is analogous to the tribal hungan, a gifted seeker of higher knowledge who journeys to the gods and then returns to make momentarily
real to tribespeople things that otherwise they could scarcely imagine.
The *hungan* (and the priestly pundit) perform for the tribe a rite of
possession that deciphers possessed esoteric knowledge into shared exoteric talk (see Kertzer, 1988).

Political priests thereby create, enhance, and preserve "terministic
screens" (Burke, 1968, pp. 44–62), a priestly vocabulary that *selects*
"what's happening," *deflects* other things that are happening, and *reflects*
the pundit's privileged status as one "who knows." Priestly pundits are
thus guardians not only of political knowledge but also of the language
of that knowledge. Their musing is not idle talk but rather the language
of power as articulated by a priestly caste. Even though bespeaking the
language of power gives them intellectual status and access to the powerful, the terministic screens of the political priesthood limit and direct
their own perspective. Political priests, like those they serve in various
establishments, develop the "trained incapacity" to think or talk outside
the linguistic perspective that they use to pundificate. Therefore, they
are not only guardians but also prisoners of the hierarchical mystery
that they are so proud to be an integral part of and to report. Ironically,
they run the risk of becoming captives of their own mystery, enshrouded
in their own bemusement. This becomes particularly the case if the
priestly quest to find out "what's happening" erodes in an era of entertainment values, only to be supplanted by a quest for the fame of
being one "who knows." Let us examine the background and emergence
of that phenomenon.

## FROM PRIESTLY SOUND IDEAS TO PRIESTLY
## SOUND BITES

In his book *The Last Intellectuals*, Russell Jacoby (1987) argued that one
of the great changes in the intellectual life of the United States in this
century has been the disappearance of the "public intellectual." By public intellectual he means politically minded intellects who ponder and
write important and weighty ideas. Public intellectuals, Jacoby argued,
are essential to a society because they articulate for educated and interested citizens a sound, well-founded sense of context: where we have
been, where we are now, where we are going, and where we should
be going. By extension, public intellectuals are vital for a political community because they provide those involved in immediate matters of
ruling with a sound, grounded political context for action. Every political
order requires a "brain trust" (i.e., brains one can *trust*). Public intel-

lectuals perform an indispensable pragmatic function by thinking about important aspects of problems of governance. Jacoby has in mind such figures of an earlier generation as Lionel Trilling, Edmund Wilson, and Lewis Mumford—few in number, but of sufficient intellectual stature to be taken seriously for their considered ideas, which are typically contained in books read by people who mattered.

Public intellectuals were not strictly speaking priestly pundits. They tended to be independent scholars working alone, striving for a disinterested comprehension of what is important and what needs doing, and largely out of the limelight. Jacoby's ideal public intellectual—largely as a byproduct of his or her curiosity and devoid of pleading on behalf of special interests—provided those involved in teaching, reporting, or governing with a larger view of things. For example, a university professor, book review editor, or government functionary could read Lewis Mumford's trilogy (*Technics and Civilization*, 1934; *The Culture of Cities*, 1938; and *The Condition of Man*, 1944) and learn about the effects of modern technology on urban life. Public intellectuals commanded deference out of the substance and independence of their thoughts, ideas that owed little to the establishment ties and confusing vocabulary characteristic of priestly punditry.

Public intellectuals are, Jacoby argued, now extinct. In part, he said, this is due to the growth of academia. Independent scholars cannot support themselves today, so they respond to the lure of university tenure and the professorial life. Being published takes precedence over being prescient, and being subsidized, over being of substance. Alternatively, they seek security by undertaking research supported financially by government agencies, private corporations, or special interest groups. In the process, they become priests beholden to colleges and universities that are funded privately or publicly, and/or move in establishments of academic and political power bent upon self-enhancement and self-preservation. (We explore the locales of these priestly intellectuals in Chapter Four.)

However, more has been at work in the eclipse of the public intellectual and the rise of the priestly pundit than the incarceration of thinkers in academic halls, bureaucratic offices, and corporate suites. The increasing role played by the mass media in this century has also pushed aside the public intellectual. Through the likes of, say, *USA Today*'s editorial page views of ordinary citizens, Willard Scott's interviews with the man in the street on "Today," calls to radio's "The Larry King Show," and "My Turn" columns in *Newsweek*, anyone with a forum to comment or complain can go public. For a brief moment, anyone can be something more important than a public intellectual, namely, anybody can be "somebody."

The drift from respect for the public intellectual to fascination with public fame came about in part because of the logical requirements of the popular media that characterized the post–World War II era (Althiede and Snow, 1979). As the pace of life quickened, so did that of the mass media, and especially the news media. Journalists created various formats as a response to the quickened pace of life and a rising demand for instant information. News content adjusted to the format for presenting it. The news media reflected the demands of an "immediate society" with interests in the here and now. The temporal context of information—a major concern of public intellectuals—was irrelevant. To avoid being boring, news formats adopted techniques of entertainment programming: short news items, provocative pictures, human interest pieces, friendly banter, bright colors, and graphics. News was restricted to the *new*, isolating information from its continuity with the past and its trends for the future.

Gradually the conventions of "news analysis" changed. Lengthy musing and reflection—in print or on the air—yielded to personalized, bemusing, entertaining writing and speech. Such changes had been hinted at long before the advent of radio or TV. For example, the development of the newspaper op-ed helped give rise to the "column" written under the personal byline of a new kind of journalist, the columnist. Political columnists pioneered a new priesthood of pundits. They were masters of news reduction: of reducing inside information and molding opinion via a few hundred words a day that appealed to a wide popular audience. This did not mean that columnists were unqualified to speak or had nothing to say; quite the contrary. However, it did mean that the columnist performed a new priestly role dictated by the realities of the media environment: be topical, not contextual; be terse, not prolix; be popular, not erudite; and be reductionist, not analytic. In addition, they must meet a deadline—daily, or two to three times a week.

### Legitimizing a Priestly Tradition: Walter Lippmann

Although not the first political columnist—a distinction often reserved by journalism historians for David Lawrence (Rivers, 1965)—Walter Lippmann was perhaps the key figure in the creation of the American tradition of the priestly pundit. Lippmann's career gave both impetus and legitimacy to the transition from public intellectual to journalistic priest. Lippmann was both. Born in 1889, he came of age in the twentieth century; before his death in 1974, he had served as an editor; adviser to presidents from Theodore Roosevelt to Richard Nixon (he was instrumental in drafting Woodrow Wilson's "Fourteen Points" that outlined U.S. proposals for peace at the end of World War I); author of books on politics, journalism, and philosophy; and the most distinguished political pundit of his era. Indeed, when publisher Henry Luce started

*Time* magazine, he used "pundit" as a courtesy title for two people: playwright Thornton Wilder and columnist Walter Lippmann (Safire, 1978).

Lippmann began his long and illustrious career as a public intellectual, yet pioneered journalistic punditry and acquired sage status as the dean of political columnists whose pronouncements were avidly awaited by politicians in Washington, D.C. Through his early writing, Lippmann was instrumental in legitimating the priestly status of journalists as intellectuals. In a series of works in the 1920s, most notably his *Public Opinion* (1922), he critiqued the new profession of journalism for the role it could, and should, play in the governing of modern society. He argued that democracy did not work in the way it was originally conceived. Public opinion was unstable and uninformed, and thus could not be relied on for forming rational judgments. The world was now too complex, decisions were too technical, and administrative direction too indispensable to leave to electoral choice or the whims of the masses.

What was demanded was a "way of overcoming the subjectivism of human opinion based on the limitation of individual experience" (Lippmann, 1922, p. 249). Since most people respond to symbols and stereotypes, news had hitherto catered to the consumer of news at that level. Journalists, Lippmann argued; must go beyond that. There must be "organized intelligence" based on quality information rather than news that was dramatized, fragmented, and out of context. Lippmann advocated a professional press corps knowledgeable of social science that could interpret, not reduce, information so that citizens could understand and be persuaded to proper courses of action. For Lippmann, professional journalists would have special status. After all, "every complicated community has sought the assistance of special men, of augurs, priests, elders". The journalist would join a technocratic elite which was possessed of skills to probe the nature of things and to communicate special knowledge to the mass public. Journalism would become not only an art but also a science. News would provide not stereotypes but a "picture of reality" on which citizens could act (p. 233).

Not everyone shared Lippmann's view of the journalist as intellectual. Philosopher John Dewey, a public intellectual of considerable reputation, thought Lippmann's notion of the public was in error. Lippmann painted the public as passive and dumb, not qualified for self-government. Moreover, in making the press an "objective" force of communication, Lippmann abrogated journalism's responsibility for provoking "conversation" among people. As summed up by James W. Carey (1989), Dewey was troubled that if Lippmann's view prevailed, the

press, by seeing its role as that of informing the public, abandons its role as an agency for carrying on the conversation of our culture. We lack not only an effective press but certain vital habits: the ability to follow an argument, grasp the point of view of another, expand the boundaries of understanding, and debate the alternative purposes that might be pursued. (p. 82)

The absence of a contentious and pluralistic press, then, would lead to the atrophy of "vital habits," and thus further reduce citizens' incentives to be politically active.

Dewey had a more sanguine view of American democracy than Lippmann, to be sure. Lippmann took a more "elitist" approach, stressing the limits and furies of mass opinion as an unstable way of governing while expressing faith in the potential rationality of elites. Carey labeled Lippmann's notions "the spectator theory." The public is "a second-order spectator: a spectator of the spectator." People are to watch and heed what other people (journalists) see and interpret. For Lippmann, knowledge rests in vision rather than speech. Citizens observe events rather than take part via talk. People watch politics through the news media and, in the process, deny themselves any active role except "to ratify a political world already represented—a depoliticized world in which all the critical choices have been made by the experts" (p. 82).

Criticisms of Lippmann's views regarding democracy aside, he prevailed in two important respects. First, schools of journalism and colleges of communication have established (as in "establishment") programs for training journalists in reporting "objective" information. At least in that restricted sense, journalism has become professional. Second, Lippmann's view of the general public, or populace, as uninformed, and of a separate attentive public, or elite, possessing a potential for absorbing objective, interpreted information left its mark. If journalists are specialists in information, which ruling elites must have to govern, then the role of the journalist is not that of a reporter so much as it is of a mediator, even an adviser, to rulers. In short, the journalist acts as a priestly pundit, representing elites to themselves and to the populace. John Dewey's "conversation of democracy" is, so to speak, one-sided: from pundits to elites and from pundits to the populace.

Lippmann continued to write thoughtful books in his long career but was more widely known in the role he helped to create: priestly pundit to elites, rulers, and the masses. During a brief thaw in the Cold War in the 1950s, the Soviet Union invited American journalists to visit, and many did so. Lippmann, however, resisted overtures and invitations for him to travel to the USSR. When a correspondent asked him why he had not taken the opportunity to visit Moscow immediately and be the first journalist to interview Soviet ruler Nikita Khrushchev, Lippmann responded, "I am not a reporter" (Rivers, 1965, p. 59).

Indeed he was not. Lippmann prized his objectivity and detachment. Columnists should not "regard themselves as public personages with a constituency to which they are responsible" or as "engaged in a public career on the stage of the world rather than as an observant writer of newspaper articles about some of the things that are happening in the world." Referring to the dictum of a journalistic mentor, he quipped that "more newspapermen had been ruined by self-importance than by liquor." Lippmann was a scrupulous professional who recognized limits to notoriety, warning that the "individual writer is not a public person-age, or at least ought not to be . . . nor is he a public institution, nor is he the repository of 'influence' and 'leadership'." Rather, the writer is a

commentator who lays before his readers his findings on the subjects he has studied and leaves it at that. He cannot cover the universe, and if he begins to imagine that he is called to such a universal mission, he will soon . . . be saying less and less about more and more until at last he is saying nothing about everything. (quoted in Steel, 1980, pp. 388–389)

Here, then, was a transitional figure. Lippmann prized the virtues of the public intellectual: detachment, objectivity, and contextual under-standing. However, his career made legitimate for a host of imitators a different set of virtues—being on the inside, speaking to and for elites, being "in the know" and "up to date," and famous. Lippmann suc-cessfully moved from public intellectual to public personage. Whether he wished it or not, he proved that one could be both a highly regarded intellect and a political celebrity. He made the role of pundit so alluring that his career expanded priestly punditry. Although few could approach his stature as an intellect and as a political force, the precedent he set provided an ideal for aspiring journalists. Which was the ideal, however: the "commentator" who "lays before his readers his findings" and then "leaves it at that," or the pundit "called to a special mission," soon "saying less and less about more and more until at last he is saying nothing about everything?"

## H. V. Kaltenborn: Priestly Punditry on the Radio

We have seen that the priesthood of pundits drew impetus from the rise of the columnist. David Lawrence, Walter Lippmann, Arthur Krock, and others perfected a formula familiar today to any newspaper or news-magazine reader. With the advent of radio there was an opportunity for new formats of punditry. Since a medium like radio reached many more people than newspapers, a radio forum for commentary had vast priestly potential.

In what today is called in nostalgic terms "the golden age of radio," there were numerous "news commentators" who, like political columnists, were not so much reporters of the news as interpreters, analysts, and opinion molders. Typically, each had fifteen minutes of daily air time commentary, five nights a week. Many of the better known commentators cut their teeth as correspondents in the 1930s and 1940s. The names of Lowell Thomas, Elmer Davis, William L. Shirer, Raymond Gram Swing, and Edward R. Murrow (see below) were regular visitors in American households via radio (Hosley, 1984).

One of the most popular radio commentators was H. V. Kaltenborn, for many years a familiar voice on various radio networks. Kaltenborn was a German-American whose distinctive accent and lively, clipped speech made his voice instantly recognizable. Even without TV, his face was also well known, for Kaltenborn was not shy of publicity, calling himself "Dean of News Commentators." He wrote books, lectured widely, and even made a cameo appearance in Frank Capra's Hollywood movie *Mr. Smith Goes to Washington*.

Kaltenborn put his priestly knowledge, voice, and face to work in the service of post–World War II U.S. foreign policy. Kaltenborn was well into his sixties and held the position of "foreign affairs commentator" for NBC radio. His listener ratings were the highest in the nation, giving him an audience in the millions, and he reached more people than any other single voice speaking on foreign policy. His broadcasts inspired newspaper editorials, letters and telegrams to Congress or the White House by the thousands, and responses to him from officials in the government whom he chose to attack.

Kaltenborn helped legitimate American foreign policy toward Europe in general, and the Soviet Union in particular, through his post–World War II broadcasts. He was extremely critical of the Soviet Union as early as the spring of 1945, well before the U.S. State Department, in the administration of President Harry Truman, voiced suspicions about Soviet intentions. By 1946 and 1947 Kaltenborn had become a leading voice in a priestly chorus arguing for a tough line against the Russians. He became the Cold War's pundit in spite of the fact that he had praised the Soviets during the war against Nazi Germany. As the international climate shifted after the war, so did Kaltenborn. This was in part because, having a priestly presence on the inside of what was going on, he sensed an inevitable shift in policy toward the Stalinist regime in the Soviet Union. Kaltenborn realized that as the Soviets pursued territorial aims in Eastern Europe at the expense of such nations as Poland and Czechoslovakia, the United States would be moved to oppose such Stalinist ambitions. Moreover, he knew well that there had been apprehensions among both elites and the populace about Soviet Communism in spite of the loyalty of the Russian allies in World War II.

By running ahead of U.S. foreign policy in 1945 and then being a major priestly spokesman for it once it had cooled toward the Soviet

Union, Kaltenborn illustrates another characteristic of the pundit as priest. As a radio commentator, Kaltenborn knew not only members of various establishments but also his audience. Through his commentaries he mediated between elites—both those elite policy officials who supported the Soviet Union and those who were in opposition—and his populist audience that exhibited a long-term antipathy toward Communism and the politicians who were charged with making U.S. foreign policy. In his priestly commentaries he put on the agenda for elite, official, and popular discussion the possibilities of a shift in policy. He thus helped make acceptable to a variety of audiences a policy position that, a few years earlier, would have been unmentionable.

Like priests of old, Kaltenborn spoke from the pulpit not only to the parishioners who listened to him but also to the hierarchy of the political church, those in power who found it prudent to heed a priest who was influential with his flock and versed in a political doctrine of "right action." If official actions are indeed "right," the priest's praise and support for the hierarchy goes a long way in legitimating policy among the faithful. Kaltenborn as priest acted to reform the church (America) to which he belonged, but as Erasmus seeking change, not Martin Luther demanding revolution. What distinguishes a media priest like Kaltenborn is a recognition that criticism strengthens rather than weakens the political order. The task of the pundit is the rectification of error by guiding those who err toward truth (Liebovich, 1987).

### Edward R. Murrow: Priestly Punditry on TV

With the arrival of television, many of the disembodied voices listened to for punditry on radio faded from the scene. Taking their place were the "talking heads" of the TV screen, persons with striking appearances or styles to complement priestly words spoken with an inspiring voice. One widely known radio commentator who made a successful transition to television was Edward R. Murrow of CBS. Murrow brought an impressive reputation from radio news, based most notably on his live broadcasts from London during the Nazi blitz. He aired numerous reports while dramatically, and dangerously, perching on rooftops where he could see and describe the bombs falling around him. What Bernard Shaw and his CNN colleagues won acclaim for in 1991 while reporting bombing raids on Baghdad from their hotel room during the opening of the Gulf War, Murrow had made routine a half century earlier. Murrow's ritual introduction to those broadcasts—"*This* [lengthy pause] is London"—became a familiar signature line during the blitz. (The pause was on the advice of his college drama coach.) Murrow had a commanding voice on radio, an articulate and authoritative aura, and a reputation for integrity. Today we would say that he possessed charisma.

Murrow believed that network journalism should be the gadfly and watchdog of the state, telling listeners what they could not find out for themselves. He conceived his role in priestly terms, as he once wrote to his parents during the war:

I remember you once wanted me to be a preacher, but I had not faith, except in myself. But now I am preaching from a powerful pulpit. Often I am wrong but I am trying to talk as I would have talked were I a preacher. One need not wear a reversed collar to be honest. (quoted in Gates, 1978, p. 15)

Murrow's priestly pulpit was broadcast news, a pulpit that was made all the more powerful when he entered the TV scene.

Murrow's evangelism as a pundit was tempered by his membership in another establishment, the CBS priesthood. Even though the network had gathered a formidable array of journalistic talent, there were still considerable internal and external constraints on what politically sensitive areas broadcasts could touch. With the advent of TV, CBS had a massive audience and could dramatize political issues on news programming in striking ways. However, CBS executives were ever mindful of going too far in politically controversial areas and thus alienating that audience. This was a major concern in the early 1950s when the fear of Communism as an alien force threatening the United States reached paranoic proportions.

Leading the charge against the "Red Menace" was U.S. Senator Joseph McCarthy, Republican of Wisconsin. McCarthy crusaded to remove all Communists, sympathizers, and fellow travelers from government and nongovernment positions on grounds that their presence might threaten the American Way. In the span of a few years in the early 1950s, McCarthy became a seemingly unstoppable force in American national politics, attacking a wide variety of people and institutions for their Communist sympathies, pasts, and ties. His targets extended well beyond government officials and included news organizations and correspondents, especially pundits who criticized and opposed him and what he stood for.

Not all pundits opposed McCarthy. Among his supporters were radio commentator Fulton Lewis, Jr., and even H. V. Kaltenborn, who supported McCarthy's early attacks on the Truman administration. The more widely publicized McCarthy's tactics were, the bolder he became; thus he became even more controversial. By 1954 the senator from Wisconsin possessed a considerable following, yet it was becoming easier to oppose him, for he was proving an embarrassment and nuisance to the new Republican administration of President Dwight Eisenhower.

Kaltenborn abandoned his defense after McCarthy attacked an army general, arguing that power had corrupted McCarthy. Other priestly pundits, such as Marquis Childs, James Reston, and Drew Pearson, openly rebuked McCarthy as his charges and antics grew more outrageous. CBS radio pundits Elmer Davis and Eric Sevareid also criticized McCarthy openly.

Throughout the time of McCarthy's rise, friends and colleagues urged Edward Murrow to use his popular television forum, "See It Now," to take on McCarthy. Murrow was the high priest at CBS, someone whose prestige might turn the tide against the Senator. Viewed from the perspective of McCarthy's admirers, Murrow became a high priest of a different sort, one who cut out their hero's heart. In March 1954, "See It Now" aired a controversial thirty-minute documentary on McCarthy that used the senator's own words and public performances to draw attention to his excesses.

The program was a breakthrough in priestly punditry. It depicted for viewers for the first time the senator in person and in action. What emerged was a depiction that was a far cry from the mythic "Joe" of self-promotion and right-wing fanfare that had been trumpeted in newspaper accounts. Murrow acted as a guide to McCarthy's demonic tactics with a priestly air of urbane disdain and condescension that contrasted sharply with McCarthy's recorded crudeness, abrasiveness, and absence of civility or compassion. Viewers witnessed a learned priest who was experienced in the folly of lesser mortals exposing a false prophet who had mocked the values of the established political church under the guise of protecting them. Here was McCarthy enunciating, all giggles and sneers, his usual array of charges and bullying, followed by Murrow's priestly correction of error and untruth. Murrow invoked the priestly authority of editorial writers whom he identified as not "left-wing," but who nonetheless had joined the opposition to McCarthy, among them the staff of the conservative *Chicago Tribune*. Here was corroborating proof that the high priest of CBS was no Jeremiah standing alone in his concern about McCarthy nor a rival political force out on a singular vendetta against a great patriot. Murrow concluded with a priestly sentence, accusing McCarthy of confusing the Communist issue to the point of causing "alarm and dismay among our allies abroad" and even, ironically enough, of giving "considerable comfort to our enemies," the very charge "the senator" used against his targets (Quoted from the CBS-TV *See It Now* of March 9, 1954, in Rosteck, 1989, p. 285).

Murrow as a TV pundit thus conducted a ritual of priestly inquisition that gave free rein to the accused to convict himself. McCarthy's words and pictures captured his undeniably questionable tactics and his offensive and untelegenic demeanor. In response to the program, McCarthy challenged Murrow's patriotism and past affiliations. CBS gave Mc-

Carthy equal time in the "See It Now" weekly time slot. McCarthy's defense, a film written in part by yet another pundit, conservative columnist George Sokolsky, attacked Murrow again. Murrow, said McCarthy, was "a symbol, the leader and cleverest of the jackal pack which is always found at the throat of anyone who dares expose individual communists and traitors" (Quoted from the CBS-TV *See It Now* of April 6, 1954, in Sperber, 1986, p. 405). The broadcast did little to restore McCarthy's dignity. Its grainy film quality, montage of scenes weaved together in an amateurish fashion, and rehash of allegations did little more than magnify the very traits that had been publicized on "See It Now." It thereby helped vindicate Murrow's public exposure of the senator's villainy and foolery.

Murrow's role in ending McCarthy's reign of terror is hard to assess. (The U.S. Senate ultimately censured McCarthy on various grounds.) Murrow came to the public fight against McCarthy late in the struggle, yet his showmanship and mastery of the priestly rites of punditry— notably condescension—conducted during a forum of prime-time, national TV added new dimensions to the role of the journalist in American politics. Murrow may not have brought down McCarthy any more than Lippmann avoided fame or Kaltenborn correctly read popular attitudes toward the Soviet Union, but he did contribute to the development of a new era of priestly punditry in an age when newspaper columnists and radio commentators were being supplanted by TV stars (Bayley, 1981; Gates, 1978; Metz, 1975).

### Eric Sevareid: The Search for a Priestly Formula

Neil Postman is an astute student of the shifts wrought in people's views of the world as a result of TV. He has offered a view that helps us understand changes in punditry that are associated with the TV age. Earlier generations of journalistic pundits came from a print culture associated with an "Age of Exposition" and the "typographic" mind (Postman, 1986, p. 63). The logic of discourse in a print culture prompts literate people to exercise reason in understanding the flow of arguments. They think not in pictures but in typescript, not in visual images but in words. Theirs is verbal communication for the eye and/or ear. A newspaper or radio pundit—since radio scripts are but printed words read out loud—caters to the typographic mind of the reader/listener. She or he instinctively attempts to make a logically coherent and sequentially readable argument out of what is written and said.

With the proliferation of television, a new, more "visual," culture, emerged. That culture reflected the "Age of Show Business" (Postman, 1986, p. 63). Broadcasters like Murrow and his boss at CBS, Frank Stanton, had misgivings about that age. Murrow fretted about "the constant striving to reach the largest possible audience for everything," hoping that television could be something other than a toy used to "distract, delude, amuse and insulate us." If that were all television could do, said Murrow, it would be seen by future historians only as "evidence of decadence, escapism, and insulation from realities of the world in which we live. . . . If we go as we are, then history will take its revenge" (Metz, 1975, pp. 289–290). Fret or not, Murrow then solidified his position as a CBS star by becoming the host of "Person to Person," a weekly show that interviewed celebrities in their homes—a forerunner of "The Rich and the Famous." Stanton worried that even CBS News might become an instrument of mass distraction. He conducted a long and losing battle to dissuade TV producers from referring to news programming as "shows," preferring the term "news broadcast" (Gates, 1978, pp. 27–28).

Both Murrow and Stanton foresaw that the news potential of television could be exploited to positive ends but that there were risks that the logic of TV might work against that. The primary mode of communication on television is not the word but the image. TV rests more on the logic of representation than print or radio's logic of argumentation. If print and radio focused people's attention on the discourse of ideas, television drew people to the discourse of images: not things said but things seen. A discourse of images calls for a different approach to news, one complementing the words of news with vivid and compelling images. Consequently, Frank Stanton's worries aside, in developing TV news formats the news broadcasts quickly became news shows.

One of the early problems that TV news producers faced was how to use punditry. Even though news commentary and editorial license were common on radio, television did not lend itself easily to open and avowed punditry. The medium's natural emphasis on the graphic rendered the "talking head" an inappropriate format for news analysis (Hirsch, 1990). However, the trained habit of journalists moving to TV was to continue the convention of punditry as a language of words. For example, consider the programs of news analysis in the 1950s. They were known as "talk shows" (for reasons we consider in depth in Chapter Five). They simply featured journalists—at first, almost all white males—discussing the news of the past week. There was little punditry in those programs. Later the "news documentary," such as "CBS Reports," came along. They consisted primarily of visual tours of selected social or political problems. Although a few such documentaries were criticized as "editorializing" or "biased" (for example "Harvest of Shame," November 25, 1960, and "The Selling of the Pentagon," February 23, 1971,), they were not chiefly vehicles for priestly punditry.

Producers experimented with other formats. They tried closing news broadcasts with reports involving commentary. Moreover, they created special programs as vehicles that would give free rein for popular anchors to express personal views (e.g., "Chet Huntley's Journal"). However, these attempts at punditry carried risks. Star anchors were the networks' valuable property. They were the "talent" that attracted large audiences; large audiences attracted advertisers and advertisers brought dollars. Why lose a portion of that dollar-delivering audience by taking a chance that an anchor might voice an unpopular opinion? Networks preferred that star anchors simply deliver and introduce the news of the day in somber, authoritative tones. At most, popular anchors and star correspondents might flirt with punditry by interviewing prominent and opinionated public figures, thus eliciting controversial views. CBS's Eric Sevareid, for example, conducted interviews with celebrated pundits Walter Lippmann and Eric Hoffer.

Of the TV networks, CBS News most doggedly searched for a correct formula for priestly punditry. It discovered it in Eric Sevareid. Sevareid (who was brought to CBS radio by Edward Murrow in World War II) replaced Howard K. Smith (another one of "Murrow's Boys"), who had air time on the "CBS Evening News" for a segment of "news analysis." Smith proved too analytic, erudite, and reasoned in discourse, a throwback to his heritage as a newspaper and radio reporter. He tended to lecture in a professorial manner. Sevareid, by contrast, was more rumpled and less austere. By nature nervous and intense in his delivery, Sevareid profited with the invention of videotape. He polished his style with retakes. He refused to use graphics (film, stills, or charts) to augment his commentary. Viewers saw only "Eric the Great's" formidable talking head (resembling, pundit James J. Kilpatrick once said, "the bust of Pericles") addressing the camera, talking about, and around, a subject. Where Howard K. Smith mused with a professorial, typographic, didactic style, Sevareid bemused in a manner that was cerebral, thoughtful, and obscure. During the 1960s and 1970s, Sevareid had many imitators but was the undisputed dean of pundits on network television.

Walter Lippmann, H. V. Kaltenborn, and Edward R. Murrow all made contributions to the development of the art of priestly punditry. They did so, however, by appealing to audiences who sought from the popular media political information first and entertainment second. Eric Sevareid successfully pioneered a different TV format for punditry, one that gave priestly commentary a legitimate part to play in the TV entertainment mix. His packaged, videotaped image as a serious and philosophical priest suited news audiences, who did not want to be lectured to yet wanted to feel informed. Audiences accepted "the bust of Pericles" as an integral part of Walter Cronkite's survey of "that's the way it is" on the "CBS Evening News," a sober and serious voice and presence in the maelstrom of the news. Sevareid's short analysis, which usually came late in the news program, was a sagely capstone essay (see Chapter

Three), a reflection on what meaning to attribute to the onrush of events that Cronkite had introduced and reported.

By combining carefully scripted words with a Nordic visual image of what a priestly pundit should look like, Sevareid made punditry entertainment without appearing to bend to TV's entertainment values. His TV presence seemed to represent solid values in a world of relativism and flux; he gave rhetorical voice to thoughtful but not threatening ideas, ideas that called for momentary reflection but not action. For the viewers of CBS—and likely, for the powers that be at the network—Sevareid served an important ornamental function as a symbolic figure voicing quiet and unargumentative thoughts that were acceptable both to the conventions of the medium and the demands of viewers of CBS News. Sevareid was the soul of priestly punditry adjusted to the brevity of television. (Bill Moyers, one of those who tried to replace Sevareid after the latter's retirement, never looked comfortable with the formula—for reasons that will be apparent in Chapter Six.)

### The Sound Bite Priests: Pundits in the Age of Show Business

As we shall see in Part Two in discussing the endless parade of political experts, technicians, talk shows, and critics on contemporary TV, the opportunities for priestly punditry flourish in the United States. Those opportunities have expanded in direct relation to the capacity of the art of punditry to be adapted to the entertainment values that drive television. Perhaps over the dead bodies of Lippmann, Kaltenborn, and Murrow, and with the impetus provided by Sevareid, pundits have made peace with the intrusion of entertainment values into news. Punditry has become a form of entertainment, both shaping and adjusting to popular expectations regarding how to keep up with and understand "what's happening."

In the TV age of immediacy where "what's happening" is happening now, the task of the pundit is to provide an instant, readily grasped analysis of the moment. As they do so, priestly pundits convert analysis itself into immediate experience: here today and gone tomorrow. Jacoby's public intellectual who resided in a land where time stood still long enough to grasp the context of events is gone. Today's priestly intellectual deals with a world where time is fleeting and context is nothing. To ply their trade, pundits must adjust to the "Headline News Service," "News Brief," and "Update"; when the working phrase of the journalist is "Give me 20 seconds and I'll give you the world," there remains no "long view of history."

The priestly rite of public discourse is a less leisurely and thoughtful pursuit than it once was, as it adapts to the contemporary requirements

of immediacy. True, Lippmann, Kaltenborn, Murrow, and their ilk had
deadlines to meet. They had to get their copy in on time or go on the
air on schedule. However, even with the constraints of a few hundred
words of a political column or a fifteen-minute commentary, they expected that audiences would pay attention. Now the pressures for "journalistic shorthand" are greater than ever.

In an era of breathless information overload and frenetic time constraints, people have short attention spans. The pressure on pundits is
to compress analysis into quickly understandable form. Priestly rhetoric
responds by translating events and processes into a shorthand that meets
demands for crisp and fleeting knowledge. Obviously, such a rhetorical
requirement challenges the pundit to say something contextual in con-
stricted ways that discourage arguments with qualifications, nuances,
and complexities. There is always the possibility under those conditions
for bad arguments to drive out the good, for short and quick analysis
to be merely glib and superficial babble. This is the age of the sound
bite. Anything to be said must be quotable, clever, and even audacious;
to enliven and entertain, even if not to inform, the pundit must be able
"to turn a phrase."

As the "sound bite" mind—to extend Postman's notion of the "typographic" mind—has replaced the typographical mind, priestly punditry has had to adjust in other ways. For one thing, not everybody
wants to hear every pundit talk. Some people listen only to pundits who
voice views they want to hear. Others insist that priests, while knowing
more of "what's happening" than they do, at least share something in
common with their TV viewers. Thus, some women listen only to
women, blacks only to blacks, Hispanics only to Hispanics, native Americans only to native Americans, conservatives only to conservatives,
liberals only to liberals, and so on. To cover all the possibilities and to
give everyone a voice and an ear—and to assure a sufficient audience
to appeal to advertisers—the sheer number of pundits has expanded
far beyond the small coterie of columnists and commentators of generations past. Now there are pundits who are specialists, dealing with
matters of concern to a particular group or with a particular issue. There
are "women's pundits" (such as Ellen Goodman and Anna Quindlen)
who specialize in writing and speaking about women's issues. Black
writers devote most of their columns to issues that concern blacks and
those interested in minority concerns (e.g., Carl Rowan, William Rasp-
berry, and Clarence Page). There are business, finance, and labor pundits; a vast array of national security, military, and international affairs
pundits; pundits who specialize in medical and health issues; and so
on, endlessly.

Specialization, one would think, tends to pigeonhole a pundit, making the priest qualified to talk about one thing but not another. However, this is not so. If the specialist builds a popular following, she or he may branch out, for example, starting as a business writer, taking on budgetary politics, and then becoming an authority on Congress. In fact, in the age of sound bites, to rise in the priestly hierarchy a pundit must be a multiarea analyst and a multimedia performer. A case in point is Cokie Roberts. Her "insider" credentials are impeccable. She is the daughter of the late U.S. representative Hale Boggs of Louisiana and Lindy Boggs, who succeeded her husband in Congress upon his death. Roberts began as a specialist in Congress for National Public Radio (NPR) after a stint as a correspondent in Greece for CBS. She soon turned to analyses of electoral politics, presidential politics, and, of course, all policy areas of congressional scrutiny. Now she not only "covers" Congress for NPR but also engages in roundtable discussion with fellow pundit Kevin Phillips (see Chapter Four) and appears as a regular on "This Week with David Brinkley" (see Chapter Five). Says Roberts: "I walk into the Capitol every single day Congress is in session and of the 535 congressmen and senators, 250 just heard me 15 minutes before on the radio. Now that's very nice, and for a reporter it means that access is total" (Porter, 1990, p. 29).

Roberts puts her finger on another aspect of priestly punditry in an era of the sound bite mind: Pundits measure their influence by their fame. Priests of previous generations were uncomfortable with fame. Stardom, however, is essential in show business; journalists who aspire to the priesthood and its priestly rewards must deal with that reality and, as Roberts hints, exploit it. Indeed, priestly pundits are creatures of the mass media, appearing in contrived forums that Daniel Boorstin long ago dubbed "pseudo-events": events staged almost solely for media coverage and not for their inherent substance (Boorstin, 1973, p. 45). A journalistic roundtable on TV, a one-minute commentary on the radio, or even a newspaper column under a byline is not something that must happen. They simply bring performers and audiences together momentarily in a contrived experience.

As a performer in a media event, the priest becomes something of a pseudo-event as a pundit. To achieve and to sustain stardom, pundits hire agents to promote their appearances, negotiate their contracts, and publicize the "pseudo-fame" derived from that promotion. Pundits and their agents deluge TV talk show producers with news clips and FAX copies of their work and credentials, and even "video press kits" with tapes showing the pundit's performance on other programs. Priestly pundits command large sums to speak to groups. A popular network news anchor or correspondent may trade on journalistic fame to build and capitalize on fame as a pundit outside the daily routines of employment. For instance, for talks averaging forty minutes, Dan Rather, Ted Koppel, and Tom Brokaw are paid $25,000; Diane Sawyer and Sam Donaldson receive $27,500; and Barbara Walters draws $30,000.

In the age of show business sound bites, print journalists require TV exposure to achieve pundit status. News organizations such as the *Chicago Tribune* routinely employ a media consultant in Washington whose job is to get the *Tribune*'s Washington bureau correspondents on TV news shows. Gloria Borger, a reporter for *U.S. News and World Report*, recalled that she had covered Capitol Hill competently for years, but when she began appearing regularly on "Washington Week in Review," it augmented her ability as a reporter: "Once I started going on that show, it helped me in terms of reporting on the Hill in many ways" (Randolph, 1989, p. 2).

"Reporter Gab" and "Chatter" are terms applied to such gatherings of pundits on radio and TV as "Washington Week in Review." We explore the punditry of that type of programming at length in Chapter Five. Paul Duke, the genial host of the establishment "Washington Week in Review," noted that TV has produced "the Hollywoodization" of news and news analysis. In order to "gain recognition in your field, it's almost not enough to be a top reporter. You have to be on TV, seen by millions. So we have reporters shopping for a breakthrough that helps them gain a certain fame and fortune from TV" (quoted in Warren, 1990, pp. 1–2). "Hollywoodization" raises problems for other reporters-cum-pundits besides Paul Duke. Michael Kinsley of CNN's "Crossfire" edited the *New Republic*, restoring it to a place of importance in Washington political circles. He left that job for CNN and nightly combat with conservative Patrick Buchanan (and a reported $120,000 a year), prompting some of his previous admirers to accuse him of selling out. Kinsley, however, does not travel the lecture circuit, which is the pecuniary motive of some reporters who court "Gab" shows; they trade on their celebrity to make paid speeches to anyone who will pay. Such exploitation makes too much of what are, according to Kinsley, fairly superficial requirements for making one's self well-known: "The only real requirements are to be recognizable from television and plausibly able to salt your monologue with a few references to what Washington insiders really think" (Adler, 1990, p. 104).

Kinsley thus cuts to the heart of priestly punditry in the sound bite era: to appear briefly but often on TV, usually identified with the label "political analyst," appearing plausible, and salting the monologue with attention-grabbing metaphors and cliches. Widely quoted pundits such as William Schneider and Norman Ornstein are masters of the sound bite priesthood. One study dubbed Schneider and Ornstein "the enterprising experts of everything." Both men are affiliated with a conservative think tank, the American Enterprise Institute (see Chapter Four), but they are rarely introduced as professing a right-wing point of view. Instead, news producers treat them as objective and learned priests who are above the political fray, and able to speak with authority on an inexhaustible array of subjects. Although their academic vitae are those of two political scientists, TV news shows identify them in film clips as leading experts on all manner of specialized areas. Ornstein has been cast in a variety of academic garments by those who consult and quote him: "economist," expert on "congressional–White House relations," "congressional scholar," "tax policy expert," "political pundit," and so on (Waldman, 1986, p. 38). He has voiced opinions on an astonishing range of subjects, not all within the purview of a political scientist's expertise, including, the National Football League (for *Sport* magazine), abortion (for the *Ladies' Home Journal*), and banking policy (for the *American Banker*). Ornstein even became a pundit on pundits: when "NBC Nightly News" ran a special segment on the proclivity of network news programs to recycle the same pundits over and over again, the segment's anchor asked Ornstein to explain that phenomenon as well (Cooper and Soley, 1990, p. 23).

Like earlier news pundits such as Eric Sevareid, sound biters serve an ornamental function but are restricted in commentary to a few short lines glibly delivered to augment a news story. As S. Waldman has noted, figures such as Ornstein are "a prop, and sometimes a crutch, for political reporters" (Waldman, 1986, p. 37). The pithy quotes often state the obvious, but that is part of the priestly ritual. In essence, TV reporters turn to the priest to pronounce a benediction on the story, blessing it as correct in thrust and detail and reducing it to the orthodoxy of the conventional wisdom. The priest's sound bites bestow authority and credence to journalistic observations, which is precisely the reason why pundits are invited for news interviews in the first place.

Thus have the sound bites of pundits become indispensable to the dramatic rituals, the pseudo-events of TV news, which is driven by the practices of show business. The more quotable the talking priestly head, the more authority the pundit has; the more authority, the more the requests for sound bites. It is a circle that has gone far beyond Walter Lippmann's call for professional journalists, H. V. Kaltenborn's warnings about foreign policy, or Edward R. Murrow's strictures regarding Joe McCarthy.

## CONCLUSION: PROPHETS WITH AND WITHOUT HONOR

We have traced selected developments in modern punditry that lead us to the priestly practices of the present. It is clear that we have come a long way from the priestly notion of public intellectuals, a small and

elite group of the learned and politically involved individuals who provide wise advice and counsel to the unlearned but politically powerful.
We have charted a movement from a restricted and exclusive priesthood
to one consisting of a vast army of liturgists who swarm out over the
op-ed pages, radio frequencies, and TV channels with pithy comments
on everything political. Like it or not, both the politically attentive and
the inattentive are beset with a cacophony of priestly voices.

Consider the punditry surrounding the Gulf War of 1991. The usual
stable of pundits on news forums were joined by newly discovered
military and strategic experts. The newly recruited priesthood did not
necessarily consist of the wisest specialists but rather the most available
individuals with reputations as "good performers" (quoted in Margolis,
1991, p. 4). As the priesthood of pundits expanded, so too did the cacophony. Experts did not always agree on when the war would start,
if it would be an air war or ground war, the likely numbers of casualties,
or anything else. A war between TV network pundits almost rivaled
that in Iraq. Viewers witnessed media pundits attacking one another's
credentials and wisdom. NBC's military consultant, David Hackworth,
attacked CNN's James Blackwell as not "qualified to talk about diddly
squat." NBC analyst Harry Summers, said Hackworth, was "shooting
from the hip" (quoted in Margolis, p. 4). ABC's pundit Anthony Cordesman was, said David Evans, ex-Marine and military affairs writer for
the *Chicago Tribune*, so much a part of the military-industrial establishment that he was a "carpetbagger for the defense industry." Some commentators on the war were air force experts who were asked to explain
ground operations, and vice versa.

The award for priestly humility had to go to CNN's retired Air Force
General Perry Smith, when he was asked about the environmental damage that might result from bombing Iraq's nuclear facilities. "I can't
comment on that," he said. "I don't have technical competence in that
area" (Warren, 1991, p. 2). Controversy over the TV and radio presence
of military pundits reached the point that Harold F. Radday, director of
communication at a major military-oriented think tank, the Center for
Strategic and International Studies, defended military priests, arguing
their views were educational and essential (Radday, 1991, p. 17).

What made punditry controversial was that almost all the commentators predicted the course and outcome of the Gulf War incorrectly.
During the Gulf War, Richard Reeves, a syndicated columnist with a
priestly reputation, wrote a column considering the problem of whether
pundits should criticize one another. He quoted a noted pundit, Ben
Wattenberg, who felt that they should: "Pundits and experts don't attack
each other publicly. They should start." However, Reeves had a different
slant. Criticism of pundits, if criticism there should be, should not hinge
on their being right or wrong; in either case, a pundit is simply exercising

a right to speak, the privilege to dissent: "The issue, it seems, was not punditry—the word means 'actual or self-professed authority'—but prognostication" (Reeves, 1991, p. 29A).

Reeves's observations about the pundit as dissenter speak essentially of political pundits in general. Another pundit, columnist David Broder of the *Washington Post*, has raised a concern more directly related to priestly pundits. By definition, the priest is an insider, speaking to, with, of, and for elites. Accepting the National Press Club's 1988 Fourth Estate Award (which is often given to priestly pundits) Broder said: "There's a developing pattern—encouraged most, perhaps, by television but visible also in print media—to create a new hybrid creature, an androgynous blending of politician and journalist called the Washington Insider." He went on, "There's a real danger in blurring the line . . . in letting ourselves become androgynous Washington Insiders." While people can vote politicians out of office who displease them, "they have no such recourse against us in the press." In a soul-searching conclusion, he noted, "If they see us as part of a power-wielding clique of Insiders, they're going to be as resentful as hell" (Broder, 1989b, p. 9; 1989a, p. 6).

Therein lies a major problem for the priestly pundit. To be on the inside means running the risk of being numbered among the "power-wielding clique." Not to be on the inside means running the risk of losing priestly status. In either event, the priesthood stands to dissolve out of its own "unbearable lightness of being," for the priest's opinion is either not disinterested or not weighty. A priest without the authority of the church that he or she serves is no longer one whose opinions "count." The flock loses faith in the moral of priestly sermons or the relevancy of the priest's secular prayers, and will no longer listen to the saintly wisdom. People must look elsewhere for authoritative answers to "what's happening." Some look to bards, if indeed they had not already been doing so for most of their political lives.

# Chapter Two

# The Bardic Tradition in Political Punditry: Speaking of, to, and for the Populace

We saw in the Introduction that the distinction between priestly and bardic pundits lies in their relationship with their respective audiences and, in some measure, the makeup and expectations of those audiences. A media bard's orientation is populist rather than elitist. The bard's followers respond to appeals to popular sentiment rather than elite rationality. Bardic rhetoric, then, emphasizes emotional appeals over the reasoned arguments that marked priestly discourse, at least prior to the era of electronic sound bites. A bard addresses common sense rather than the "uncommon sense" typical of priestly deliberation. Whereas priestly logic tends to the abstract and analytical realm of concepts applied to history, bardic logic tends to the palpable and specific realm of folklore which is derived from stories of everyday life.

Bardic language smacks less of dispassionate analysis than gut reaction. Bards engage in plain speaking. Bardic rhetoric employs emotional devices largely abjured by priests; they exploit the jeremiad, the diatribe, satire and irony, and even the peroration. The reputation and influence of the priest reside in the conduct and expression of thought; those of the bard reside in passion, a passion expressed to and shared with the populace. While the priest is a realist, the bard is a romantic. If the mood of the priest is serious, then the bard is, by contrast, circumspect and wistful. The priest is comfortable with elites and often enthusiastic in the elite exercise of power, while the bard is suspicious of, and even cynical about, those who rule. Bards speak of and even with elites, but they certainly do not speak for them; they are more likely to speak ill about them.

Bards claim to speak for popular interests or sentiments, and they are anti-establishment, although not revolutionary. Rather, they express popular revulsion at the way in which elites run things. Their romantic strain brings out a Jacksonian belief that anyone with common sense could rule better than the fools and scoundrels in charge at the moment. Bards differ over where common sense lies. For conservatives it is on Main Street, and for liberals, in the life of ordinary working people. In either case, wisdom rarely, if ever, resides among life-styles of the rich and famous, who merit only scorn and pity.

In this chapter we look closely at the tradition of bardic punditry that informs an important, and popular, segment of political commentary. We begin by considering key characteristics of bardic punditry beyond those reviewed to this point: chiefly, bardic humor and bardic story-telling. To that end, we profile three representative pundits in the heritage of bardic political commentary—Mark Twain, Will Rogers, and "Mr. Dooley." We then consider a forerunner of bardic punditry on radio and TV, Walter Winchell, and a current radio commentator in the bardic tradition, Paul Harvey. Finally, we illustrate the tenor of contemporary punditry in the bardic tradition by exploring examples of puckish and acerbic pundits.

## THE HUMOROUS AND COMIC MUSE IN BARDIC PUNDITRY

The bardic attitude helps explain why one of their rhetorical strengths is humor, while as a rule, the serious priestly task precludes it. The canons of the priesthood largely exclude humor except when there is a somber purpose that can be illustrated by sophisticated, and often esoteric, comic touches. The priest is often critical of the ruling class, but there is little levity in the critique. One can peruse many political columns of David Broder or George F. Will and find little of the lighthearted touch. There may be mockery, but it is penned with a furrowed brow. Typically, priestly pundits confine their comic relations with politicians to ritual settings, such as National Press Club "roasts," where "fun" consists of polite humiliation that in no way threatens the pundit's insider status. This good-natured bantering is clublike, and not really intended for public consumption or entertainment.

Bardic humor, by contrast, is very much for public display and is directed at officeholders, aspiring politicians, and other establishment members. Bards may well move in elite circles but, as they are devoid of the high seriousness of priests, bardic pundits are reluctantly accorded a grudging tolerance. Established elites respect bards less for what they do than for the popular following they command. A bard's influence on popular opinion rests on popularity, and popularity rests on the bardic talent for placing politics in a humorous, whimsical context. Many bards avoid elitist contacts altogether. They avoid the nation's capital in Washington, D.C., as fish avoid an unbaited hook. A few flaunt the superiority of provincial life and their own humble origins as a counterpoise to the corruptions and highfalutin life in "Capital City." Others, in order not to have their bardic status threatened by revealing elitist connections to popular followings, trumpet their isolation from the movers and shakers. Humorist and bard Art Buchwald, for example, publicized the fact that he had never been invited to the White House. (He was, however, a luncheon fixture at fashionable Washington restaurants such as Sans Souci and Maison Blanche where power-brokers dine.)

As popular communicators, bards extol their populist connections, employ humor, and tell stories, as well. Priestly pundits pontificate via serious, abstract, and conceptual analysis, namely; the Logos we mentioned in Chapter One. The bard is a storyteller, a weaver of humorous narratives that give humane and empathic force to unfolding events and processes. The bard's appeal is that of pathos. The priest may, to be sure, relate stories, but they are usually elite stories that validate a conceptual framework or argument; the bard, by contrast, uses popular stories to validate mass responses to events, casting the moment as individual experience writ large and making each representative anecdote a lesson for ordinary folks (Burke, 1969a). For the priest, the story is subordinate to ideology and defined as the logic of ideas. For the bard, the story *is* the story; it is one of "human interest," not representative of ideology but of folklore.

### Mark Twain and the Tradition of Bardic Humor

It is tempting, but beyond the scope of this discussion, to trace American bardic punditry back to Benjamin Franklin and, later, to the Jacksonian orators who excoriated and ridiculed the Washington establishment of John Quincy Adams. One of the progenitors of bardic punditry who must not be ignored, however, is Mark Twain. If, as Ernest Hemingway remarked, all American literature derives from Twain's *Adventures of Huckleberry Finn*, it can be argued with equal justice that the bardic tradition of humorous punditry derives from Twain as well. Twain was not only a great novelist but also an essayist and lecturer who was widely known and read in the popular press of the nineteenth century. He grew wealthy and consorted with sophisticates of the Gilded Age yet retained his bardic status by harkening to his humble and rustic origins in Hannibal, Missouri, and by exploiting the guise of a country bumpkin to invoke the bardic muse.

In his time Twain not only invoked but also embodied the bardic muse, expressing nostalgia for the fast-disappearing frontier life, poking fun at the garish pretensions of the newly rich, and touting a populist political stance. His remark that in the United States, "there is no permanent criminal class, save Congress" both delighted and instructed because it spoke to the popular belief in social mobility that condemns no group to perpetual poverty and crime: The real criminals are elite politicians who preside over and benefit from the looting of the public treasury. Twain did not espouse anything revolutionary or radically egalitarian; he merely portrayed established pretension and misconduct in comic ways, leading a popular cheer at the outrages of the rich and powerful.

We have said that bards engage in plain talk and plain writing and dislike the use of overblown and flowery language, which they associate with self-important elites speaking the esoteric languages of "academese" or "bureaucratese." Twain's own style was exemplary. Even with his bitterly satirical and even misanthropic tone, he was so readable and amusing that he enjoyed a wide audience. However, like many bards, he was partisan and openly opinionated about current events and would take a public stand. For instance, he was outraged by the U.S. military intervention in the Philippines and used his considerable reputation to condemn it. In a scathing speech he said that the American flag should be altered to have "the white stripes painted black and the stars replaced by the skull and crossbones" (Tebbel, 1974, p. 300). People expect analysis of major events from priests but reactions from bards, and Twain reacted. In the bardic tradition, Twain offered emotional guidance, and not priestly, detached analysis.

Twain's bardic storytelling, both in fiction and in responses to political fact, made him a prototypical American bard. His humorous reputation gave him a forum for bardic rhetoric, both funny and serious. More important, the mythic stature he achieved during his mature lifetime and after his death raised bardic punditry to a level of acceptability and respectability equal to that of priestly utterances. After Twain, priests alone no longer dominated political commentary. Reputable bards, not lecturing from the pulpits of the priesthood but spinning yarns from the ostensibly humble and unbroken circles of the multitude, spoke for, of, and to the people.

## Will Rogers: Spokesman from the Heartland

One such bard was Will Rogers. Like the classic bard Aristophanes, Rogers thought that elites, both intellectual and political, were so high in the clouds that they had lost touch with the common ground of ordinary American life. Nonetheless, Rogers, like Twain, moved easily among the powerful while making critical fun of them. Today, the political comedy of Mark Russell, the piano-playing satirist and columnist who appears frequently on TV, and Garrison Keillor, with his tales of

"Lake Wobegon," reflect the continuing heritage of Rogers's bardic tradition. Rogers became such a familiar and indispensable part of American life that his untimely death in an airplane crash in 1935 brought about national mourning. A week after his death there were memorial services across the country; on one evening twelve thousand movie theaters observed two minutes of silence in his honor before the evening show.

Rogers came from relatively humble, although not starkly impoverished, circumstances in Oklahoma. He grew up on a prosperous ranch, attended a private military school, and finally sold the ranch to travel abroad extensively. He ventured into show business performing an act of cowboy rope tricks accompanied by his wry and homespun comments about virtually everything, including American politics. He talked about what was happening in politics, provoking laughter; in typical bardic fashion, he claimed no insider's expertise but just widespread common sense in judging the antics of the mighty: "I would just read the newspapers and tell everyone what Congress had done that day, and they all would laugh." By the 1920s Rogers was a familiar figure who had entered movies, was on radio, lectured widely, wrote a daily syndicated newspaper column, and was the author of popular books. At the time of his death, he was undoubtedly the country's leading bard, a combination of cracker-barrel philosopher and shrewd observer of the modern American scene.

Rogers exemplifies one of the primary functions of the bardic pundit: He had a talent for mediating popular experience, not only by what he said but also because of a commanding public persona. Rogers was a heartland voice and icon, from the nostalgic past of the frontier and the rural culture that was rapidly being superseded by the city and urban milieu as a way of life and a center of political power. Rogers seemed to live in both worlds, retaining the values and sensibilities of the old and lost yet living and starring in the new and unfamiliar. As modernity brought a new sense of uprootedness and complexity, Rogers symbolized reassurance that the roots of the past were still relevant to the present and that the present could be understood in simple, cherished ways. He demonstrated that the provincial and rustic could be interwoven into bardic rhetoric in an age of mass mediation, appealing to audiences who shared Rogers's sense that the brave new world had not made popular, basic, folkish beliefs obsolete.

As a down-home pundit, Rogers played a latter-day version of the old frontier act of the "wise fool," the holy innocent of American democracy whose familiarity with the soil or the street qualifies him or her to see things clearly and think with the power of common sense. The wise fool, noted literary anthologist E. Veron (1976), "speaks with authority on subjects that concern the ordinary citizen. . . . Often, despite poor education and low social status, he presumes to be the counselor and colleague of men of affairs," speaking the "language of the naive wit that identifies him as 'just folks.' " Mark Twain, he noted, "slipped into the role of the plain-talking, untutored literary critic in a classic satire of the early American novelist James Fenimore Cooper" (pp. 63–64).

Will Rogers, like all bards, became a voice and tribune of the people precisely because of his amateur standing. Any pundit takes pride in being a member of a loose guild of qualified observers of society and politics who practice a profession as a dignified and important vocation. Whereas the priest observes politics from the perspective of a professional political science, the bard practices popular science which is derived from the canons of common sense and folklore. The bard feigns being an amateur who spins casual observations as an avocation. From the bardic viewpoint, professionalism itself is suspect, since that claim to status smacks suspiciously of putting on airs. Rogers reflected an understanding that audiences identify with the amateur status that makes the bard one of them. Since many people view professionals (whether doctors, lawyers, politicians, or elite journalists) as conspiracies against the laity, anyone who pricks the professional bubble is a welcome friend and ally.

Will Rogers, the "cowboy philosopher" or "homespun philosopher," had the common touch of bespeaking amusement and astonishment of politicians for the benefit of his audiences. For instance, one of his classic routines concerned a favorite target, Congress: "The way to judge a good Comedy is by how long it will last and have people talk about it," Rogers said. "Now Congress has turned out some [comedians] that have lived for years and people are still laughing about them." Congress is like the movies: The House of Representatives is like the studio Scenario Department, with bills much like a comic script. Representatives ponder what "will make a good Comedy Bill or Law, and they argue around and put it into shape." Then it goes to the Senate, the "Cutting and Titling Department," where "Gag Men" add amendments, or Gags, since the Senate "has what is considered the best and highest priced Gag men that can be collected anywhere." Bard Rogers concluded: "Now, Folks, why patronize California-made Productions? The Capitol Comedy Company of Washington, D.C., has never made a failure. They are every one, 100 percent funny, or 100 percent sad" (quoted in Weiss and Weiss, 1977, pp. 86–87).

Rogers deliberately used bad grammar and inappropriate capitalization, a drawling style, and a folksy intimacy. He bonded with audiences by telling them that they were correct in thinking what Congress does is essentially frivolous, comparable to the production of a movie comedy. The bard thus confirms the popular suspicion that elite behavior is so sad that it is funny; we the people should once again not expect much worthwhile to come from the fools that run things. Typically, bards like Twain and Rogers do not express the view that elites are evil but rather assert that they are simply foolish. In the populist tradition, wisdom and competence reside with ordinary people; the bard appeals to that prejudice but avoids the more threatening argument that the people at the top are agents of satanic forces (which some populist writers have argued). The bard makes people feel good by casting elites in a comic drama that reveals them as buffoons. Bards frame the outrages of politics as ludicrous, a result of bumbling and not cunning. Rogers was an important bard because his punditry appealed to the democratic bias that flattered his readers by juxtaposing their common sense and solid values with the idiocies and corruptions of the powers that be. As one reviewer of a Rogers movie said, he gave "the impression somehow that this country is filled with such sages, wise with years, young in humor and life, shrewd, yet gentle. . . . He is what Americans think other Americans are like" (quoted in Rollins, 1988, pp. 92–93).

Rogers voiced a principal bardic theme: this too shall pass; the people will endure if they have a sense of humor. Their wisdom can be witnessed in the bardic power to express contempt for the mighty through the comic muse. Since a bard like Rogers is of the country and not the capital, his influence emanated from the bardic voice he gave to the country. It may have been a mythic country produced by nostalgia and democratic folklore, but bardic celebration gave a sense of pride (and self-congratulation) to the common culture and a modicum of power to the bard who sang the cultural song.

If the bardic pundit tends to express the feelings of the common culture toward its rulers, whom it feels are a group whose cant and pretense produce social malodor, there is also a tendency for the bard to view the democratic society for which she or he speaks in positive and even epic terms. Rogers could direct his satire toward popular institutions and habits, but nonetheless there was always an undercurrent of good will toward the country and its people, expressed most succinctly in his motto that he had never met a man he did not like. His hilarious little essays on the divorce mill in Reno, Nevada, and the "modesty" of Californians are masterpieces of satire but expressed in a way that suggests that he finds these places remarkable and not disgusting. They are simply variants of Americana, part of the grand comic epic of a continually astonishing and delightful people in mad pursuit of happiness.

Similarly, Rogers's satires on politics are biting but not savage. He finds politicians truly comic and not demonic. If President Calvin Coolidge, whom Rogers loved to lampoon, had not existed, Will Rogers would have invented him. Rogers was a bard of wonderment and not cynicism, finding both people and politicians to be wonderfully comic.

In a sense, he performed well the bardic function of mediating between the elite and the masses, representing to each the wonderful follies and foibles of the other and reminding everyone that they are part of an epic story of a comic people. In so doing, the wise fool demonstrated his grasp of both the wisdom and foolishness of the democracy of which he sang.

### Urban Punditry: Mr. Dooley Says "Politics Ain't Beanbag."

Will Rogers spoke for the mythic America of the hinterland, giving bardic voice to the people who populated the farms, ranches, and small towns of the country. Rogers was a part of the tradition of Jacksonian oratory that celebrated the nabob democracy of the frontier, was suspicious of elites, and political elites in particular. However, punditry obviously could no longer be confined to rustic and parochial traditions as the United States became an urban nation with a large immigrant and ethnic population. The urbane and the cosmopolitan gave rise to bardic voices uttering concerns about and responses to modern life and politics.

This is not to say, of course, that a rustic bard like Rogers did not appeal to urban folks; quite the contrary, he appealed precisely because he was not a sophisticate. However, Rogers and his ilk did not foreclose the emergence of urban pundits, especially actual and fictional characters rooted in urban streets who were conversant with the folkways of city life in bardic tongues. Today the rustic bard speaking from a remote and humble place, such as Rogers's Claremore, Oklahoma, has all but disappeared. (Garrison Keillor's Lake Wobegon is a state of mind and not an actual locale.) Now urban-based bards are the rule, numbering among them stand-up comics like Jay Leno, cartoonists such as *Doonesbury*'s Gary Trudeau, popular culturists in the fashion of Bob Greene, and a host of newspaper columnists.

One of the notable forerunners of today's urban bards was a fictional character named "Mr. Dooley," the creation of a Chicago journalist named Peter Finley Dunne. Dunne created Mr. Dooley in 1893. The character was an Irish immigrant who had been in Chicago politics; he decided to turn over a new and more respected leaf—politics, after all, was scarcely a reputable trade—so he adopted the upright life of a saloonkeeper. Dunne's Mr. Dooley spoke in the vernacular with a thick Irish brogue, discussing current events and politics with a good friend and patron, "Hennessy." "From the cool heights of life in the Archey Road," wrote Dunne, "uninterrupted by the jarring noises of crickets and cows, [Dooley] observed the passing show and meditated thereon" (quoted in Veron, 1976, p. 94).

Standing outside his saloon in Bridgeport (the area close to Comiskey Park in Chicago that produced the two mayors Daley), Dooley engaged in bardic amusement regarding the passing show of politics. His was the world of scrap iron politics of Chicago and rough-and-tumble power plays in back of the "yards." For three decades, through Mr. Dooley, Dunne acted as an urban bard, analyzing politics with wit, insight, and "a sense of Celtic gloom that while things might be hopeless, they were never serious" (Schaaf, 1977, p. 1).

Although at first glance Dunne's Mr. Dooley might seem very different from Will Rogers, in fact they had much in common. Both affected the bardic persona of humility based in simplicity that was far removed from the temples of power and privilege wherein reside priests and politicians. Both the unlettered cowboy and the saloonkeeper "merely" knew what they read in the papers. Theirs was the discourse of the jester, to be sure, mocking the gravity of serious political events. The guise of the wise bumpkin or holy innocent, however, fooled the unwary reader into thinking that truth does indeed spring from the mouths of babes. Nevertheless, Dooley differed from Rogers in one key respect. Given the lingering remnants in Rogers's time of the Jeffersonian myth that true wisdom lies in the rural yeoman, the appeal of the Bard from Claremore is understandable. Dunne's achievement was to relocate that source of wisdom in a figure who was not a tiller of the soil nor an Anglo-Saxon Protestant but rather a creature of the city streets.

As a political bard, Dunne spoke to all Americans caught up in the life of the new and turbulent cities of the land and the rapidly changing politics of the new century. Mr. Dooley seemed to have an Old Country peasant wisdom that underscored his role as a Celtic bard able to bespeak of things beyond his ken. Rogers's roots in rural culture qualified him as a bardic pundit to voice popular opinion; Mr. Dooley's intimacy with both the peasant culture and the burgeoning urban culture made him uniquely qualified to speak to the politics of the times. For Dooley, politics was a comic epic, a spectacle of vibrant and growing cities in a young nation at the brink of awesome new power. Both city and nation were governed by such an array of characters that they could only be properly understood in comic terms, be they the "lords of the levee" of Chicago's notorious First Ward or the pretensions of William McKinley and Theodore Roosevelt.

The Spanish-American War over Cuba gave Mr. Dooley status as a national pundit. Mr. Dooley's skeptical and sardonic comments on the wars in Cuba and the Philippines appealed to readers, Dunne believed, because beneath the public displays of war fever and patriotic hysteria was a lingering feeling that these bloody interventions were neither noble nor worthwhile. Dooley punctured the images of the ballyhooed heroes of the Spanish-American War. On Admiral Dewey, the hero of

Manila Bay: "Whin we come to find out about him, we'll hear that he's ilicted himself king iv th' F'lipine Islands. . . . He'll be settin' up there under a pa'mthree with naygurs fannin' him and a dhrop iv licker in th' hollow iv his arm, an' hootchy-kootchy girls dancin' befure him." When Theodore Roosevelt published his war memoirs, *The Rough Riders*, Mr. Dooley dubbed the book "The Biography of a Hero be Wan who Knows . . . Th' Darin' Exploits iv a Brave Man be an Actual Eye Witness," and thought it mistitled: "If I was him I'd call th' book 'Alone in Cubia' " (quoted in Schaaf; 1977, pp. 24–27).

Bards such as Mr. Dooley voice skepticism about warfare; they suspect manipulation by cynical elites to whip up mass support for dubious enterprises. Dunne's Dooley joined Mark Twain before him, the Twain who condemned the bloody suppression of the Filipino insurrection as "some little war away off" that divided that nation into "half-patriot and half-traitor, and no man can tell which from which" (quoted in Tebbel, 1974, p. 300). Dunne refused to continue the Mr. Dooley column during World War I despite the satire's continuing popularity. He argued that such mass insanity as the Great War did not lend itself to humor. Other bards, however, have been jingoistic promoters of war, stirring up populist sentiment for the martial spirit or simply voicing a perceived widespread consensus supporting a war. For example, during "the good war," World War II, journalistic bards (as well as the movies, radio, and comics) extolled the democratic virtues of the "GIs" against the Germanic "master race" and the treacherous "Japs." However, by and large, warrior bards find war's heroes not in politicians and generals but in ordinary soldiers and their stalwart families and friends back home. In World War II, for instance, bards such as columnist Ernie Pyle and cartoonist Bill Mauldin depicted the life and death of ordinary soldiers, canonizing the GI, or "Willie and Joe," while criticizing politicians in charge. The bard typically identifies with the common experience of the many.

## BARDIC GOSSIP AND POLITICS IN PRINT AND ON RADIO

Media oracle Marshall McLuhan (1964) drew a distinction between "hot" and "cool" media (pp. 259–268). Radio, he wrote, is hot because it is a highly defined and informative medium that demands little active participation by the listener; radio offers a great deal of information along with a sense of intimate, private experience that links the individual to a world of voices and sounds. The growth of radio in the 1920s and 1930s gave pundits an active forum for propagating opinions. As we have seen, priests such as Edward R. Murrow and H. V. Kaltenborn made use of radio.

If McLuhan is correct, radio was, and remains, a medium more suited to the bard who speaks to and for a populist audience than the priest preaching to the choir. The radio bard beats the "tribal drum," appealing across the airways with sonorous and involving messages (McLuhan, 1964, p. 259). This is not to say that actual preachers of religious doctrine do not beat radio's tribal drum. Many noted ones have done so with great fluency. In exploiting radio, however, they have adopted bardic, rather than priestly, tones. Thus, Father Francis Coughlin, a Catholic priest, capitalized on radio to become a nationally known political bard with a following of millions in the 1930s, preaching a message of elite betrayal and conspiracy and the virtues of common goodness. Pioneering evangelist Aimee Semple McPherson initiated her "Cathedral of the Air" program in 1924, broadcasting the "Foursquare Gospel" with her sermonic blend of evangelical hopefulness and enthusiasm and a dramatic portrait of what awaited the believer in her marble-and-gold heaven. Her bardic talents glistened in sermons with titles such as "What Would Jesus Do if He Were a Great Film Director Like Cecil B. de Mille?" (Lothrop, 1988).

Whereas priestly rhetoric is predominantly a serious elite affectation of responsible prose, the bard is usually more poetic and colorful. The language of a Father Coughlin or Aimee Semple McPherson appealed to romantic and comic impulses. Coughlin was a Catholic romantic telling a bardic tale of elite power and betrayal, and finally invoking one of humankind's oldest romances, the myth of the Jewish conspiracy. McPherson embraced the joy of the evangelical romance of the believer and church that was easily triumphant and made herself and her religion into a comedy of faith that amused the faithful into devotion. The bard's communion with a popular following is emotional, not rational. Hence, Coughlin and McPherson could combine the serious and ludicrous in ways that appealed to radio audiences. Although both dealt with the eternal, radio gave them a tribal drum for bardic appeals to the internal longings of popular theology.

Bardic radio is consistent with what James W. Carey (1989) called the ritual view of communication. The bard (or some other agent of the cultural community) constructs and projects cultural ideals by creating "an artificial though nonetheless real symbolic order that operates to provide not information but confirmation, not to alter attitudes or change minds but to represent an underlying order of things, not to perform functions but to manifest an ongoing and fragile social process" (p. 19). Bards perform rhetorical rituals that evoke a symbolic order for communities, confirming what the common culture wishes to believe about itself and its relation to the world. Priests typically engage in "the sermon, the instruction and admonition," while bards conduct "the prayer, the chant, and the ceremony" (p. 18). The priestly drama is conducted within an elite proscenium, with a curtain drawn across the back of the staged public drama behind which the audience may not venture and from which the priest addresses his or her auditors, whereas, the bard identifies with popular forums outside the formal theater, speaking openly in informal theaters to people who are "soilwise" (the country store) or streetwise (the corner bar). The priestly theater of sermon and proscenium are for the eye and are admirably suited to TV; prayers and chants of soil and street are for the ear and are better suited to radio.

### Walter Winchell: Bard of Print and Radio

Few political bards have exploited the hot qualities of radio for political ends as fully as did Walter Winchell. Winchell came to radio after building a popular following as a newspaper columnist. Winchell was no ordinary columnist, and he was not a political columnist. Rather, he was a "gossip columnist." Steven Aronson (1983), wrote of gossip that "all of us indulge in it privately and idly" but that "there are many who practice it publicly and professionally." Today, "the business of minding other people's business is practically an industry" (p. 233). In the early days of radio, that was not the case. There were few gossip columnists in newspapers and fewer still on radio. Winchell was one of the most celebrated.

A bard is a chronicler of the tribe and tribal lore, a repository of wisdom that enables him or her to expose the faults and foibles of the great. Hence, oddly enough, the gossip columnist carries on the bardic tradition of the Hebrew prophet. A major task of the prophet was to uncover and condemn wickedness in high places. "Thanks to today's license to billboard the secret side of public lives," wrote Aronson, "gossip is more aggressive than ever in breaking reputations, careers, marriages, even governments" (p. 233). Winchell understood that aspect of gossip and made a career out of purveying it. Since, as Aronson noted, we all engage in gossip privately and idly, what could qualify Winchell more as a bard than openly and purposely to gossip? Winchell as bard was, after all, "one of us."

Winchell added to his bardic credentials by adopting a tactic employed by Mark Twain and Will Rogers. As noted, although both Twain and Rogers were sophisticates, they posed as rustic men of the prairies. Winchell affected a different pose but one just as bardic, namely, that of "working reporter." Popular legend in the early decades of this century extolled the virtues of the tough and worldly-wise reporter whose wisdom derived from the hard-bitten grubbing for a story that goes along with covering night courts, morgues, and gangland murders. No member of the effete elite, the working reporter's curse, has had the rough-and-tumble experience required for bardic status. Harvard and Yale may be suitable training grounds for priests, but only the "school of hard knocks" teaches the truths of the common life that a bard must share with audiences.

As newsroom bard, Winchell cultivated an air of "healthy cynicism," and a deep distrust of human, and especially elite, motives, pretensions, and actions, along with a mild pessimism about the chances for "truth, justice, and the American way" to prevail in the absence of public scrutiny. The "working news bard" is not misanthropic but just attempting to unmask the "Big Shots" who run things. The image of the "working reporter" possesses romantic notions of the virtues of the much-put-upon common people who are always victimized by the general incompetence or malevolence of "the system." In his guise as reportorial bard, Winchell's self-appointed mission was to report the comedy behind the elite proscenium. Such a bard could—and Winchell did—cross the proscenium and mingle with elites, and then "return," as it were, from the halls and palaces of the gods to renounce uncovered misdeeds. Winchell capitalized on the condition that in a democratic society the many do not defer to the few, nor do they seek to overthrow the few; rather, they are voyeurs of the few. Thus did Winchell as gossip columnist, and then as gossip broadcaster, perform the democratic function of reducing the stars of stage and screen, politics and government, to a glimmer of a lesser magnitude. The bard Homer revealed that the hero Achilles had a vulnerable heel; Winchell revealed that many politicians *were* heels. Winchell, and many bardic imitators who serve as talk show hosts such as Phil Donahue, David Letterman, and Morton Downey, Jr., are uncomfortable with the priest's mantle of "responsible reporting" (see Chapter Five). Responsible reporters do not point out that the high and mighty are heels. However, in its relationship to elites the bardic role is, by definition, irresponsible.

Walter Winchell virtually invented the gossip column and the idea that political news was gossip as well. During the height of his popularity, an estimated fifty million people read his newspaper column; one of every seven Americans listened to his Sunday night radio broadcast. Billed as "America's One-Man Newspaper" (Fang, 1977, p. 257), and acknowledged as the "wizard of America vicarious" (p. 257), Winchell revealed and reported the foibles of presidents, governors, mayors, legislators, bureaucrats, admirals, generals, and kings and queens. Winchell was also one of the first reporters in the "media age" to recognize that one did not have to be consistent or even coherent; indeed, what the bard said did not necessarily need even to be true. It just had to be colorful, gripping the audience in a high drama that readers and listeners could vicariously enjoy. Michael Herr's fanciful novel-screenplay about Winchell sums it up well. According to Herr, the young Winchell learns the mass appeal of amusement: "You call it schmooze," he says to a friend, but "I say it's news" (Herr, 1990, p. 34).

Winchell's scoops, revelations, and "schmooze-news" derived in part from his intimacy with "cafe society" where stars, the idle rich, and the politically influential gathered. He passed along his bardic gems of gossip, rumor, and innuendo by employing a variety of devices: embarrassing fact ("Fanny Brice is betting on the horses at Belmont"); hints of deplorable elite behavior ("Blind Item": "What glamorous movie star was seen 'that way' about a notorious gangster at the Stork Club?") (Fang, 1977, p. 254); the oblique allusion, equivocal reflection, and parenthetical insinuation. It was as if every statement were followed by a wink, a knowing smile, and a cynical "Know what I mean?"

Winchell's staccato writing and speaking style earned the sobriquet of "Winchellese" in the press. His broadcast sign-on exemplified it. He spoke rapidly, saying: "Good Evening Mr. and Mrs. North and South America, all the ships at sea! Let's Go to Press!" Promotional photos of Winchell featured the bard at the mike, coat off, tie askew, wearing a hat, enveloped in a cloud of cigarette smoke, and surrounded by the paraphernalia of the newsroom—a typewriter, a bank of telephones, teletype copy, and empty coffee cups. Winchell spoke as he wrote, at a fast and furious pace, punctuated by quick dots and dashes from an accompanying telegraph key. The Winchellese voice gave the impression of world-weary cynicism yet a frenetic and keen interest in the panorama of the seven deadly sins that the bardic reporter has come to know all too well. It was an urbane voice, one easily associated with both New York's penthouses and its prisons. It was not a voice that could be silenced; like Job's servants, Winchell alone had escaped to tell all.

In print and on the radio, Winchell proved that a bard too can be an "inside-dopester." Unlike the journalistic priest, who uses "inside dope" to ratify elite status, the bard uses inside dope to serve as the lyrics of the bardic song warbled for mass culture. For the priest, the information that is inside dope centers around responsible action of respected elites; for the bard, the information centers on the irresponsible action of elites who deserve and, in the words of stand-up comic Phil Foster, "get no respect." Winchell had many imitators and was the spiritual ancestor of "tabloid TV" (of Geraldo Rivera, Maury Povich, and others), expose biographies (e.g., Kitty Kelley's works); and the bravado talk host (such as John McLaughlin or Robert Novak). In all cases the bardic message is patently antiheroic: "Mama, don't raise your sons to be politicians."

Bardic gossip, however, is more than "factoids" of inside dope. Schmooze is only news if it is related in a normative and evaluative context, encouraging audiences to feel morally superior to wrongdoers. Winchell put gossip in the context of narrative moral amusement, revealing the shocking news of the moral degeneracy of the powerful. The characters in bards' tales are a sorry lot of drunken sots, philandering husbands, unfaithful wives, hedonists, liars, criminals, corrupt politicians: an endless litany of human wickedness and transgression that would impress St. Augustine. As a popular moralist, Winchell communicated a sanctimonious quality felt by many in his audience toward their alleged social betters and masters. His gossip appealed to the powerless whom he made feel powerful through the rhetoric of sanctimony. For instance, Winchell mocked "the lifted pinky set" and the "idyll rich"; he carped about the American "swastinkas," "swasticooties," "Hitlerooters," or "ratzis" who were apologists for Adolf Hitler. By contrast, Winchell always found some ordinary person who exemplified democratic virtue ("Captain Ben Gomez proved what sort of American he is. He left something for us all on Mindoro, in the Philippine Islands—both his legs"). (Fang, 1977, p. 254).

Winchell stepped up his schmooze about politics with the advent of the New Deal. Franklin Roosevelt (FDR) was a popular leader, and Winchell was unabashed in his admiration and praise of him. He saw Roosevelt as a "friend of the common man"; Winchell's praise of FDR furthered the broadcaster's role as a friend of the common citizen as well. Winchell also sensed that Nazism was a sinister force and invited isolationist criticism for his condemnation of the "swastinkas." As a practicing bard, Winchell's reaction to politics and politicians tended to be visceral and instinctive, based on likes and dislikes and showing a modicum of opportunism. It was easy to dislike Hitler and to like Roosevelt in the 1930s, and Winchell's political preferences, expressed in tough street language, were attuned to the popular ethos of the age. Nonetheless; true to his bardic credentials, Winchell had to be willing to attack any political leader, even Roosevelt: "I am not a premier, a prime minister or a president. I am merely a reporter who must follow the truth wherever it might lead, whomever it may hurt, and however unpleasant it may be to read and hear" (Fang, 1977, p. 257).

At the height of his power, Winchell was such a nationally recognized bard that people in the public eye feared being ignored by him as much as they fumed over his attacks. He held court at New York's Stork Club, where politicians, celebrities, and press agents who were eager to plant an item in his column paid their respects. One story will illustrate: Winchell reported that Bette Davis had entered a hospital (which was true) and that she had cancer (which was not). Furious, the volatile Miss Davis demanded a retraction. The danger in such a challenge was that Winchell could retaliate by attacking the star or politico in print, or worse, adding one to his "Drop Dead List" (i.e., he would not mention the public figure in print or on the air at all). That was the kiss of death for those whose careers depend on fame. When Davis protested, one press agent bluntly remarked, "If Bette Davis doesn't have cancer, she's in real trouble." Being a Winchell unmentionable was almost a worse fate than having cancer.

The bardic vocation is fraught with one great danger that also seems worse than cancer: a loss of popular notoriety and attention. If no one wants to hear the lyrics of the bard's song any longer, then there is no reason to fear or heed the bardic melody. Always the public patriot, by the time of the Cold War Winchell had become a red-baiter, joining in the clamor to find domestic scapegoats and succumbing to the irrational fear of Soviet power. Perhaps Winchell calculated this as the "popular" thing to do, but it cost him part of his following. Worse, radio was being eclipsed by television. Winchell was losing his audience and his influence; no one heeded or feared him any longer. He attempted a TV show, complete with hat, loosened tie, telegraph key, and punchy talk, but he looked ridiculous on the cool, priestly medium and soon disappeared as a television presence. Although he continued on as a columnist and on occasional radio broadcasts for Mutual Broadcasting, he became increasingly a marginal and forgotten figure before his death in 1972.

## Paul Harvey: Five Decades (and Counting) of Bardic Punditry

Walter Winchell was an important bardic talent who made innovations in reporting news. He was a new kind of bard, one whose modern urban voice found a wide and receptive audience in the heyday of tabloid newspapers and radio. Winchell failed to make the transition to television, no doubt for many reasons, but that failure raises an intriguing question. Media researcher John Fiske has asserted that television is the modern American bard, performing functions for the culture that were performed in traditional societies by other types of bards. These functions include articulating the main currents of the "established cultural consensus about the nature of reality," communicating to audiences the "dominant values systems" of the culture, and assuring the culture of its "practical adequacy" in relation to a changing world (1990, pp. 75–76).

Fiske's metaphor of television as bard is a useful one but it does not explain why the medium of television is so devoid of bards, whether like or unlike Winchell. Is it because television is, as McLuhan (1964) asserted, a "cool" medium and bardic communication is inherently "hot"? Do TV pundits, for instance, have to be "cool"? If so, how do we explain the success of confrontational talk shows such as "The McLaughlin Group" and "Capital Gang" (see Chapter Five)? Alternatively; is bardic communication basically oral and aural, an interplay of voice and ear? Since television is a "visual medium," favoring the image over the voice, does it discourage bardic talk, or, if Fiske is correct, perhaps TV is *the* bard in our lives; hence, figures like Winchell are expendable?

It would be hasty to say that no bards remain who practice the tradition of Walter Winchell. Popular radio newscaster and commentator Paul Harvey is clearly in this bardic tradition. One observer of pundits has rated Harvey as one of the "the ten most powerful voices" in each decade from the 1940s through 1980s (Mankiewicz, 1989). He is still going strong in the 1990s. His is a familiar and folksy voice and his radio shows are consistently in the top five network programs in ratings. He even has a boulevard in downtown Chicago named after him—while still alive! His patented phrases, "And now, the rest of the story" and "Good *day!*" are as familiar to today's audiences as Winchell's signature "Good evening Mr. and Mrs. North and South America and all the ships at sea" once was. Like Winchell, Harvey intersperses his stories with commentary and personal reaction, including his own views on politics and politicians. He also has the bardic quality of being unpredictable, responding to events in ways that frustrate efforts to classify him as a "conservative" or "liberal." Although Harvey is not a gossip, his news has a gossipy air as if he were telling his tales to a bunch of fellows at a local restaurant in a kind of heartland vernacular. His style offers a bit of glib polish without sounding too sophisticated (he broadcasts from Chicago, he says, to keep in touch with the heartland). Like Winchell, Harvey has a bardic penchant for making the listener feel morally superior to the many miscreants in the news. He is a public patriot who views events from a nationalistic perspective and scores politicians on their failures and follies.

As a bardic pundit, Paul Harvey eschews "straight news," intermingling the event or fact with comment, weaving in the important and the seemingly mundane, and inserting his personality as a vital part of the tale being told. The news is distinctive in the voice of a master bard such as Winchell or Harvey, who impose on the disparate events a cultural unity through Homeric narration. Harvey, unlike Winchell, has not faded, perhaps because he has avoided TV and stuck to his nasal "generic American" radio voice which wafts across the country as an unseen presence tied to no city or urban edge such as Winchell. Harvey's is a voice of American pastoral and small town myth, reaching an estimated twenty-three million listeners a week through thirteen hundred radio stations (Siegenthaler, 1990). His "combination of showmanship and little-guy relevance has kept him on top," and "he seems to find stories no one else can that confirm the traditional American mistrust of authority, particularly government authority" (Mankiewicz, 1989, p. 86).

## BARDIC PUNDITRY IN CONTEMPORARY POLITICS

We noted earlier that the bardic muse favors popular forms of drama of high entertainment value: comedy, satire, farce and spoof, and melodrama. Figures such as Will Rogers and Mr. Dooley were bardic satirists who were adept at spoofing the pretensions and inanities of politicians; Walter Winchell and others of his ilk engaged in melodramas of exposure, controversy, and emotional gestures. Contemporary political talk show hosts (see Chapter Five) carry on the bardic penchant for the dramatic ''by creating a political melodrama, replete with heroes, knaves, fools, and conspirators. American history becomes a morality play, a cataclysmic struggle between good and evil'' (Levin, 1987, p. 150). The colorful rhetoric of the bard places events and personalities in the poetic motifs of popular theater rather than the expository and conceptual prose of the priest's temple. Let us examine the bardic comedy theater in greater detail.

## The Puckish Pundits: Buchwald, Baker, and Barry

The puckish bards are comic amusers who offer themselves and their works as impish and whimsical exemplars of the experience of the common culture. They are mischievous spirits, humorous gadflies attached to the body politic. As self-styled ordinary observers of the American scene, they are forever astonished by the elitist facility to foul things up. Moreover, bardic pucks are wary of the "system"—bureaucratic or professional establishments of power. The puckish bard claims to be a free spirit who is able to see the system for what it really is, namely, a bane on all of us.

Moreover, the puckish bard is an incongruous figure in an absurd world who writes of the world's absurdity. Puck is a comic exemplar who represents our universal experience with the system and our quizzical amusement at the absurdities of those who profess to lead us. Pucksters remind us that comic absurdity is probably the only sane attitude in an insane world. Laughter is a means of survival. Like all little people, the puckish bard defends those who are otherwise defenseless through absurd insight into the folly that incapacitates us. Contemporary pucks are in the grand American tradition of Charlie Chaplin, Buster Keaton, and the Marx Brothers. They provide us with an individual's perspective on political insanity, letting us share their effort to impose order on chaos, or, perhaps, chaos on elitist order.

### Art Buchwald: The Dean of Pucksters

The dean of columnar pucksters is undoubtedly Art Buchwald. For many years, Buchwald has written a thrice-weekly syndicated column (for 550 newspapers around the world) with great success. His rhetorical approach is decidedly puckish, with its air of irreverence and astonishment that things could always go so wrong. Like Will Rogers, he claims that all the material he needs is available in the newspapers and all he has to do is compress it into a column and present it for the reader's delight. He argues that he is not satirizing but merely dramatizing the idiocies of the ruling class: "*I'm* supposed to be the clown. And now, the people who are running this country are all clowns. . . . [T]here's an anarchy going on and you just wonder after a while how much the people understand or can take, or can do about it" (quoted in Piantadosi, 1982, p. 28).

The puckish bard searches for, and revels in, anarchy, gleefully pointing out its presence, sources, and consequences. Buchwald agrees with the proposition that contemporary American satire is barely a match for the folly of our politicians. Buchwald recalls what U.S. Senator Paul Douglas of Illinois told him: "America gives out two or three hunting licenses a generation. And they say, 'You're OK, you can make fun of us or you can do anything you want, we're not going to get mad at you.' Will Rogers was somebody like that." Pleads Buchwald, "I didn't ask for the license, but having it—I accept it" (quoted in Piantadosi, 1982, p. 34).

Puck, then, is a court jester that ruling elites can tolerate, or at least ignore. (Buchwald admits that many thin-skinned and big-egoed politicians do not find him funny.) In either case, because of his popular following as a puckish bard, they cannot deny him the status that allows him the right to spoof. Nonetheless, as William Zinser has noted, puckish columnists are "not just fooling around. They are as serious in purpose as Saul Bellow—in fact, a national asset in forcing the country to see itself clearly. To them humor is urgent work" (quoted in Piantadosi, 1982, p. 33). Politicians and priestly pundits may dismiss the puck's reduction of politics to low comedy or farce, but the message remains: Politics is a joke, and a bad one at that. The puckster's pie-in-the-face attitude, so well exemplified by Buchwald's columns, exposes politics as a major form of human silliness and politicians as an especially base example of human ineptitude and stupidity. The court jester turns out to be wiser than the monarch when the puck proves that the true clown is the one on the throne.

The puckish Buchwald has often amused his audiences with his imaginative tales of the naked emperor. For instance, he once contrived a diary allegedly kept by Ronald Reagan during one of the president's numerous extended vacations ("I went to California and had a great time . . . I cut brush, cleared out trees, hiked with my best girl, Nancy, and shot down two Libyan airplanes. I was sleeping when we shot them [Libyan air craft] down and my best friend Ed Meese didn't wake me up at the time. But it was fun hearing about it") (Piantadosi, 1982, p. 32). Such writing satirizes a particular politician's (in this case Ronald Reagan's) habit of maintaining a languid life-style and casual attitude toward everything, including warfare. Buchwald depicts the president as childish and foolish; puck, by contrast, possesses the innocent wisdom of an impish god who sees mortals, and politicians too, as the puerile, self-important figures who both invite and deserve ridicule. A popular puck such as Buchwald performs the rhetorical task of reminding the nation who the real clowns are.

### Russell Baker: The Melancholy Puck

Russell Baker is a more serious, and even melancholy, writer, yet he too has a puckish streak in his orientation toward politics. He contrasts himself with Buchwald: "Buchwald is writing a humor column. I do . . . whatever I feel like. He's got to make you laugh, I don't worry about whether anybody's going to laugh." Nonetheless, Baker shares the puckish view that the political world is chaotic and the people who run things are both contemptible and funny: "Given the state of government, and the parlous condition of the world, the whole country's going down in a quagmire of seriosity" (quoted in Piantadosi, 1982, p. 33). Like Buchwald, Baker's task is to drain the swamp of the official nonsense that creates quagmires.

The grave danger of the politician's (and priest's) gravity stems from the elite delusion that politicians are both wise and benevolent. Politicians desperately need to create a myth of wisdom and compassion to enhance their own sense of self-worth and to mobilize support and admiration from the press and the public. Politicians get neither support nor admiration from Baker, a bard who cannot resist puckish digs at the astonishing panorama of elite misrule in an even more deeply ironic, and melancholic, motif than Buchwald. Whereas Buchwald is more urgent and immediate, Baker is more thoughtful, with his humor a little saddened. (Perhaps this stems from the fact that Buchwald's base of operation is the *Washington Post*, which publishes in the midst of the political hothouse of capital news, while Baker writes from the magisterial *New York Times*, a more "intellectual" newspaper which invites a calmer and more reflective analysis.) However, Baker is not a priest; his identity lies with the fate he shares with the rest of us who are undone and misruled by a pathetic elite who are largely responsible for the perilous condition of the government and the world. It is not that he has any particular heartfelt sympathy for the people who run things; as a bard, he holds them at fault for perpetuating the insanities of the world. However, more than Buchwald, Baker has an existentialist streak which extends the point of fatalism: "We live in an age of irony. . . . [I]n the twentieth century, nobody's responsible. . . . Everybody is the victim of circumstances and position, so all you can have is comedy, really" (quoted in Grauer, 1984, p. 38).

Baker's comic muse leads him to puckish writing, sonnet-like columns that are both topical and philosophical and that amuse with "serious humor." Buchwald has his serious intentions, but Baker is sardonic, mocking the world of power and wealth with a melancholy bitterness that belies a barely contained ethical outrage informing the humor. Baker displays an amused disdain for elites, presidents included, who seem to be able to commit what to Baker are either calculated infamies justified as necessities or colossal errors presented as triumphs.

Baker has also criticized the priggishness of "the new Puritanism," the contemporary attempt to forcibly purify every American in mind or body, be it by imposing politically correct speech or an acceptable cholesterol count. He noted gleefully, for example, that not so long ago medical "experts" touted—in all the health books in public schools— the undeniable benefits of a "good breakfast" consisting of bacon or sausage, eggs, buttered toast, whole milk, and caffeinated coffee. Now, however, the "health police" consider yesterday's "good breakfast" poison; other foods such as oat bran, yogurt, wheat germ, and alfalfa sprouts are the "magic bullet" to eternal life.

Russell Baker is a wry and unassuming puckish bard, due in part to his rural Virginia origins and experience in having been a beat reporter. Baker has worried, though, whether his bardic idiom will continue to appeal to a changing nation. With the pessimistic undertone one might expect of him, Baker has charted a decline in American politics: The Eisenhower normalcy of the 1950s was "probably as close to an Augustan Age as we'll ever have . . . which began to come apart almost as soon as Kennedy was elected, and it has been shattering ever since" (quoted in Grauer, 1984, p. 45). What Baker has forgotten is that the bardic satire, especially of the bitter and melancholy variety, is quite appropriate for periods of imperial decline. He actually works in the tradition of the second century A.D. Roman satirist Juvenal (Decimus Junius Juvenalis), whose portrait of the corrupt and decaying Roman empire of "bread and circuses" bears many similarities to the sad but amused perspective of Baker on the contemporary United States. Baker seems to agree with Juvenal, who said of his time that it was hard *not* to write satire.

### Dave Barry: The Cheerful Hopelessness of It All

Perhaps even more directly in the Juvenalian tradition of savage satire is Dave Barry, whose syndicated column is entitled "Notes on Western Civilization." Barry shares the "decline and fall" pessimism of Baker but little of the undercurrent of gloom: the American world deserves ridicule but not scorn. It is a delightful challenge to observe and record the descent into a state of inert chaos of what remains of civilization. Like Buchwald and Baker, Barry does not find fault with the average person who must cope with an existential nightmare in surviving everyday life; rather, our condition is a result of systems of power, and the power of systems. Baker tends toward the sardonic while Barry tends toward the sarcastic; Baker conveys a sense of resignation while Barry displays out-right enthusiasm for the awesome spectacle of societal decay and anarchy.

Barry's sense that nothing works anymore is apparent in his many pieces about coping with bureaucracy, the most obvious manifestation of systemic inertia. The common assumption is that systems of power work for people's betterment, but any sentient being can observe, after experience with toll booths, tax collectors, university registrars, checkout lines, the post office, the department of motor vehicles, the emergency room, or any other bureaucratic agency, that the idea that these institutions serve the public is a hopeless delusion. Barry delights in observing that we have perfected a democracy where no one is in charge, a condition so terminal that our leadership can be justly proud of its accomplishment for rendering leadership nonexistent. Everyone is simply following orders yet no one is giving them. It obviously, hints Barry, has taken real genius to "advance" society to its current rapid decline into organizational gridlock and elite ineptitude.

Like Buchwald and Baker, Barry has made himself into a well-known bardic personality whose opinions and books inspire popular interest and press coverage. Dave Barry, like the other bards, carries the bardic burden of articulating the extent and depth of our misrule. Buchwald and Baker, who are of an older, World War II–era generation, include a subtext of seriousness and even occasional optimism. Barry, who is of a younger generation, has no such lingering vestiges of progressivism. His is an air of cheerful hopelessness that may become a common bardic motif as the United States devolves.

### Mike Royko: The Liberal Cynic

Syndicated *Chicago Tribune* columnist Mike Royko, like the puckish bards, possesses a popular public persona. However, being streetwise, he is also a throwback to the "front-page," "working reporter" tradition of American journalism. His persona is thus also that of the ultimate urban journalist in the quintessential American city, Chicago. Chicago was, after all, the city of legendary journalists such as Ben Hecht and Charles MacArthur, which gave rise to the myth of hard-line and shameless journalistic competition. Hecht, for example, once concocted the "Great Chicago Earthquake" hoax by employing a crew to dig a jagged ditch in Lincoln Park, photographing the ditch, and then running the photos on the front page to suggest a fault line under banner headlines of "Earthquake in Chicago."

Royko is the not totally unwitting recipient of that scrap iron image of the city with "the big shoulders." Many of his columns focus on the everyday life of the metropolis. His character "Slats Grobnik" is as famed, and as real to readers, as Mr. Dooley once was. However, Royko also writes about national politics, responding with his characteristic tough-mindedness and street-schooled skepticism. It is a skepticism welcomed by his vast army of readers. When, for example, Royko went on vacation in the weeks before the launching of Operation Desert Storm which preceded the 1991 Gulf War, he was deluged with letters from avid readers who felt his absence and missed his guidance.

It is fair to call Royko's rhetorical style one of measured, if amused, cynicism. It is also an informed and comic cynicism. Royko is no cheap misanthropic or peevish cynic. He finds virtue in the lives of ordinary folk, especially city dwellers. What he *is* cynical about are the systemic wrongs that perpetually plague his city and the world of power in general. He is contemptuously mistrustful about the motives and actions of those who rule, assuming, and demonstrating, that they are motivated by self-interest, and, in consequence, that they do not serve the public interest. However, there is a decidedly liberal quality expressed through Royko's five-day-a-week syndicated column. His cynicism is thus also a liberal cynicism.

Royko's political values are generally liberal, including support for civil rights and opposition to racial discrimination (which is not always a popular attitude in racially divided Chicago). However, he is no "limousine liberal" or "wine and cheese" liberal. He scorns such phonies in his columns (he hates "Yuppies" too). His liberalism stems from a populist sympathy for what he feels is the Democratic party's true constituency: the majority of working stiffs, the hard-up, the put-upon, the average Joes and Jills, all of whom are forgotten by elites, the press, and priestly pundits. Royko's liberalism appeals to the cynicism that many people feel about established systems of power that seem to care little about them and actually exploit them. Royko combines his working-class and streetwise liberalism with a cynical disbelief in established elites and their allies, appealing to the feeling among many people that they are being "had" (see Kanter and Mirvis, 1989).

Royko's urban roots—humble origins, ethnic background, school-of-hard-knocks education, working experience (like Russell Baker) covering the city at night, and hard drinking at the Billy Goat Lounge—enhance his bardic reputation and working-class liberal credentials. His liberalism celebrates the romance of the populace, especially city dwellers, who survive in spite of the system. Royko argues for an authentic rather than a phony liberalism, the latter being the fashionable, and upscale, liberalism of intellectuals espoused in (he believes) such exotic causes as feminism or racial quotas. He despises special treatment and privilege in the spirit of an old-time Jacksonian Democrat and constantly excoriates insensitive bureaucrats, television news personalities, professorial obscurists, and celebrities in politics. For Royko, liberalism has abandoned its hard edge in social reform which benefits the unheralded many in the working class and, thus, its natural constituency. Liberalism is thus no longer liberal.

Royko's indignation comes out in poking fun. For instance, by making fun of a mythical professor, "I. M. Kookie," he caters to populist anti-intellectualism by spoofing the obscure language and preposterous ideas of campus eggheads. "Slats Grobnik" attacks with cynical glee the practices of banks that give preferential interest rates to corporations and the wealthy and charge exorbitant rates to ordinary folks trying to buy a house or start a small business. Royko voices doubts about, and downright opposition to, war without sounding like a pacifist or appeaser. He became an opponent of the Vietnam War and a doubter about the wisdom and outcome of the Gulf War. However, he has no sympathy for "war wimps"—members of the political and social elite who are hawkish but at some point in the past avoided rubbing elbows with combat, including political notables such as 1988 presidential aspirant Pat Robertson, conservative Pat Buchanan, congressman Newt Gingrich, and vice president Dan Quayle. Korean War veteran Royko has only contempt for the "great patriots" who are willing to fight to the last drop of somebody else's blood. During the buildup to the Gulf War, Royko proposed that the draft should be reinstated to guarantee that in the front lines would be the offspring of the members of the Bush administration, of those in Congress cheerleading for the war, of those companies executives that had sold Iraq arms and munitions, and so on. Royko would have exempted from the draft the survivors of Vietnam veterans.

At a Washington awards dinner in 1990, Mike Royko said that his milkman father never got "milkman's block," (Royko, 1991, p. 86) referring to laments some news people have about writer's block. Associated as he is with the common world of work, he said, he has never had a case of writer's block just as his working father did not have milkman's block. Royko's punditry thus continues a bardic romance with the urban working class and the plebeian virtues he celebrates, even though that class and its virtues are passing into history. Royko is the heir to the myth of those "huddled masses yearning to breathe free," a bard of a mythic tribe. Royko is a master of the bardic vernacular, attacking in street language the patina of phoniness that envelops society. He is a combative bard who wears his cynicism like a badge: As a liberal, he sympathizes with the plight of the many and hopes for social reform, but as a cynic, he holds out no such hope. His is a liberalism of hopelessness. Like Dave Barry, Royko sees hopelessness in the human condition. Unlike Barry, he does not celebrate it. By contrast, for a priest like, say, David Broder, of the *Washington Post*, the political condition is serious but not hopeless; for a bard like Royko, the situation is hopeless but not serious.

## CONCLUSION: THE MAGIC OF THE BARDIC SONG

"When bards talk," wrote Thomas Lessl, "it is our own voice that we hear, the faint murmuring of a collective consciousness amplified in poetic utterances and often recognizable as myth" (1989, p. 184). From Mark Twain to Mike Royko, we have surveyed various bardic appeals to the American collective voice. Bards articulate a belief in the goodness and continuity of the tribe against all odds and largely without the aid of tribal chiefs. The rhetoric of the bard is a form of sympathetic magic in that it invokes the power of language to celebrate the community and its common heroes, thereby magically preserving tribal goodness and continuity.

One writer spoke of the ancient role of the "satirist-magician" whose satirical powers "may contribute to the richness and coherence of his culture by virtue of being a constitutive element of ritual" or "may be employed in straightforward and warlike defense of his tribe against threat from without" (Eliott, 1965, p. 329). We have seen both forms of bardic magic: the ritualized celebration of the myth of community and the romance of the common life as well as the bellicose defense of that community against threat, both from elites and foreign foes. The magic of the bardic word makes sacred the rites and observances of the invoked mass community (as the magic of the priestly word renders sacred the rituals and ideologies of the invoked elite community, whether the priesthood or the king). Even if we do not really believe in the magical powers of the bard to guarantee our community sovereignty, we enjoy the popular aesthetic of bardic punditry as it evokes the comic muse. Bardic power is from the bottom (populace) up rather than from the top (elite) down, as is priestly power. Bards are spiritual descendants not only of troubadours and storytellers but ultimately of tribal magicians, whose mastery of the language of ritual made indispensable. The bard makes "We, The People," exist, and reminds us that "We, The People," are sovereign.

Some scholars argue that the collective search for identity is central to the human condition in the modern world; the "story of the loss and regaining of identity is," wrote Northrop Frye (1964), "the framework of all literature" (p. 54). For many people living with the anxieties and insecurities of modernity, a bard expresses what it is we all have and what it is we all lack. The bardic pundit identifies our common predicament as something we all share and articulates a common response to it. That response may be more ironic and cynical than hopeful, but the bardic muse is there to identify rather than to glorify. As our world grows increasingly problematic, we may well require not the priest but the bard to remind us of our identity as a people and how we might lose, or regain, what the bard tells us has always been rightfully ours.

# Chapter Three

# Sages and Oracles: The Pundits of the Larger View

The political roles of priestly and bardic pundits persist in the modern world, albeit in different guises than in previous epochs. In neither ancient nor modern societies, however, have priests and bards been the only members of the learned class with pundit-like roles. There is also the venerable tradition of sages and oracles. In the United States we virtually canonize sagely status. For example, the Mount Rushmore National Memorial in the Black Hills of South Dakota bears the sixty-foot busts of four of this nation's most revered sages: George Washington, Thomas Jefferson, Abraham Lincoln, and Theodore Roosevelt. Our oracular pundits are not always so well treated, however. Remember, for instance, that abolitionist John Brown ("Old Brown of Osawatomie") had a vision of the end of slavery that was so powerful that it inspired his attack on Harpers Ferry, where he was captured, tried for treason, and hanged. Other oracles have done better. Astrologer Jean Dixon's annual forecasts of the political fates that will befall the nation and its people are always featured "predictions" as New Year's Day approaches.

In this chapter we examine sagacious and oracular punditry. We begin by considering the ways of sagacity; then we examine specific sages and their political advice. From there we move to reflecting on sages who add reputations for oracular wisdom to their credentials as pundits.

## THE SAGACIOUS MUSE IN POLITICS

The sagacious pundit plays both a derivative and a primary socio-political role. Sages usually rise from the ranks of priests and bards, yet their activities as pundits are distinct from either priestly or bardic pundits. A sage is often a former priest, versed in the lore and learning of the temple and exalted to the rank of sage by virtue of possessing among members of the elite (and, more rarely, the populace) a reputation for demonstrated sagacity, discernment, prudence, and acumen over a long period of time. A sage is "wise" in the ways of politics and has experience and reflective powers that have proved valid and reliable across the years. Sages are respected, mature pundits whose utterances command deference, even awe; they are pundits who are considered distinguished by elderly peers and by a youthful following.

Here, then, is a proven font of profundity and sound judgment. Age gives the venerated personage the air of thoughtful maturity, at least as long as there is a widely shared belief that the powers of astute discernment and judicious—rather than senile—counsel increase with aging. It is prudent to heed a sage who "always has something worthwhile to offer," or at least so it is thought by those elites with whom the sage exerts intellectual or political influence. An outsider might consider the sage a pompous, conceited fraud, but as long as the reputation for sagacity persists within the community, the elders return over and over again for advice and counsel. A sage performs different rhetorical functions depending on what the community expects. For instance, a venerable sage versed in the lore of the tribe which has been developed over the decades passes along accumulated wisdom to younger generations. Another sage, having been virtually "present at the creation," paints the "Big Picture" which articulates the overarching and persisting meaning and purpose of community. However, another sage can play the elder statesman or stateswoman, the embodiment of inherited wisdom of the body politic.

Whatever the rhetoric, the sage is the carrier of myth, the story of the tribe as it has been, is, and will be. This distinguishes the sage from priest and bard: A priest tends to be an ideologist, communicating in the forensic context of ideas in the present institutional setting; a bard tends to be a folklorist, communicating in the popular context of feelings responding to events and processes; and the sage tends to be a bearer and creator of myths, communicating in the group context of mythos, the high narrative of the historical group as manifested through time. A priest deals in abstract concepts and a bard in folk wisdom, while a sage communicates in the myth and mythic inferences derived from the wondrous story of the community.

Sages are rooted in two distinctive rhetorical traditions: the heritage of *maximology*, and the art of the essay. The tradition of maximology involves the formulation and expression of maxims derived from the received wisdom of the ages, the generalizations inferred from the community mythos. We recognize it in popular form in such widely held views as "Murphy's Laws," for example, "Nothing is as easy as it looks,"

"Everything takes longer than you think," and "Whatever can go wrong will." The political sage is a walking lexicon of "words to the wise," those general truths and rules of conduct deduced from myth and condensed usually in proverbial form.

The sagacious expression of proverbial wisdom goes back at least to Aristotle, but in political theorizing the most obvious example is Niccolò Machiavelli. In exile Machiavelli wrote *The Prince*, essays on the princely use of power; in so doing, he gave impetus in the modern world to the ancient tradition of political maximology (Born, 1973). The received maxims enunciated by the sage are eternal verities, or at least are interpreted as such, to be employed regardless of the uniqueness of current circumstances. Sagacious pundits confide what "principles" have worked in the past and, being transcendent, will work in the present and future.

Maximology, however, does not insulate the sage from contemporary affairs. Columnist Walter Lippmann (discussed in Chapter One), for instance, moved from priest to sage status but never became a remote and forbidding figure who expounded paradoxical truths from a Himalayan cave. His priestly origins could scarcely permit such isolation. A priestly pundit is decidedly tied to the immediacy of the present, at least in the sense of voicing ideas derived from and pertaining to current, and even fashionable, problems. The bard is a member of the community and derives truth from the collective folk wisdom of that community, truth that is applied to matters of the moment. The sage is simply a bit more detached, but not totally so. Here is the tribal elder bringing to current circumstances the informed and experienced circumspection they deserve, and that only the seasoned sage can provide. The priestly muse articulates the logic of elite rationality, the bardic muse propounds the folk wisdom of the mystic community, and the sage enunciates the wisdom of the ages. In parallel fashion, the priest regards the priesthood as a sacred drama of responsible realism, the bard harkens to the drama of folk romance and comedy, and the sage (and oracle) observe with detached interest the historical reenactment of political verities and the cyclical laws of history, which are the stuff of tragedy. Rather than the immediate focus on what is happening currently in either temples or towns, suites or streets, sages are concerned with what always happens.

Their tragic muse informs sages that people in power keep making the same mistakes because they simply ignore the verities of the ages. Historian Barbara Tuchman achieved sagely status during her lifetime, speaking to awestruck audiences in lectures and at the Army War College. She did so, in part, because she kept asking why there was so much "wooden-headedness" among politicians. In her book *The March of Folly* (1984) she documented repeated instances in recent U.S. policymaking where politicians were only repeating the ancient errors of the past. As sage she reminded rulers that historical lessons of both errors and truth can be applied to the present in the spirit of pragmatic sagacity. However, the sage hedges. Recognizing the immutable laws of history mean that ultimate human control over the forces of destiny is an illusion, sages also remind rulers that their moment in the sun will pass all too soon. All rulers can do is to bask a few moments more, and then only if they learn the sagacious lessons of history. The tragic fall of both rulers and regimes is inevitable. Sagely maxims thus combine pragmatic and cautionary political advice.

The sagely tradition, along with a mastery of historical and experiential maximology, also includes the sagacious talent for expressing advice in essay form. The term *essay* comes from the Latin for "the act of weighing"; the sage is the agent of weighty expression, the pundit whose breadth of perspective and depth of knowledge qualifies him or her to weigh matters. The essay format offers sagely pundits a vehicle for expressing the everlasting verities of their wisdom. Priestly sermons and bardic anecdotes may come and go, but the essay is etched in stone—or in the computer's memory.

Consider again Walter Lippmann. He remained a columnist almost to the end of his long life; his columns had the style of essays, of seasoned experience brought to the present, as well as a sense of historical overview and a treasure trove of generalizations from the heritage of political lore. He had entered the Washington priesthood many decades before, demonstrating his attention to both events and the development of his thought toward a mature synthesis. By the late 1950s and 1960s, Lippmann was not merely another priestly columnist with a limited audience; rather, he was an essayist in the tradition of Richard Steele and Joseph Addison of *The Spectator*, or Alexander Hamilton, James Madison, and John Jay of *The Federalist Papers*. In 1963, Lippmann (who was nearing the age of 74) signed with the *Washington Post* syndicate to write two columns a week for the newspaper and sixteen articles a year for *Newsweek* (Steel, 1980, p.539). The addition of the now sagely Lippmann to its roster of writers increased circulation to the point that *Newsweek* eventually became competitive with *Time* (Steel, 1980, p. 540). Lippmann's subjects remained topical but he included a "thoughtful" quality in his essaylike columns. Each reflected the enormous fund of knowledge he possessed and deigned to share with his readers.

The essayist offers the rhetoric of personal composition and discourse supported by the credence of considered and sound judgment. The essay displays the rhetoric of weighty discernment, displaying the funded power of maximal and historical knowledge. Depending on any given pundit's variation on the basic format, the essay may at times border on the ponderous or be the expression of mature thought and insight. Being relatively short, Lippmann's essays were not the outpourings of the public intellectual that we discussed in Chapter One. Rather, they were "pseudo-essays" that provided a largely middlebrow readership with the impression of a sagacious muse descended from a highbrow heaven to elevate elites and populace alike. Exploiting the essay form, the sage is a civilized voice attempting to signify universal and comprehensive values and solutions in an immediate and piecemeal world. When rulers accept the sage's lofty position and thought, the pundit-politician relationship is warm and cordial; however, if sages feel that their advice is being ignored or, worse, exploited, the result can be a monumental conflict between the sage and the politician.

### Cooptation and Conflict: The Sagely Muse Confronts the Committed Politician

When Lyndon Johnson (LBJ) suddenly became president in 1963, Walter Lippmann was the undisputed dean of Washington pundits. Johnson was a highly persuasive and manipulative politician who had courted Lippmann for years, and as president, he was determined to have the most renowned and influential journalist in the country on his side. Johnson was delighted that Lippmann, who was not always an enthusiast of new social programs, supported LBJ's "Great Society" initiative. Lippmann received numerous invitations to the White House, where Johnson and his aides dutifully listened to Lippmann's advice and counsel. Sagely, Lippmann supported Johnson's civil rights policies, confided his views on major policy matters, and endorsed Johnson over Senator Barry Goldwater in the 1964 presidential election.

As we noted in Chapter One, Lippmann had known and counseled many presidents, most notably Woodrow Wilson during World War I. None, he thought, had been all that one might hope, and many had proved disappointing. Hence, he shied away from becoming LBJ's crony. Nonetheless, by 1965 he was close to being a sage at LBJ's court, a latter-day Voltaire declaiming to a ruler who was certain of grasping destiny by the forelock. Certainly LBJ thought himself so destined. The sage, however, has a higher and nobler calling: to be true to sagacious maxims and principles no matter what the circumstances. A sage cannot be an apologist; sagely advice and counsel is, by contrast, often what the powers do not want to hear. Sagacious pundits run the risk of being at odds with power: It is the nature of the calling. The exercise of power in the here and now is often ill-informed and wrong-headed, and the sage has the duty to "remind" those in power of the folly of their ways. The sage speaks for a level of political perfection and historical foresight that are denied to most politicians, many of whom are just trying to get through the political day, surviving in the palace and squeezing by in the next election. Sagely pundits reside in the political present but are not of it: The sage belongs to the ages while the politician belongs to the particular age.

Walter Lippmann resisted LBJ's attempts at cooptation but not without generating considerable ill will between the pundit and president. The break came over the Vietnam War. Johnson doggedly pursued, and eventually became consumed by, the war. However, as early as February 1965, Lippmann warned that it would be a "supreme folly" to get involved in a land war in Asia (quoted in Steel, 1980, p. 558). Johnson continued to be solicitous toward Lippmann but the pundit's views did not change. Estrangement eventually solidified into open hostility between the two. The beleaguered Johnson administration regarded Lippmann's opposition to its policies as tantamount to betrayal.

The sagely columnist was unperturbed: "A primary vital interest is one in which the security and well-being of a nation are involved. Our security and well-being are not involved in Southeast Asia or Korea and never have been." The administration, wrote Lippmann, did not understand that history is "like a geological phenomenon, like the subsiding of the earth and the return of the waters after a great upheaval"; unless officials grasp that lesson, they will continue to beat "our heads against stone walls under the illusion that we have been appointed policeman to the human race." The sage advised caution and humility: "A mature great power will make measured and limited use of its power." A great power, Lippmann argued, eschews the notion of possessing a global and universal duty that commits it to "unending wars of intervention" and "intoxicates its thinking with the illusion that it is a crusader for righteousness." The biggest illusion of all, wrote Lippmann as he drew on his World War I experience with President Woodrow Wilson, is that each war is "a war to end all war" (quoted in Steel, 1980, pp. 564–565).

Having staked out a position informed by the maxims of rule ("measured and limited use of . . . power") and a philosophy of history (the "geological" metaphor, with subtle movements that only the sage can glean), the sagacious pundit offers an exalted perspective from Parnassian heights. The major attribute of sagely advice is, of course, that history eventually provides a check on its wisdom. Lippmann's sagely status was enhanced as the American adventure in Southeast Asia became a nightmare vindicating the essayist's general counsel that involvement violated sagacious maximology. As opposition to the war widened to include not only student antiwar protestors but also prestigious and sober members of the national political elite, Lippmann stood as the sage who had correctly defined the rational and enduring reasons for opposition. LBJ's critical remarks referring to Lippmann as a "political commentator from yesteryear" (quoted in Steel, 1980, p. 578) did nothing to diminish the sagacious luster. This Cassandra warning of the disaster that would befall the nation if it pursued the lethal combination of imperial misadventure abroad and neglect of festering social injustice at home had been right.

In his later years, Lippmann added an oracular quality to his sagely advice by placing current events in the context of speculations about the future. He regarded the late twentieth century and beyond as having revolutionary potential. However, he prophesied a "much less pleasant world to live in" than when he was a youth. Thus far, the mid-twentieth century had not been a "great progressive age" despite advances in human rights; rather, it presaged the onset of a "minor Dark Age." The United States and the world were growing decadent and barbaric; the sheer numbers of people that required governing and the problems of the environment and nuclear weapons seemed beyond the capacity of rulers to comprehend or solve. Toward the end of his life Lippmann wrote of the "inherited code of civility." He prophesied that "society won't last, will be overthrown, if that code is violated" (quoted in Steel, 1980, p. 593).

Few priests have taken on the role of sagacious pundit with such renown as Walter Lippmann. Nonetheless, throughout his long career of providing presidents with sagely advice, he often fretted that they would not heed his views. Perhaps that is a plight of all sages, especially those that begin with professions of hopefulness, but who, like Lippmann, witness in the end the same sad, slow drama of recurring error that has always marked the course of geological history.

## Paths to Sagely Status: The Brains and Bloodlines of Aristocratic Sages

The priestly pundit Walter Lippmann acquired sagely status in the late 1950s. He earned sagehood through decades of experience as an editor, political adviser, and columnist. His insider role gave him the ear of politicians and his column gave him the eye of readers. In short, Lippmann took the path to sagely pundit via the roles of the working journalist, the priestly insider, and; finally, the astute counsel.

There are other paths to sagehood. For example, the sage, like the priest, claims special access to knowledge that is not only special but universal and secret (i.e., truths hidden from others). In that sense the sagely tradition derives from such ancient ancestors as the wizard, sorcerer, soothsayer, prognosticator, and others whose mastery of cryptographic codes gave them access to cabalistic and mysterious doctrines and systems. The esoteric knowledge kept secret by such fabled sages as alchemists, astrologers, and theosophers presaged the more familiar modern disciplines of the natural sciences and theology.

Since sages claim this special and secret knowledge, another path to sagehood is to acquire a reputation for such knowledge. In earlier times that meant by apprenticeship to sorcerers, alchemists, and similar individuals. In today's world, acquiring secret knowledge involves formal academic training, such as studying with and at the feet of a scholarly sage reputed to have insights that ordinary teachers do not possess. In fact, that was yet another route to sagehood that was taken by Walter Lippmann. As an undergraduate, Lippmann attended Harvard. There he met the distinguished philosopher William James. The sixty-six-year-old James was a sage in his own right. His works in psychology and pragmatism revealed insights into the workings of the human mind that were provocative and controversial. Moreover, James's lectures, which were actually verbal essays, combined weighty thought with a breezy, colloquial style that caught the attention of scholars and lay persons alike. Lippmann went to James's residence for tea, an experience he termed "the greatest thing that has happened to me in my college life" (Steel, 1980, p. 17). It became a weekly ritual that taught Lippmann a great deal about thinking, writing, and life.

Men of learning such as James pass along the sagely tradition to their disciples. Notable intellectual aristocrats such as philosopher John Dewey, comparative anthropologist Joseph Campbell, and political scientist Charles Merriam (see Chapter Four) have performed as sages and have trained future generations of pundits. However, there are other aristocratic gateways to sagehood outside the academic. Self-styled social aristocrats can add the quality of sageness to their pedigree if they have long-standing access to a public forum and conduct themselves in the aristocratic manner expected by audiences. Being "to the purple born" provides the social standing and the wherewithal—especially resources to be educated at the "best" schools—to claim special and secret knowledge possessed by only those who are "born to know." Once aristocratic sages acquire that knowledge, they reveal it in guarded ways out of a sense of noblesse oblige. Noble blood brings noble bearing and eventually noble thoughts. It is a tradition of aristocratic sagacity that found an American voice in Thomas Jefferson, the "Sage of Monticello." Two contemporary sages illustrate the persistence of the tradition in American politics: William F. Buckley, Jr., and Lewis H. Lapham. Lapham stands to become for liberals what Buckley has long been for conservatives.

Both are from families who acquired wealth through enterprises in America's West and then became part of the establishment elite in New England. Both had the advantages of wealth and an Ivy League education. Finally, both became intrigued with politics as young men and brought their own moral convictions to their political perspectives. Buckley and Lapham are practiced writers who pen their essays in an elegant, if aloof, language that avoids pandering to the crowd. Each has acquired a forum for the propagation of his views: Buckley with his journal,

*National Review*, and Lapham with the editorial page at *Harper's* magazine. In his respective forum each has championed a political ideology at precisely the period that other pundits were dismissing the relevance of that ideology to the age.

Buckley and Lapham share something else in common: a rhetorical style that befits a sage. Both are able to operate within journalistic constraints but still communicate a sagacious sensibility, mainly by transcending the passing scene and locating the present within a grander and more sweeping scheme of human experience and values. Buckley and Lapham practice the sagacious habit of the higher seriousness; they write and speak with a philosophical air and a sense of axiological grounding. The distinguishing feature of their rhetoric is that it places the discussion in a larger and more universal set of values that, when traced to its roots, demonstrates philosophical sophistication. This produces an "educated" tone and a weighty consistency that enhances the writers' claims to pass judgment for the benefit of readers. Priests, as we said in Chapter One, often "talk down"; Buckley and Lapham practice the sage's refusal to do so. Their writing is not deliberately opaque or difficult but does demand intellectual effort on the part of readers. Each assumes a grasp of history and the humanities and peppers essays with quotations. For Buckley the quotes come from writers such as John Donne and Edmund Burke; Lapham's *Harper's* editorial columns favor quotes from, say, Oscar Wilde, Ralph Waldo Emerson, John Maynard Keynes, William Hazlitt, and even an "old Arab saying." The erudition is not a cheap ploy for recognition; rather, it simply reflects the company that the sage keeps. Such references remind readers that the sage is conversant with the big ideas of the big names and expects acknowledgment of that fact.

Unlike priests and bards, sages are not overly imbued with the problems of the moment. From the perspective of the sage, historical periods anywhere and anytime have a tangle of problems. Some can be addressed by political intelligence, while others are intractable and endemic. Buckley and Lapham express the sage's philosophical inclination to see the problems of our time as but another episode in the grand march of folly that seems always to characterize and torment. This is not to say that the problems of the present are insoluble and that one must therefore be fatalistic and quietistic. Rather, solutions, such as they are, must derive from the accumulated experience of humankind, the precedents and precepts of history. For Buckley, conservatism "is the tacit acknowledgement that all that is finally important in human experience is behind us, that the crucial explorations have been undertaken, and that it is given to man to know what are the great truths that emerged from them" (quoted in Grauer, 1984, p. 144). The long, slow, and painful discovery of these "great truths" is what Buckley undertakes, even in the wake of the unfortunate and often disastrous trends of the twentieth century.

Lewis H. Lapham seems to share this sagacious attitude toward the present. Even though his specific political choices are very different from Buckley's, nevertheless, he reminds readers that they share with people at other times and places conditions of contention and travail: "Freedom of thought brings societies the unwelcome news that they are in trouble, but because all societies, like all individuals, are always in trouble of one kind or another, the news doesn't cause them to perish" (1990, p. 371). Even though Lapham's political instincts are liberal rather than conservative, he retains the sage's skepticism about "progress" and "program." He dislikes "parties of transcendence," preferring "parties of experience" that speak the language of "conjecture and speculation." If we heed "voices of experience," we court "the last, best, and only hope of mankind" through recognizing "that the world is not oneself" (1990, p. 383).

Although Buckley at times has sounded jingoistic and militaristic, he has sagely cautioned that we should learn from history "how useless it is, how dangerous it is, to strut about ideologizing the world when we need to know it was born intractable and will die intractable" (quoted in Burner and West, 1988, p. 63). Lapham has repeatedly uttered a similar caution to those who would exercise power: We live in a period of "imperial masquerade" wherein "the man who can make wrong appear right must first be dressed up in the veils of innocence" (1990, p. 224). Buckley and Lapham exemplify a sense of moral indignation about power as reflected in the growth and dangers of a Leviathan state. Buckley's reservations about state power stem from his ideological position; Lapham's come from a more fundamental political skepticism born out of his reflections on the past. If the ultimate lawgiver for Buckley is Edmund Burke, for Lapham it is more likely Thucydides.

Buckley and Lapham are both scions of an elite that nurtured, enriched, and educated them, thus opening a gate to sagehood not readily entered by the working journalist or the intellectual aristocrat who has reached priestly status. From their common social backgrounds, Buckley and Lapham have developed similar sagely styles even though they voice different sagely judgments about the conservative or liberal persuasions. The former became a sage as a longtime spokesman for, and later a defender of, the political triumph of conservatism, especially in the presidency of Ronald Reagan. The latter trumpets no triumph but is a political outsider who is skeptical of all forms of power, including programmatic liberalism. The two sages share a common problem, however: Buckley's instincts remained decidedly conservative, although as time passed with conservatives in power in Washington it was not at all clear what of value they had conserved; Lapham's instincts are generously liberal, although it is no longer apparent what liberalism can ever accomplish.

Sages, then, are rhetorical masters of the everlasting nature of things, the sense that there is nothing new under the sun. For them, civilization is always problematical but never unique; the present will knot itself into the same kinds of problems as it always has and solutions will follow knowable patterns of action. With sages like Buckley and Lapham, there is always a humbling undercurrent: the unspoken notion that not only is our age not unique, it also is not nearly as important as we would like to think. The sage understands that all ages are ages of crises, and, like Merlin, we must live through it all yet again.

### Havens and Subsidies for Sagacious Punditry

To practice their craft, political sages, like other pundits, require public forums for pundification. Walter Lippmann had his published columns. William F. Buckley, Jr., has his journal, *National Review* (founded in part with large amounts of his own considerable wealth), as well as a syndicated column and his Public Broadcast System (PBS) talk show "Firing Line" (see Chapter Five). Lewis H. Lapham has the editorship of *Harper's*, occasional syndication, and a PBS show about current books and issues called "Bookmark."

Along with an outlet for their punditry, sages require some means of support. Lippmann received handsome royalties; Buckley and Lapham had their own family fortunes. More commonly, however, we detect a pattern that is a throwback to an earlier tradition of sagehood. Once sages traveled from one imperial court to another, seeking to be cared for in a royal manner in exchange for their sagely advice. Alternatively, they visited monasteries for shelter and food to sustain them in their travails. Today there are few royal courts or monasteries, yet there are institutional settings that provide safe havens and finances for those sages who are not of independent means. They do not resemble medieval or classical monasteries in the sense of involving religious vows or pledges of celibacy and poverty, but they do mimic them in the sense that they are set apart from the world for some high intellectual purpose.

These havens may have governmental sanction, such as the Federal Reserve Board (FRB) or the Council of Economic Advisers, or they may have private but highly regarded status, such as the Brookings Institution or the American Enterprise Institute. Here we consider those with governing sanction; in Chapter Four we address the privately funded think tanks. In either case there is a monastic quality, with small but selected collections of learned individuals pondering ideas in a cloistered atmosphere far from the "madding crowd" or the pressures of political or academic life. Although sagely pundits sequester themselves away from the world to concentrate on deep thinking, there is no oath of silence. Modern-day sages are not by nature reclusive hermits or Trappist monks habituated to shyness or reticence. Quite the contrary, they eagerly share with the outside world pronouncements and judgments. As we have seen with Norman Ornstein (Chapter One), many have ready access to the mass media. Others publish books or studies that become "must reading" for policymakers. Finally, pundits-in-residence at such temples of knowledge take no vows of poverty; many are handsomely rewarded for their thoughts (Weaver, 1989).

With comfortable surroundings for thinking and adequate-to-lavish budgets for doing so, it is small wonder that many sagely pundits develop an assertive and self-confident rhetoric. Although sometimes self-serving, it is not always so. Rather, the air of self-confidence is essential to providing audiences with a sense that the sage indeed possesses special and secret knowledge. For example, consider the chair of the Federal Reserve Board. The chair's task is to convey economic wisdom in ways that assure people that diagnosis and prognosis of and for the economy is informed yet skeptical, timely yet grounded in past experience, confident yet cautious, and certain yet vigilant.

"The Fed Chief," the keeper of "the secrets of the temple" (Greider, 1987) appears before public forums (say, the U.S. House or Senate Budget Committee) and typically speaks in tongues. For example, this hypothetical statement is commonplace: "As best we can judge, the latest data contain some hints that the effects of last quarter's downturn have largely worked their way through the system and that the downward pressures on activity may be lessening." Similarly, "The uncertainties in the current situation are great, and the risks of making policy mistakes are high." This self-confident language preserves the secrets of the temple by hinting at mystical knowledge of the Fed priesthood of secret "data" (econometric data open only to interpretation by sages in the same fashion that the entrails of pigeons are read by witch doctors or horoscopes by astrologers). The sagely chair of the Federal Reserve Board is a wizard of the economic universe, the very soul of institutional knowledge and responsibility, who presides over the most exalted American temple, worshipping the God of Money.

In the American economic order, the Federal Reserve Board joins other sagacious institutions such as the Council of Economic Advisers and, more notably, the Business Cycle Dating Committee of the National Bureau of Economic Research. The committee has the sagely task of being the arbiter of business cycles, determining when they begin and end. It was founded in 1920 and is funded by corporate, government, and foundation grants. The chair receives de facto sage status in news accounts as the person who passes public judgment on the history and future of the current business cycle.

As we shall see momentarily, since it is the duty of such economic sages as those in the FRB or the Dating Committee to predict the economic future, they have an oracular aura. The chair of the Federal Reserve or the Business Cycle Dating Committee not only reports with an informed analysis of the economic past but also provides a more secretly informed foresight. This is a difficult task which is performed with rhetorical flourishes that preserve the secrets of the economic temple. With an appropriately cautious but confident demeanor, the economic sages note what seven lean years (or seven fat years) likely augur—barring, of course, "unforeseen circumstances" and "scenarios we cannot contemplate or anticipate," and "all other things being equal." The economic sages thus depart their monasteries to let Pharaoh and his court know whether prosperity or poverty is to befall the kingdom.

Such punditry is important in a political culture that values economic prosperity. Certainly, economic prediction puts the sage to the test, and it is understandable if the sage hedges toward seeing the seven fat years; however, overly rosy and wrong predictions dispute the sage's credentials. Witness the great stock market crash of 1929 and the subsequent Depression: The "reputations of the most respected and luminous economic and financial figures of the time suffered badly from their repeated predictions that it would very soon be over" (Galbraith, 1991, p. 22). Similarly, many of the Wall Street gurus of the highly speculative 1980s were eclipsed by their failure to predict the crash of 1987. Respected and luminous economic pundits lose not only credibility and luster when investors, or nations, bet in an ill-advised way on their oracular prognostications. Gone as well are the safe havens and subsidies that sustain the modern-day wise and worldly pundits in the style to which they have become accustomed.

## THE ORACULAR SAGE: A PUNDIT FOR ALL SEASONS

We noted in our introductory chapter that an oracle is a special type of sage. Sages bring audiences the wisdom of the ages; for them, the present is but a fleeting revisit of the past. The oracular sage goes farther and offers the wisdom of the future, or what he or she predicts will be the future. An oracle is a sage who ponders the time*ful*ness of things rather than the time*less*ness of things. While a sage deals with the discovery and mastery of eternal truths manifested in the present, an oracle deals with the discovery and mastery of temporal truths discovered in every aspect of the present. The sage's power resides in a talent for discovering the morality of the maxim; the oracular status stands on an ability to sway and soothe the inexorable force of time.

### The Oracular Tradition

The sagely tradition derives from such figures as Niccolò Machiavelli and Michel Montaigne; the oracular variation on that tradition derives from philosophers such as Giambattista Vico, Georg Hegel, and all those, to use Jules Michelet's phrase, who "have looked for and thought to see the secret play of history" (quoted in Wilson, 1972, p. 22). Oracles transform the temporal flow of human experience into a knowledgeable prediction. As masters of ritualized procedures for "divining" the future, oracles are metaphysicians claiming access to a secret knowledge of a pattern in history that makes the future fathomable and predictable. Divination is not a haphazard exercise of wishful thinking or casual prediction ("the Cubs are bound to win the pennant this year") but rather a systematic, reflective analysis of signs, trends, cycles, and forecasts. Oracularism may range from the sweeping and apocalyptic predictions of a Nostradamus to the precise and data-based models of econometrics. Whether a necromancer or an econometrist, each transforms information into a prediction, a prediction couched in the mystery of *la technique* of analysis (see Chapter Four) and enunciates it in a language that conveys the authority both of the oracle and of the wisdom (if not the accuracy) of oracular knowledge.

There is a problem with such oracular punditry. As has been pointed out about econometrics, prediction involves such a high level of interpretation, mystification, and rhetorical barriers to falsification that it becomes difficult to prove the oracle wrong. Being right or wrong, however, is not necessarily the basic point or task of oracular punditry. It is not accuracy or inaccuracy of prediction that is the oracle's magic; rather, it is the rhetorical prediction itself that is important. Divination fosters the myth that the future is knowable and thus controllable, relieving anxieties about uncertain and often fearsome outcomes. Right or wrong, the oracle says have no fear; just the attempt to predict offers hope of removing the element of chance from the future.

Hence, like the ancient oracle at Delphi, it is the ritual aspect of oracular communication that lends it social credence. Oracular rituals provide ceremonial verification of our control of individual and social destiny. The economic predictions of the Council of Economic Advisers serve that Delphic function, assuring audiences that econometric data inform with certainty about fate and reassuring them that governing elites are informed and in control. Through Clio, the muse of history in Greek mythology, the oracle places the elites and/or the masses on the side of the gods. Whether correct or incorrect, the same oracle basks in the limelight of publicity.

### The Oracle and Cycles: Ravi Batra's "Great Depression"

Such a view, of course, seems to fly in the face of John Kenneth Galbraith's statement (quoted above) regarding the loss of credibility suffered by economists after the Great Depression of 1929. However, that was over six decades ago and the rhetoric of punditry has changed remarkably in the "age of show business," as we argued in our Introduction. To illustrate this point let us examine the case of Ravi Batra, an economist whose book, *The Great Depression of 1990*, was a best-selling example of oracular prophesy. "Anyone who ignores this book does so at his peril," intones a message on the front cover of a paperback edition (1988). Let us, therefore, not do so. Although Batra is an economist, his methods are not those of econometrics. Instead, he studies broad, sweeping social trends, the type of timefulness data of the oracle. From it he extracted as early as 1980 the forecast of a "great depression afflicting the world at the end of the decade" (p. 6). In the ensuing years he repeated that forecast in the first edition of his book (1985), in public lectures, on talk radio shows, and on televised news and public information programs.

Batra relies heavily on P. R. Sarkar's (1967) "Law of Social Cycles." The law assumes historical determinism. Societies consist of four social classes. "Warriors" are persons of superior bodily strength who excel in physical pursuits. Those who try to rule by might are of a warrior mentality. "Intellectuals" have superior mental capacity and skills; they solve problems by brains rather than brawn. "Acquisitors" have the talents and capacities for accumulating wealth: land, goods, services, and so on. They covet wealth not only for material betterment but for its own sake. Money makes their world go around. Finally, there are the "laborers." They lack physical vigor, intellectual acumen, or the acquisitive instinct. Being unskilled, and lacking guidance, they are exploited by the other social classes, in other words, they are the grunts of society.

Over time, social order develops in each era, with different eras emphasizing different social classes: "Sometimes warriors, sometimes intellectuals, and sometimes acquisitors dominate the social and political scene. Laborers never hold the reins, but at times the ruling class becomes so self-centered and corrupt that a large majority of the people are reduced to poverty" (Batra, 1988, p. 30). What adds oracular punch to this analysis is the theory that as society develops, it follows a definite cyclical pattern: An era of laborers precedes an era of warriors, followed by an era of intellectuals, and an era of acquisitors follows that of intellectuals. Acquisitors grow self-centered and corrupt, people are impoverished, and they revolt; warriors make peace; intellectuals end the arbitrary rule of warriors; acquisitors eventually buy the consciences of the intellectuals, and the cycle begins again.

With the law of social cycles as a baseline, Batra applied his analysis to other cycles: the long-term cycle of money growth, of inflation, and of regulation of the economy. By bringing to bear on his analysis of these cycles data pertaining to the concentration of economic wealth in the United States, Batra carefully analyzed a succession of economic depressions in the era of acquisition (in the 1780s, 1840s, 1870s, and 1930s) and the likelihood of the Great Depression of 1990–96: "The message of cycles must now be crystal clear. Since the 1960s escaped a great depression, the 1990s will experience another cumulative effect–the worst economic crisis in history" (1988, pp. 150–151).

Of course, 1990 has come and gone without a cataclysmic economic disaster. That, however, means little or nothing. Batra's forecast extends beyond any given year; indeed, it encompasses almost the entire decade of the 1990s. The verdict is not yet in on Batra's accuracy. Moreover, Batra has offered tactics for avoiding the Great Depression, so forewarned is forearmed. Acquisitors may yet preserve their society from the anarchy that will certainly ensue if conditions are allowed to deteriorate, thus provoking the revolution of the impoverished laborers. (Our account of Batra's theory is far too brief to do it full justice; those wishing a more detailed understanding should consult his very readable book.)

In any event, we point to Batra's forecast not to dispute or demean it. He is following in a tradition of forecasting on the basis of cycles that is as old as Plato, Karl Marx, Oswald Spengler, and Arnold Toynbee, and as current as political scientist James David Barber (see Chapter Four) or itinerant oracle Kevin Phillips (see Chapter Four). Batra succinctly illustrates the role of the oracular pundit: prediction qua prediction is the oracle's stock-in-trade, be the prediction bright or dismal. As Lester C. Thurow, another economist with an oracular bent—albeit different from Batra's—noted in his Foreword to Batra's *The Great Depression of 1990*, "One can learn a lot about events by thinking about them in terms of cyclical regularities" and "Batra gives a novel and brilliant exposition." Then, in appropriate oracular style, Thurow concluded, "Certainly it is unnecessary to agree with all of Batra's conclusions in order to see the *appeal* of his analysis" (emphasis added; 1988, p. 5).

## Prophets of Gloom and Doom

This bright side of the oracular muse is accompanied by a darker and more negative vision, the prediction of disaster. For many people the prediction of a future of uncontrolled and ghastly outcomes is as seductive as rosier predictions of control and prosperity. The educated imagination of disaster has always had a curious grip on people, who often enjoy dire predictions of a descent into poverty, disease, conquest, and other assorted woes. The sixteenth-century French astrologer Nostradamus, after all, continues to fascinate readers with his dire, if obscure, predictions of unfolding and unmitigated conflagrations, a slightly more secular version of the ancient biblical tale of the Four Horsemen of the Apocalypse.

An example of oracular forecasts of disaster occurred during the Gulf War of 1991. Many military and strategic analysts, having learned the timely lessons of the Vietnam War, predicted that in the event of a ground war, American soldiers would be returning home "in body bags" by the thousands or even tens of thousands. Antiwar protestors used such doomsday forecasts to whip up opposition to U.S. involvement in the conflict. Officials supporting the war exploited the same forecasts to lobby for more funds to supply additional troops, weaponry, and services (medical facilities, housing, airlift systems, postal services, toll-free numbers for family members, etc.) to cope with the likelihood of huge losses. In fact, casualties of the coalition forces fighting against Iraq were remarkably low.

The politically powerful, no less than the populace, are also seduced by forecasts of gloom and doom. President Ronald Reagan and First Lady Nancy Reagan were both interested in oracular knowledge: Mrs. Reagan harkened to the hopeful tradition of astrology, consulting astrologers and horoscopes that promise knowledge of one's future and the certainty, therefore, of control over it; President Reagan was drawn to the dark oracular prophecies of biblical and contemporary apocalypse (Regan, 1988).

As we approach the millennium (2001), it is likely that apocalyptic ocularism will increase. The Gulf War provided renewed impetus to the story of Armageddon, with prophesies of foreboding, breathless predictions of a final nuclear war bringing worldwide destruction, and glee at the prospect of carnage at the end of the world. An entire apocalyptic industry has developed around the battle of Armageddon. Prophesies differ over the identity of the anti-Christ and the scenario of the final chapter. Less lurid, but no less apocalyptic, is selected literature in the oracular trade known as "futurism." Beginning in the 1970s, futurists started to envision apocalyptic scenarios of a tomorrow characterized by either total destruction through nuclear and environmental disasters or postcivilization chaos with a reversion to barbarism. Considerable scientific talent, aided by computer projections, concluded that the world society and economy would collapse in the twenty-first century. If present trends of expansion, land use, oceanic and environmental pollution, population growth, and so on, persist, then certainly the end is in sight.

Not all futurists, and certainly not all politicians, agreed. As rhetoric, however, the futurists' forecasts serve a function similar to the visions of religious apocalypse. Translated into popular oracularism, apocalyptic futurism takes on a prophetic tone: We must change our way of living or all will be lost. In addition, there is an undertone of puritanism: It is our own personal pursuit of worldly pleasures—greed, avarice, display, ostentation, leisure, and other follies—that has brought about the waste and destruction that impels us to doom. The futuristic oracle is a prophet of doom, appealing to political interests that are dissatisfied with a consumer economy, gigantic organizational capitalism, and concentrations of economic and political power. Like the church father who argued that one of the chief pleasures of those in Heaven would be watching the torments of the damned in Hell, those drawn to apocalyptic oracularism anticipate the voyeuristic joy of watching the ruination while reminding the doubters that they told us so.

A wide variety of established organizations engage in futuristic oracularism, including the Worldwatch Institute and the World Future Society. As long as typical organizations restrict themselves to trends (predicting an extrapolation of what might happen if present trends continue) and forecasts (what life will be like if certain innovations, such as robots, occur), their approach is often as sound as that of the social scientist (predicting, say, that if the birth rate continues to fall, society will change) and the journalistic forecaster (e.g., if the Cubs get good pitching, they have a chance at the pennant). When they cross over into the oracular realm of the vision or model of the future, they are on shakier ground, involving the invocation of an encompassing image of the future which involves a positive or negative valence: will the future be a dream or a nightmare, a garden or a desert, utopia or dystopia?

Many oracular sages attempt to be as specific as possible regarding trends and forecasts and to avoid apocalyptic (and utopian) visions. Worldwatch publishes regular reports on trends (such as environmental refugees and alternative transportation) and makes proposals (for example: taxing products and activities that harm the environment). The World Future Society (through their *Futurist* magazine) acts as a clearinghouse for trends and forecasts made by the worldwide futurist community, including some of their more intriguing forecasts (multipurpose robots will replace nearly the entire work force in the country and people will receive a salary not for work but for play). Eminent futurists exercise a limited oracularism, avoiding the apocalyptic visions that characterized earlier forecasting. Alvin Toffler has spoken of future shocks (major social upheavals) with the world of "powershifts" (Toffler, 1990); Robert Theobald, of the need for a "social entrepreneurship" to manage future crises (Theobald, 1987); and John Naisbitt, of "megatrends" (Naisbitt and Auburdene, 1990).

## CONCLUSION: BACK TO THE FUTURE VIA A RETURN TO DELPHI

Sages and oracles, like priests and bards, stem from rhetorical traditions dating back to ancient times. Even in the extraordinarily changed world of modernity and mass media, such traditions of punditry survive with the energy and persistence of cockroaches. They do so because they meet a variety of human needs. All such figures are authorities of one kind or another, meaning that all are heeded by those who believe them, and believe in them, out of an act of faith. Priests, says the faith, possess a special knowledge that circulates among elites; bards, says the faith, possess mystic insight into the soul of the simple folk; sages, it says, master the wisdom of the ages, a wisdom that is timeless and hence all the more relevant to our troubled times; and oracles, it says, see the future as well as the past, a future that is benign or, as Pogo the cartoon character says, That doesn't work.

To the degree that priestly, bardic, sagacious, or oracular pundits become for others authoritative sources of truth, human susceptibility to the pundit's claim to special knowledge has changed little since the ancient people who climbed the mountain at Delphi to consult the oracle. What has changed considerably, however, are the means available to pundits for conveying special knowledge. If anything, the age of show business has opened new vistas for pundits of priestly, bardic, sagely, and oracular origins to cultivate and exploit. If the dollar is the coin of the American economic realm, punditry is the coin of the political realm. To explore how this is so, let us turn to a detailed examination of the current practices of political punditry.

*PART II*

# CURRENT TRENDS IN POLITICAL PUNDITRY

# Chapter Four

# The Technician as Pundit: Campaign and Policy Experts

We do not know how citizens view the surfeit of priestly, bardic, sagacious, and oracular punditry that tells them what to think about and what to think. No polls as yet tap their feelings on that topic. What we do know comes from fragmentary evidence. There is, for example, always *TV Guide*. In the June 11, 1988, issue we find the blue collar worker's author, Studs Terkel—a pundit himself, and a bardic one—airing his gripes about television's pernicious ways: "Eliminate all those flatulent TV pundits telling us how they feel about things when they know as little as we do" (quoted in Townley, 1988, p. 5). Similarly, there is the working people's sports columnist, Blackie Sherrod, a self-proclaimed disciple of "philosopher W. C. Fields." Fields awoke one morning to find that his wallet was missing from the center of the parlor rug where he had left it the previous evening. Realizing his loss, Fields stuck his head out the window and yelled, "The countryside is fraught with marauders!" Paraphrasing Fields, Sherrod bemoaned:

The countryside is fraught with experts. . . . At no time in history have we been blessed with so many citizens with so much loud confidence in their own judgment in regard to other citizens' beeswax. If our experts are not counseling cops on what brand of kid gloves are proper for handling muggers, then they are instructing professors on the compassion required in grading a defensive tackle. (1990, p. 1C)

What upsets people like Studs Terkel and Blackie Sherrod is not only that there is so much punditry and expert advice but that it is so inconsistent, even contradictory. It reminds us of the story of "The Dragon of Alca" in Anatole France's political satire *Penguin Island* (1909). "The

Penguin people were enjoying the fruit of their labors in perfect tran-
quility when suddenly a sinister rumour ran from village to village (p.
61)" A frightful dragon was ravaging farms, carrying off maidens, and
perpetrating all manner of mischief. The Penguin Elders assembled to
take counsel by inquiring of all who had seen the dragon what it looked
like. After hearing about the claws of a lion, wings of an eagle, tail of
a serpent (some Penguins said tail of a fish), a bristled back, yellow
scales, and the size, variously, of an ox, merchant ship, man, fig tree,
and dog, the Elders asked a final question. What was its color? "Red,"
said one Penguin (p. 63). "Green," said another (p. 63). "Blue," shouted
a third (p. 63). "Yellow," claimed a fourth. "He has no colour," concluded a fifth. Small wonder that "the dispute was lengthy and the
Elders dispersed without coming to any resolution (p. 64)."

   This chapter is about a variety of pundits cum experts who, like the
penguins describing the dragon's appearance, frequently disagree.
However, we shall see that in the end, they concur that there *are* dragons.
These are the experts who make a claim to authority on the basis of
possessing skilled techniques. Their punditry is priestly: serious, sober,
even somber; elderly, elitist, and even establishment. We look at two
types of political technicians in their pundit roles, namely, technicians
who advise candidates in election campaigns and technicians who advise
public officials on policy.

## THE PUNDITRY OF TECHNIQUE

   In a trilogy published in the 1960s, French philosopher Jacques Ellul
(1964, 1965, 1967) set forth a thesis intended to explain the nature of
contemporary politics. Ellul's argument is as cogent today as it was three
decades ago. It suggests possible reasons why political punditry flourishes. Ellul believed that modern societies had been seduced by what
he called *la technique*. By *technique* he did not mean the hands-on know-
how that we normally associate with those who repair automobiles,
program computers, design freeway traffic systems, or fire antiballistic
weapons. "The term *technique*," he wrote, "does not mean machines,
technology, or this or that procedure for attaining an end." Rather,
"*technique is the totality of methods rationally arrived at and having absolute
efficiency* . . . in *every* field of human activity" (1964, p. xxv) (emphasis in
original). Technique has an imperative, a logic and life of its own that
drives people to seek and find increasingly more efficient means to
achieve controlled, perfected results. That imperative makes technique
autonomous, an end in itself.
   As a state of mind that dominates every field of human knowledge,
technique creates a social reality apart from people, the reality of "the
technological society" (Ellul, 1964) which gradually subsumes individ-

uals. All problems, all relationships, and all encounters become technical in nature. Thus, a solution for crime is to improve the means of detection, reporting, apprehension, incarceration, and rehabilitation. Sexual relations lose the human touch and become perfections of techniques of intercourse: the mastery of "erotic zones," the "turn-on," and so forth. If a person strives for social success, then it is well to practice the six "infallible rules of friendship" listed in Dale Carnegie's best-selling guide *How to Win Friends and Influence People* (1948). Carnegie's social bible was first published in 1936 and within a dozen years had sold well enough to put a copy in the hands of one of every ten American families (Hart, 1950).

In a technological society, the technical expert rules: Dale Carnegie on influencing people, John Madden on the ins and outs of National Football League (NFL) play, Dr. Ruth Westheimer on sex, Dr. Timothy Johnson of "Good Morning America" on health, "The Frugal Gourmet" on cooking, or ABC's military expert Anthony Cordesman on the Gulf War. In politics no less than other areas, the technician's role dominates. Politicians turn to technical expertise to better win elections, formulate policies, balance budgets, plan model communities, fight wars on drugs, and so on. Believing in the old adage that the expert is "on tap, not on top," politicians take one of two courses, either of which removes politicians from direct accountability to the citizens. First, politicians may try to delude themselves into believing that technicians serve them and they do not serve the technicians. Ellul thought otherwise. "The more the technician's power grows," said Ellul, "the more technological foresight . . . grows with it—but always at the expense of political foresight" (1967, p. 195). Ellul added, moreover; it also grows at the expense of political control. That politicians govern at all, and especially that politicians who are accountable to the public govern, is *The Political Illusion* (1967).

The alternative to relying on technicians yet not being able to hold them accountable is for "the modern politician . . . to become a specialist"; hence, "the politician becomes a technician" (Ellul, 1968, p. 40). When this occurs, politics itself becomes technique: It becomes "the technique of techniques" whereby politicians pose problems with rigor and engage in minute and comprehensive analysis. This includes the problems of how to get elected and how to convince the electorate that the politician is acting in an accountable and responsible fashion. In short, whatever alternative for reining in *la technique* the politician may take, the result is—as we saw the puckish Dave Barry arguing in Chapter Two—no one is in control.

Politicians, however, can scarcely admit to citizens that technicians, and not elected leaders, govern, or that politicians see accountability to the citizenry as purely a technical matter. Why should we have elected

*3b↓*

leaders at all? Hence, politicians try to create the greater public illusion that they do govern and are truly accountable. For this they use propaganda, but propaganda is *la technique* too. It has its own logic, skills, and imperatives: "The progress of technology is continuous; propaganda must voice this reality, which is one of man's convictions" (Ellul, 1965, p. 40). Here enters the technical expert of propaganda, who elects and defeats policy officials, makes and breaks policies, promotes and demotes decisions, heaps praise and blame, and points with pride and with alarm. The punditry of technique is in large measure the punditry of propaganda and counter propaganda (Ellul, 1967).

## CAMPAIGN TECHNICIANS

We explore first the punditry surrounding the technique of modern electoral campaigning. The role of the campaign consultant, and of the campaign industry that consultants represent, has been widely documented in a variety of scholarly works (see, for example, Kelley, 1966; Nimmo, 1970; Rosenbloom, 1973; Sabato, 1981). Moreover, such popular movies as *The Candidate*, starring Robert Redford, and *Power*, with Richard Gere, have both romanticized and vilified the wizardry of the campaign consultant. Both scholarly and popular accounts deal with what diverse specialists, such as media consultants, fund-raisers, speech writers, legal staffs, pollsters, vote mobilizers, and advance personnel do to get candidates elected. Our concern here is not principally with how campaign technicians advise and elect candidates but with what they do in their capacity as pundits creating and interpreting political realities for the public at large. In their public punditry they play priestly roles: They rub elbows and speak with candidates who are office-holding elites or aspiring officeholders; they speak to candidates, advising them on messages that will work with voters; and they speak to voters on behalf of their client-candidates.

Campaign pundits "go public" in a variety of ways. Campaign consultants appear on talk shows (see Chapter Five), in TV and radio interviews, in feature profiles in major dailies, on op-ed pages, and in all the other media where political experts achieve priestly status. Moreover, consultants have their own professional/trade organizations that sponsor newsletters, journals, conferences, seminars, and competition. These garner publicity for the consulting priesthood and prominent consultants. The two leading organizations are the American Association of Political Consultants and the International Association of Political Consultants. The former publishes a newsletter, *The Politea*, and until recently was involved in the sponsorship of a bimonthly journal, *Campaigns & Elections*. These publications, along with *Campaign Magazine*, provide regular outlets for the received wisdom preached by consultant pundits.

## Media Consultants as Pundits

Consider a notable example of a priestly media consultant in the era of *la technique*, namely, political consultant Roger Ailes. Ailes has been actively involved in presidential politics since the 1960s. He played a leading role in the election of Richard Nixon to the White House in 1968. He produced a series of live one-hour TV programs that featured Nixon in the middle of a group of people, as though in an arena, responding to questions. Ailes insisted that the Nixon programs be conducted not as press conferences in the manner of conventional politics but as entertaining television designed to capture audiences. His background in TV, where he worked his way up from prop boy to producer of "The Mike Douglas Show," taught him lessons about entertainment TV; moreover, it prompted his first widely quoted political pundification: "Television is not a gimmick" (quoted in McGinniss, 1969, p. 66).

Since 1968 Ailes has worked on behalf of other successful presidential aspirants, namely, Ronald Reagan and George Bush. He is clearly one of the high priests of churched consultants, and is skilled at making TV the focus of the campaign rather than a "gimmick." Much of Ailes's reputation lies in his technical mastery of negative political advertising, namely, TV ads that attack an opponent. He was instrumental in 1988 in devising the "Willie Horton" ad which attacked the Democrat Michael Dukakis's stand on the furloughs of imprisoned felons and the "Boston Harbor" ad which denounced Dukakis's record on cleaning up pollution. Hence, it is no surprise that his punditry frequently revolves about negative campaigning and the electoral system that encourages it.

Ailes draws a distinction between personal and issue attacks in campaigns: "There's something about the American people," he told an interviewer:

They have such an innate sense of fairness that the red light goes on and the bells go off the second you approach that line [of personal attack]. . . . Any kind of personal attack is verboten. You shouldn't do it; it's not worth it. It will backfire. But anybody's position on an issue, anything they've said about an issue, and any way they've voted on an issue is fair game. You have every right to question that and go after it aggressively. (Ailes, 1988, p. 26)

Ailes recognized that there is room for improving political advertising but does not see it happening: "When you are getting banged around by an opponent and the press is interested in pictures, mistakes, and attacks[,] . . . it ain't ever going to change, folks," Ailes has said, adding, "It's going to get tougher" (quoted in Runkel, 1989, p. 265).

Like Ailes, Ray Strother, a Democratic media consultant, has fashioned negative campaigns. However, Strother's technical expertise lies elsewhere, and so does his punditry. For Strother, the preparation of political TV spots requires the eye of an artist and the sense of a poet. Strother shares with Ailes sufficient fame in the campaign industry that when he speaks, people listen. What they hear are priestly utterances about art that have bardic overtones: "Good politics can be good art. But good politics can be obfuscated by bad art. That's why the cinematographer is so important to me. It is a symbiotic relationship. . . . The cinematographer's eye must become an extension of my eye (quoted in Fletcher, 1991, p. 10).

Ailes and Strother are not part of the first generation of political consultants to reach pundit status. Matt Reese is. Reese's technical expertise lies in targeting voting blocs and individual voters with the technology available to reach people: direct mail, telephones, and so on. After securing the election of several clients who had been expected to lose by large margins, Reese achieved the reputation of a guru or wizard. He plays to his technical strength when commenting in a pundit role: "All of us [consultants] sell magic; that's what the client wants to buy. He's not terribly aware of the elements of a campaign and what should go into it, but he's looking to win and he's looking for a magician" (Reese, 1987, p. 18).

The views of media consultants such as that of Ailes on what constitutes negative politics, Strother on artistic TV spots, or Reese on sound wizardry, do not go unchallenged. According to Ellul's vision of a world dominated by *la technique*, the technique of punditry sparks counterpunditry. We can illustrate one such instance by examining how the technique of negative campaign advertising in the late 1980s gave rise to countervailing surveillance techniques among journalistic pundits in 1990.

In 1990 newspapers across the country, including the prestigious *Los Angeles Times* and the *Washington Post*, and regional dailies such as the *Cleveland Plain Dealer* and the *Dallas Morning News*, assigned staff members to monitor and review TV ads for truth or deception in that year's key elections. The *Post*, according to its national political columnist and priestly pundit David Broder, was responding to the role that TV spot ads played in the 1986 and 1988 campaigns. Said Broder, "We should treat every ad as if it were a speech given by a candidate himself" (quoted in Dessauer, 1990, p. 11).

Although a *Post* reporter had regularly covered campaign ads in earlier elections, as had reporters from other major dailies, the intensified coverage in 1990 produced criticism of the Washington daily. That provoked a conflict among pundits akin to that between Anatole France's Penguins. Among the critics were Greg Schneiders, a Democratic consultant, who called Broder the "William Bennett of negative advertising," referring to the czar-like role assigned to Bennett to combat illegal drugs. Instead of having a czar of negative ads, Schneiders believed it better to "focus on candidates rather than consultants" (Dessauer, 1990, p. 11). Other critics thought the *Post*'s articles were commentary and not reporting; would make the newspaper an issue in campaigns; and actually relieved candidates themselves of the task of crying foul about their opponents. If TV journalists get into the act, "the viewer hears more of Sam Donaldson and less of the candidate" (Oreskes, 1990, p. 21). Bill Monroe, the pundit editor of the *Washington Journalism Review*, a publication devoted to critiquing press performance, took a positive view: "For the first time in most places, a referee in the form of a political reporter is showing up in the campaign arena with the savvy to call fouls and a voice that's being heard. A game with a referee is a different kind of game" (1990, p. 6).

The master technician of negative ads, Roger Ailes, provided the most scathing criticism of the "experts" of political ad critiques. He found the reviews "boring" and "biased" and charged that "many journalists have little or no confidence in the public." Voters are perfectly capable of making their own judgments of campaign ads without journalistic advice. Reviews, he urged, "offer an opportunity for journalists to voice their own opinion in a forum which presents them as 'experts.' " However, "these instant experts have little or no experience in advertising, risk no public backlash and take none of the risks that consultants do." Reviewing ads is not bad in itself, but consultants should be permitted time and space to respond to reviewer-critics. That is unlikely, thought Ailes, for journalists "control the ink barrel." Ailes's final priestly judgment was that since reviews switch few votes, as "journalistic self-gratification" the practice is "not necessarily harmful" (1991, p. 27).

## Pollsters as Oracular Pundits

The expertise of the media consultant is, of course, not the only skill that constitutes *la technique* of contemporary campaigning; hence, the media consultant is not the only campaign technician wearing the robe of political pundit. Another key technician-pundit is the opinion pollster. Pollsters have worked on behalf of political candidates since at least 1932 the year in which George Gallup contributed a survey to the campaign of his mother-in-law for secretary of state in Iowa. Polls paid for by a candidate entered the picture in 1946 when Elmo Roper surveyed for New York congressional candidate Jacob Javits. In 1960 pollster Lou Harris held a position of trust in the successful campaign of John F. Kennedy for the presidency. Today, pollsters such as Peter Hart, Pat Caddell, Greg Schneiders, William Hamilton, Robert Teeter, Richard

Wirthlin, Arthur Finkelstein, Lance Tarrance, and many others are syn-
onymous with major campaigns. The list of pollster notables keeps growing. For example, in its review of pollsters' performances in the 1990
election, *Campaigns & Elections* raised a pollster to national pundit status
by awarding the top position in its "consultant scorecard" for Democratic
pollsters to Thomas Kielhorn, whose reputation previously had been
little more than regional (Beiler, 1991, p. 32).

Like media consultants, celebrated pollsters parlay their technical success at reading the tea leaves of public opinion into reputations for
knowledge and wisdom. Unlike media consultants, the pollster's punditry is more oracular than priestly. Through interviews, syndicated
columns, books, and other media they offer their insights. One oracle
with a long and distinguished career is pollster Lou Harris. As an adviser
to John Kennedy, a beneficiary of government contracts for survey work,
a syndicated columnist, and an author, Harris probed the tenor of the
times from the 1960s through the 1980s. For example, in 1973 Harris
prepared a book-length treatise that analyzed 436 separate surveys conducted over thirteen years (1960–1973). Harris's (1973) words speak el-
oquently of the role of the oracular technician as pundit. The book, he
argued, did "not represent" his *opinions about the country and the
people."* Instead, "it represents my *conclusions as a professional analyst* on
the subject, a distinction that is critical in this day of so-called new
journalism" (emphasis added; p. xii). Harris's conclusions were that
Americans were deeply concerned and worried about the future; demanded social, economic, and political change no matter how painful;
and, unless their leaders drastically changed national priorities, "the
people will not rest easy until they throw them out and put a new
generation at the helm" (p. 288). Seven years later, Harris's oracular
forecast was tested, but the confirmation was not precisely what Harris
had in mind. Ronald Reagan, who was born in 1911, won election as
president of the United States.

Pollsters, as do media consultants, receive criticism for their punditry.
For example, in reporting poll results as though they were handicapping
a horse race, pollsters too often "steer some members of the electorate"
with clues of how to vote for the winner; "no one would argue this is
a socially or politically useful function for them to serve" (Traugott, 1988,
p. 64).

A former president of the International Association of Political Consultants has criticized his own profession and singled out pollsters. Michael Rowan argued, "I believe the failure of political leadership in the
United States is directly related to the political consulting industry."
Why is this so? The industry, he said, has promoted big-money campaigns dominated by political action committees serving special interests, an "unholy alliance" between all of the following—lobbying and

politics, nonvoting and antivoting, single issues, instant polls, and voter segmentation. Moreover, he stressed, "the pollsters are worse." Through their research they frame "words" (called "Power Phrases" by pollsters) "through which policy for a nation must emerge." Pollsters trap politicians in cliches that "don't have a long half-life" with a "fickle public." He concluded, a "combination of ignorance and arrogance in some American political consultants . . . makes you wonder whether our democracy will survive" (Rowan, 1991, p. 19).

Rowan's stricture is severe, perhaps overly so. Nonetheless, he is correct at least in one respect. Campaign technicians have moved from campaign politics to advising on how government should be run. The presidential administration of Ronald Reagan was a striking example. Reagan's media adviser, Michael Deaver, maintained throughout his tenure, as he stated in an interview with PBS's Bill Moyers (Moyers, 1989) for "The Public Mind" series (see Chapter Six), that instead of actually addressing social problems through material, substantive actions, a president could instead leave an impression of doing so by staging a TV spectacle. For instance, Deaver arranged Reagan's visit to a class of grade-school students. Pictures of the president chatting with the children appeared on all the network nightly TV news shows, thus underscoring Reagan's "concern" for improving education. The fact that his administration did not back that concern with a policy for adequate funding of education was forgotten in the limelight of the intimate TV picture. Similarly, when the construction industry took a downturn, Deaver stage-managed a shot of Reagan in a hard hat walking through a construction site to provide visual proof of White House sensitivity to the ills of the construction industry and to give silent testimony to the success of the Reagan administration's policies.

Presidential pollsters also became policy advisers in the Reagan White House. Richard Wirthlin explained to Bill Moyers on PBS's "The Public Mind" (Moyers, 1989) that the practice of selecting which network TV news anchor Reagan would grant an interview to for nationwide broadcast. Using a polling technique to measure the "feelings" of viewers toward ABC's Peter Jennings, CBS's Dan Rather, NBC's Tom Brokaw, or CNN's Bernard Shaw, pollsters matched the president with the anchor that would, according to viewers' perceptions, best allow Reagan to promote the administration message. The "winner" was Brokaw.

Borrowing the technique of Reagan's advisers, pollsters for George Bush in 1988, decided that an on-air confrontation between Bush and CBS's Dan Rather (who was perceived as "cold" by audiences) would bring an abrupt end to the vice president's image as a "wimp" and "lap dog." The highly controversial Rather-Bush exchange on CBS's "The Evening News" of January 25, 1988, was the result. It may have made Roger Ailes's point on behalf of the vice president, namely, that Bush "gets up for the fight, and he's the kind of guy who creates a tactical advantage" (quoted in Runkel, 1989, p. 67). It may also have accounted for the fact that "after their acerbic exchange over Bush's role in the Iran-contra affair, his good press took a nosedive on CBS" (Lichter, Amundson, and Noyes, 1988, p. 89).

## POLICY TECHNICIANS

In shaping campaign punditry into policy advice, media consultants, pollsters, and other campaign technicians join a host of experts who play the role of priestly policy pundits. *The Idea Brokers* are what political scientist James Smith calls "the new policy elite" (1991, p. 23). An age-old concern of governance has been how to bring to bear in formulating policies the research, insights, knowledge, and wisdom of those who make a living out of learning—or at least have a reputation for being learned—namely, scholars. Plato (427–347 B.C.) prized knowledge as crucial to governing; he proposed that only the most enlightened should serve as philosopher-kings of his ideal republic. Aristotle (384–322 B.C.), Plato's pupil, took another course; instead of practicing governance he served as tutor and adviser to a noted ruler who did, Alexander the Great. Centuries later the English philosopher Thomas Hobbes (1588–1679) did the same for the young prince who was to be crowned Charles II.

Other members of the learned class proposed other ways to influence policy affairs. Two Florentine scholars with experience in political matters, Niccolò Machiavelli (1469–1527) and Francesco Guicciardini (1483–1540), wrote sagely guides to impart to princes the timeless lessons of prudent politics. The politically ambitious English philosopher Francis Bacon (1561–1626) foreshadowed current approaches to wedding the political and intellectual arts by proposing that scholars be brought together in a single place where they might study and impart their advice to rulers. The French satirist and historian Voltaire (1694–1778) added a peripatetic dimension to his role as enlightened policy consultant by traveling to the royal courts of France, Prussia, and Russia, offering his wit and insights in exchange for lavish treatment. This made Voltaire the Henry Kissinger of the Enlightenment.

In his study of the evolving relationship between the politician and the scholar in the United States, Smith (1991) has pointed to a paradox. The political culture, which emphasizes the competence and independence of each and every citizen, has had an "avowed democratic disdain for experts." Nonetheless, "Americans have typically been obsessed with expertise and specialization." In words that might have been written by Jacques Ellul, Smith argued that "we have felt an elemental urge to bring social science and technical skills to bear on policymaking, and our politics has been shaped and reshaped by a yearning to govern ourselves more intelligently—even if doing so means escaping the political process" (p. 3).

This urge received a marked impetus during the Progressive Era at the beginning of this century. For example, President Woodrow Wilson showed no restraint in expressing skepticism at the role that university-trained experts could play in government, yet he frequently consulted such experts for advice. Moreover, in his desire to make governing more efficient, Wilson drew a distinction between politics and administration. Politics he viewed as the partisan-ladened formulation, deliberation, and choice of policy alternatives; administration consisted of the execution of the chosen alternative in an efficient and business-like manner, well above the hurley burley of partisanship. Politics was the province of politicians; administration required the expertise of the technician. Thus, the expert who was barred at the front door of politics was ushered in warmly through the back door of the Wilson administration.

Smith (1991) charted the steady emergence and steadily increasing influence of policy experts through successive phases. (We need not repeat his detailed discussion.) Each phase produced a different form of political punditry for both the consumption of policymakers and for general audiences. At the turn of the twentieth century, the "first experts" (Smith's term) concerned themselves with social reform. Much of their advice, and the motivation for giving it, was couched in the language of medical science. Their task was to diagnose, cure, and prevent social ills. Frequently backed by wealthy philanthropists who practiced what they labeled the "science of preventive philanthropy," researchers alerted themselves to the symptoms of social and economic problems, probed their causes, and proposed cures. Their primary tool was the social survey. Technical experts gathered data on the state of housing, sanitation, employment, education, recreation, public health, crime, and other conditions in various cities and locales. The policy pundits exploited every vehicle available (pamphlets, newspapers, books, exhibitions, etc.) to publicize survey findings to enlightened citizens who in turn were to mobilize public opinion on behalf of reform.

What the first generation of policy pundits discovered, however, was that data alone did not produce reform. The complexities of social and economic life required more detailed, technical probing and interpretation. Policy scientists gradually became more specialized in their concerns and methods. Moreover, they shifted the focus from curing social ills to the promotion of social efficiency. Studies of the workplace, production and distribution, local governments, the civil service, and management of all varieties of organizations aimed at removing cumbersome processes. Replacing these unproductive practices were the efficient techniques of accounting, cost–benefit analysis, and reporting. Along with everything else, citizenship too would be engineered for efficiency. Government was too complex for average citizens to understand. Hence, pundit experts should step in to help officials govern rationally and to explain to citizens the wisdom of technical solutions to human problems.

The promises of efficiency no longer had much appeal to politicians or citizens once the Great Depression began in 1929. It was too late to practice the preventive medicine of reform on the millions of unemployed and too presumptuous to urge the hungry to eat more efficiently. A new phase of policy expertise and punditry arose. What the experts turned to were the cataclysmic changes in the social, political, and economic psyche; pundits recommended means of "adjustment." The adjustment phase of policy punditry, however, was brief. The Great Depression yielded to World War II, and soldiers in foxholes cared little about "adjusting" to getting shot. Moreover, following the close of World War II, social scientists mastered new tools of quantitative analysis in hopes of better understanding how social processes worked. Instead of acting as physicians, efficiency experts, or adjustment psychologists, they cast themselves as "social engineers." By designing, evaluating, and tinkering with complex systems and social experiments, policy experts occupied key roles in the Cold War, urban reform, and LBJ's Great Society initiative. This phase too proved short-lived. In the wake of retreats in the Vietnam War and the War on Poverty, policy experts and their critics alike questioned the legitimacy of social engineers' claims to scientific rigor and control.

The current phase in the relationship between the partisan politician and the scholarly expert has two emphases. One stresses that scholarly ideas are weapons in a war to restore conservative, fundamental ideals and values that had been pushed aside by the policy advice of preventive social medicine, efficiency experts, adjustment proponents, and social engineers. Policy should be sagely; in other words, as we saw in Chapter Three, it should be based on permanent truths, not faddish diagnoses, technical criteria, self-help guides, or social experiments. Parallel to the contemporary view of the policy expert as ideological sage is the second emphasis; namely, the expert as entrepreneur. The marketplace rather than the battlefield is the testing ground for ideas. Policy experts sell their ideas to those who are in a position of sufficient influence to consume and act on them: legislative staffs that brief congressmen, administrative appointees competing with civil servants for the boss's ear, celebrity journalists reaching audiences made up of policymakers and citizens, radio and TV talk show hosts, even Hollywood stars and starlettes with penchants for political causes. Whether contemporary policy pundits are ideological warriors or policy entrepreneurs, their place of residence is the "think tank."

## The Punditry of Think Tanks

We discussed in Chapter Three the safe havens where sagely pundits reside and think. Our focus in that discussion was the havens of government: for example, the Federal Reserve Board. Now we turn to other pundit residences not mentioned in Chapter Three, the "think tanks" and the cloistered "halls of ivy." Although *think tank* is a widely used term, there is no single definition of what a think tank is, does, or should do. Safire (1978) used the term to refer to "the brain; or a group of advisers; or specifically a research organization developing plans and projects for government and defense-connected industries" (p. 722). The "brain" reference Safire attributed to former president Harry Truman, who said on his eightieth birthday that he might live until ninety "if the old think tank is working" (quoted in Safire, 1978, p. 722). The "group of advisors" reference harkens back to advisers surrounding President Franklin D. Roosevelt. The press called them a "brain trust."

A more current definition of *think tank* is the usage of "research organization" or William Plowden's (1987), definition: "an imprecise term" applied "loosely" for "a wide range of different types of institutions engaged in public policy analysis and/or research" (p. 611). In the discussion that follows we employ Weaver's (1989) practice and speak of think tanks as a type of "service industry" consisting of private, nonprofit research organizations (p. 563). More than a thousand such think tanks operate in the United States (Smith, 1991), with about one hundred being "inside the beltway" surrounding Washington, D.C. (p. xiv). Although the types of research and/or analysis performed by the policy experts housed in think tanks varies widely, what many have in common is that they "spend much of their time competing to get their name in print," a view held by journalist Peter Kelley (quoted in Weaver, 1989, p. 564). Not only do researchers advise governing officials of their findings and recommendations, they also seek outlets for their views in newspapers, on radio and TV, and other popular media.

Weaver described three major categories of think tanks. The first he labeled "universities without students (p. 564)." Here the researchers are academics (social scientists employed by the think tank and/or moonlighting from regular teaching positions). Funding for these studentless universities derives from private philanthropic foundations, business and industrial corporations, and individual contributions. Books and quasi-academic journals are the principal media for their findings. Although think tanks in this category set out to be rigorous in their scholarly research, objective, and nonpartisan, over the years they acquired a reputation for their political colorings.

The granddaddy of such think tanks, for example—the Brookings

Institution—has successively been known for conservative opposition
to the New Deal, liberal support for the Great Society, and its current
centrist hue. The American Enterprise Institute (AEI) for Public Policy
Research has a conservative reputation. Moreover, it became a refuge
for scholars who, in the 1960s and 1970s, felt that the Democratic party
had departed its liberal calling. Such scholars as Jeane Kirkpatrick, Philip
Moneypenny, and Ben Wattenberg moved into the AEI orbit. Affiliated
with AEI also are the ubiquitous Norman Ornstein and William Schneider, who were discussed in Chapter One. In contrast to the Brookings
Institution and AEI, the Cato Institute asserts classical liberal and libertarian views in its policy pronouncements.

Weaver's second category of think tank is the "contract research organization (p. 566)." Researchers here are under contract with specific
governmental agencies for specialized studies. The Rand Corporation,
for example, has long performed contract service for the U.S. Department of Defense; the Urban Institute, which was once tied primarily to
serving the U.S. Department of Housing and Urban Development and
the U.S. Department of Transportation, now contracts to meet the research needs of over three dozen federal agencies and state governments
that are concerned with domestic policies. Although the findings of
researchers at such think tanks enter primarily into the writing of government reports, many analysts also advocate their policies on radio and
TV public affairs programs.

Finally, Weaver identified "advocacy tanks" (p. 567). These "combine
a strong policy, partisan or ideological bent with aggressive salesman-
ship in an effort to influence current policy debates" (p. 567). What
"universities without students" have been to the technology of reform
and efficiency and "contract research" has often been to social engi-
neering, advocacy tanks are to the ideas-are-weapons and entrepreneu-
rial schools of policy advising. Among the most notable of such tanks
is the Heritage Foundation, the source of many ideas that provoked
policy orientations of the Reagan Administration. In 1988 several aspirants to the presidency founded their own think tanks; the tanks supplied their candidates with research, position papers, and a means of
exploiting loopholes in Federal Election Commission regulations and
Internal Revenue Service codes regarding campaign contributions.

It is appropriate to add another category of think tank to Weaver's
classification. A few pundits operate private think tanks as cottage industries. These cottage industries, which are not quite "Mom and Pop"
operations, consist of an individual with a reputation for expertise and
technical insights who works for no organization but operates instead
as a free-lance pundit. Perhaps the leading example is Kevin Phillips.
Phillips was a political analyst working in the presidential campaign of
Richard Nixon in 1968. After that he spent a brief time in the U.S.

Department of Justice as an aide to Attorney General John Mitchell. In 1969 he published a controversial study of partisan politics based on a detailed historical analyses of patterns of support for the two major political parties (Phillips, 1969).

In his book *The Emerging Republican Majority*, Phillips acted as an oracle. He argued that the fortunes of the two major parties come and go in thirty-six-year cycles. In this century, for example, the Republican party was dominant until 1932, controlling both the presidency and the Congress for most of the period 1896–1932. Democrats were the dominant party from 1932–1968 in the period of the Great Depression, the New Deal, World War II, the Fair Deal, and the Great Society. Neither a Republican victory in congressional elections in 1946 nor the two terms of the presidency of Dwight Eisenhower seriously negated the overall Democratic dominance. Phillips saw the 1968 victory of Richard Nixon as ushering in a new cycle of Republican dominance (1968–2004) which would be very different from the Democratic era that preceded it.

Phillips left government service and became a full-time independent newspaper columnist in 1970. For a score of years he has written a syndicated column and published tomes of political analysis. He appears regularly during election seasons as a guest analyst for CBS News, airs his views periodically as a commentator and political critic on National Public Radio's "Morning Edition," and moves across the spectrum of cable TV on such channels as CNBC and C-SPAN. Phillips's broadcast punditry, like his books, covers both campaign and policy matters (foreign and domestic), and he is wont to invoke the sagely "big picture" of sweeping, global analyses. Thus, in *Mediacracy* (1975) he painted with a broad brush the impact of the mass media on an America that had become a "post-industrial society." In *Post-Conservative America* (1982) he used a similar broad brush to sketch the sweep of changes in ideology in a "time of crisis." More recently, in *The Politics of Rich and Poor* (1990), Phillips has argued the pernicious effects of Reagonomics in the 1980s that left the very rich richer but improved the lot of no other Americans.

Research into the performance of think tanks and/or pundit cottage industries, no matter what their type, testifies to the major role that punditry plays as an activity engaging researchers (Smith, 1991; Weaver, 1989). Think tank pundits appear on TV and radio talk shows (see Chapter Five) as "authorities," "experts," "consultants," and "specialists" on programs including the "MacNeil-Lehrer Newshour," C-SPAN call-in shows, "Meet the Press," "Face the Nation," and National Public Radio's "Morning Edition" and "All Things Considered." One think tank, the Center for Strategic and International Studies, reported in 1988 that its staff members had been cited forty-five hundred times in print and broadcast media in the previous year (Weaver, 1989). Satellite and cable TV, WATS lines offering literally almost 1-800-Dial-a-Pundit technology, and other means make it unlikely that citizens can hide for long from the free advice of think tank punditry.

### Savants as Policy Consultants

Dictionaries tell us that the savant is a learned scholar. The principal residence of the learned scholar in the United States has traditionally been the ivy-covered walls of the nation's colleges and universities. Since the outpouring of funds to construct and open new institutions of higher learning in the 1960s, the walls are, to be sure, more likely to be barren brick or concrete blocks than crawling with ivy, yet such places still house large numbers of savants who think of themselves as learned experts in various academic disciplines with relevance to politics. There is, therefore, no shortage of academic savants performing as political pundits.

By far the largest portion of such savant-like pundits are teachers that are relatively unknown to those outside their immediate surroundings. They are what the Russian dramatist Anton Chekhov (1860–1904) wrote about derisively as "parochial celebrities" (quoted in Joyce, 1988, p.147). Chekhov found them intolerable, petty, and conceited. However, in modern America most of the newspapers, radio, and TV stations located in towns and hamlets that are home to colleges and universities are more appreciative. Whether it be on election night or a time when local military reserve units mobilize for war, the president of the United States comes to town, or a local politician demands a change in the tax structure, the news media turn to these provincial pundits for analysis and commentary. Many such academics limit themselves to speaking only about their area of expertise; for example, a student of Eastern European politics may restrict remarks to the possibilities of a breakup of Yugoslavia or a specialist in state politics may confine comments to a gubernatorial race. However, other analysts are not so reticent. An assassination attempt on a leader, war in the Persian Gulf, student unrest in China, or famine in Africa: all are grist for the mill of academic pundits who are eager to bring their knowledge to bear on the world's ills.

The professorial pundit, however, need not claim fame only in the locality of town-and-gown. There are college and university savants who have transcended their own institutions and localities to win national reputations for political commentary. We speak here not of such scholars as political scientist Woodrow Wilson, who actually entered the rough-and-tumble world of politics to win, first, the governorship of New Jersey and then, the presidency of the United States. Nor are we speaking of such savants as political scientist Charles E. Merriam, who left the confines of academe to accept such public positions as membership on the National Resources Planning Board during the administration of President Franklin D. Roosevelt, or political scientist Henry Kissinger, who served as national security adviser and secretary of state for president Richard Nixon. Our focus is rather on those academic savants who continue to wear their mantles as teachers while offering punditry on matters both inside and outside their domains of teaching expertise. They neither engage in government service nor join think tanks. In a sense, they are the heirs to a tradition that has been taken for granted since at least the time of philosopher John Dewey (see Chapter Three).

Purely by way of illustration, and certainly not to be exhaustive, we single out three from among the many such savant pundits courted by the national news media for pithy quotes and sound bites. A leading example is Kathleen Hall Jamieson, a communication scholar and dean of the Annenberg School for Communication at the University of Pennsylvania. Jamieson's reputation rests on several book-length studies of mass media's role in politics. Her study of the history and state of TV advertising in presidential campaigns (1984) was widely reviewed and praised. She followed with treatises on how television has worked changes in presidential oratory (1988) and the nature and limitations of televised presidential debates (Jamieson and Birdsell, 1988). Jamieson's critical, almost caustic, manner in presenting her analyses, both in writing and in speaking, has made her a favored source for media interviews. Given her expertise in presidential communication, she has commented both on campaign politics and on policy matters—foreign and domestic—as they involve the presidency. She frequently appears on National Public Radio, nightly network TV newscasts, and documentaries.

Media critics (see Chapter Six) also regularly use Jamieson as a source of expert insights. For example, media critic Ed Bark of the *Dallas Morning News*, in preparing a five-part series on the global role of television in the conduct of foreign policy, featured a catchphrase he attributed to Jamieson. Writing about how Iraqi ruler Saddam Hussein had used television as a tool of foreign policy prior to the Gulf War of 1991, Bark noted that such "tele-democracy" was actually, in Jamieson's phrase, "tele-oligarchy" which might even become (as it indeed did) "tele-hostilities" (Bark, 1990, p. 26A). Leading political columnists also pay tribute to Jamieson's views. David Broder, national political columnist for the *Washington Post*, bestowed on Jamieson a compliment that only one pundit can pay another. Reviewing the role that Peggy Noonan, speech writer for Ronald Reagan and George Bush, played in presidential politics, Broder began his column with homage to Jamieson:

Kathleen Hall Jamieson, the whip-smart professor of communications at the University of Pennsylvania, does a shrewd, funny monologue on the rhetorical devices in George Bush's acceptance speech at the 1988 Republican National Convention. Mocking its male braggadocio, she quotes Bush's assertion of his readiness for the presidency: "I am that man!" And then, after the slightest pause, Jamieson adds "Peggy Noonan wrote." (1990, p. A-13)

Few things are more potent in the creation of a pundit than being designated so by another pundit, particularly one of Broder's stature.

A second academic pundit who has transcended parochial celebrity is political scientist James David Barber. While Jamieson's pronouncements derive from her technical criticism of presidential communication, Barber's derive from his expertise in analyzing presidential "character." In a series of books (1978, 1980, 1985) Barber has developed a reputation for an oracular analysis of the personality factors and styles of occupants of the White House and the role that the news media should play in alerting the American public to character traits and/or flaws. After Barber correctly assessed, based on an analysis of a life history, the type of presidency that Richard Nixon would have and the problems he would encounter, Barber made appearances on prominent TV news programs, documentaries, and talk shows and served as a continuing source for news columnists and commentators. Of course, since character touches all aspects of the presidency, and since presidential character has consequences for so many areas of American life, Barber's punditry ranges over a wide variety of political issues.

Far more of a specialist than Jamieson or Barber is Edward Said, a third academic pundit of national repute. A professor of English and comparative literature, Said's approach is that of a literary critic who reads texts for meanings that are not always apparent to the casual observer. He concentrates his political punditry on issues involving the Middle East, especially views expressed in the popular news media about such matters as Islam, the Israeli–Palestinian conflict, and the 1991 Gulf War. His 1981 book *Covering Islam* analyzed the unexamined and hidden assumptions contained in U.S. news accounts and in documentaries about the nature of Islam. Given the focus on the Middle East in the 1980s it is not surprising that the national news media seek out Said for interviews, panel discussions, and commentary. He appears frequently on National Public Radio's "All Things Considered," nightly network TV news, and "The MacNeil-Lehrer Newshour."

Whether Jamieson, Barber, Said, and the many other examples of academic savants who fill airwaves, news columns, and op-ed pages with punditry add to or detract from the quality of public discussions about politics is not the issue here. Rather, we simply point out that academic savants are but one more variety of those individuals whose technical expertise in a given subject area provides the wherewithal to project them into the national limelight and portray them as having special insight into the problems of the times. Expertise and insight alone, however, are not enough. What these individuals must also possess is the capacity to voice their views in a style suitable for consumption and distribution by the mass media. They must develop *la technique of* performing for the media.

## CONCLUSION: THE CENTRIST DRAGON OF *LA TECHNIQUE* OF PUNDITRY

Janet Steele, a communication scholar who has also taken time off from her teaching to work in the broadcast media on such TV productions as NBC's "Today Show," points to what the performing technique of punditry requires (Steele, 1990a, 1990b). In doing so, she implied a reason why the Studs Terkels of the world will not get their wish of removing "the flatulent pundits" from TV. Steele argued that by and large, TV journalists do not see themselves as experts with voices of authority on the stories they cover. Moreover, whether or not they are "objective" in reporting, they refrain from too much analysis and interpretation of opinion. Nonetheless, they need to convince themselves and their audiences that their work is significant and that they are doing a professional job of reporting. Consequently, TV journalists turn to academics not simply for expertise but also to legitimize the news enterprise.

TV news departments, of course, have their own agendas. From a TV producer's viewpoint, technical and academic experts help advance those agendas. Producers seek an aura of academic authority, but only by calling on professors who are telegenic: presentable, personable, adept on camera, and capable of speaking in sound bites. TV news particularly prizes the quick, pithy remark, preferably an appealing metaphor or with a biting humorous tone (for example, " 'I am that man!' Peggy Noonan wrote."). To guarantee the appearance of the appropriate academic pundit, TV producers plan the story script and then undertake a talent search. For example, in sounding out academics for the "Today Show," according to Steele, network producers search newspapers and magazines for potential "experts." When a story breaks that demands expert testimony, it is a simple matter to let the fingers do the walking through the Rolodex to screen possibilities for follow-ups. In effect, producers know the sound bite they want and recruit the expert who will voice it. According to political scientist Stephen Hess, a think tank (Brookings Institution) rather than purely academic pundit: "A producer calls to check me out, asking enough questions to know whether I am likely to say what he or she is after." If the expert does not offer to comply, "they say they'll get back to me, which they won't." Said Hess, "someone else is sure to have the magic words they are looking for" (quoted in Steele, 1990a, p. B2).

Talent searches, screenings, and tryouts assist TV journalists in their craft, but what of the punditry that is evoked? One of its characteristics, thinks Steele, is that academic commentary becomes predictable and even trivial. In selecting academic experts whose remarks conform to stereotypes built into a "canned" news script, TV (and other media as well) "chooses academics in exactly the same way it chooses public officials. The academics who appear are centrists." The academic pundits,—Steele calls them "mandarins"—repeatedly "make their reputation by staking out mainstream intellectual positions" (1990a, p. B2). Steele includes among such mandarins Edward Said, the academic pundit discussed above. He is, she said, "a typical example of television's use of expertise." By representing a Palestinian view, on the surface he appears extreme. Nonetheless, "as Palestinians go, he's a centrist: and as academics go, he's establishment" (1990a, p. B2).

Moreover, the technique of punditry and the technician as pundit produce a self-fulfilling practice: "The more their names appear in the mass media, the more apt they are to make it on to a news show as an 'expert' " (Steele, 1990b, p. 29). That practice serves the news media in two ways. First, as already noted, it provides journalists with "Rent-an-Expert" files to tap as stories break. Second, it assists journalists in enhancing a reputation for objectivity. By turning to academics whom they deem "balanced" in their grasp of issues, news programs and newspapers delegate the task of opinionated analysis and interpretation to savants. Rarely do news viewers or readers know the political persuasions of academics; presumably, they have none. If there is an acknowledgment of the biases of academic pundits, news organizations retain the impression of balanced coverage by matching a savant or think tank expert of one viewpoint against another.

Such a balancing of opposites, however, does not negate Steele's overall assessment that the pundit's dragon seldom wades outside the mainstream. Eric Alterman is a think tank pundit from the World Policy Institute; the institute favors world economic growth rather than military buildups to promote peace. Alterman has pointed out that the mainstream punditocracy during the Reagan administration allowed the president "to define his program in such a way that it negated the possibility of a principled, patriotic alternative" (1988, p. 35A). Pundits on confrontational TV talk shows such as "The McLaughlin Group" or "This Week With David Brinkley" (see Chapter Five) or on news programs like ABC's "Nightline" or PBS's "The MacNeil-Lehrer Newshour" put on a good show of disputing Reagan's policies. They hurled insults, invectives, and criticisms; they baited and bashed one another. However, in the end they presented the world as a straightforward, simple, uncomplicated place whose problems could be alleviated by equally simple bromides—or simply ignored altogether.

Steele noted one other characteristic of TV punditry that derives from the talking heads, sound bites, and pithy quotes of the technician performing as pundit: It is seductive. Few scholars, she noted, can pass up the opportunity to court celebrity by lecturing to a national audience. It serves the professorial ego, and at many institutions desirous of projecting a "public service image," it looks better on a resume than a listing of stodgy scholarly tomes or academic articles that one might write. However, in that seductive quality of punditry lies the danger. The otherwise ignored "prophet without honor" in his or her own country pays a price for a national forum. That price is manipulation: by journalists, by politicians, and by the pundit's own ego.

For pundit professors at colleges and universities there is another problem. Television and radio stations, newspapers and news magazines are in business to turn a dollar's profit, or if not a profit, then at least—as in the case of National Public Radio and the Public Broadcast System—to attract financial sponsors in the form of private and public corporations. Broadcasters deliver audiences to advertisers and financial backers. Is it the proper province of the academic to be used in such corporate enterprise—to help produce profits or raise money, even indirectly, to sell products and produce consumers? To the degree that savants' expert technical commentary for the media does so, the professorial pundit shares something in common with the "scholar-athlete" playing big time athletics at big time schools. Both are revenue-producing agents delivering audiences for big media. Let the audience members they deliver, and allegedly inform and entertain, beware.

*Chapter Five*

# The Chattering Pundits: Talk TV and Radio

As she walked through Wonderland, Alice discovered "a table set out under a tree in front of the house, and the March Hare and the Hatter were having tea at it: a Dormouse was sitting between them." Alice sat down in a large armchair at one end of the table. Shortly, the Hatter asked: "Why is a raven like a writing-desk?" Alice, thinking the Hatter sought an answer to a riddle, said, "I believe I can guess that." There followed this exchange:

*March Hare*: "Do you mean that you think you can find out the answer to it?"

*Alice*: "Exactly so."

*March Hare*: "Then you should say what you mean."

*Alice*: "I do. At least—at least I mean what I say—that's the same thing, you know."

*Hatter*: "Not the same thing a bit! Why, you might as well say that 'I see what I eat' is the same thing as 'I eat what I see'!"

*March Hare*: "You might as well say that 'I like what I get' is the same thing as 'I get what I like'!"

*Dormouse*: "You might just as well say that 'I breathe when I sleep' is the same thing as 'I sleep when I breathe'!"

*Hatter*: "It *is* the same thing with you."

Here the conversation stopped. Shortly the aimless chatter picked up again, marked by argument, rude behavior, and even personal attacks. Unsettled by it all Alice vowed, "I'll never go there again. It's the stupidest tea-party I ever was at in all my life!" (Carroll, 1960, pp. 93–104).

In this chapter we consider places where political pundits—priests, bards, sages, and oracles—frequently congregate to exchange and argue conventional political wisdom, rumor, and gossip. The pundits are members of America's "Chattering Classes." Their venues are the ever-growing number of political talk and call-in shows that glut the air waves of television, cable TV, and radio. Although refreshments are not always served, in many respects they invite comparison to the Mad Hatter's tea party. We leave it to readers, after considering what we have to say about a few sampled shows, to agree or disagree with Alice whether these are "the stupidest tea-parties" they have ever witnessed in their lives.

According to Alan Watkins (1989), a political columnist for the London *Observer*, the phrase "the Chattering Classes" came into use in the mid-1980s. Watkins did not originate the phrase but he takes credit for having made it popular: "What I was trying to do was to popularize a phrase which comprehended the new media intelligentsia of the seventies and eighties—together with their subsidiary—some might say client—groups." Prominently numbered among this new media intelligentsia were "journalists, television people, media folk generally." As the phrase grew in popularity, said Watkins, it "got quite out of hand" and became a derisive expression applied to anyone invited to TV shows, panel discussions, and interview sessions to offer views on all manner of matters, political and nonpolitical. It was not long, said Watkins, until the Chattering Classes were identified with the "marginalia" rather than the "nitty-gritties" of politics and viewed by critics as persons of no influence at all (p. 25).

In the United States the phrase is less popular and, perhaps for that reason, less derisive in application. As Martin Walker (1990) noted, the phrase refers to "the political junkies inside the Washington Beltway" who "tend to watch C-SPAN as a matter of course" (p. 8). They not only watch but also appear on local and national TV and radio public affairs programs that are aired on all networks. Through their public visibility they either are, or aspire to be, opinion makers. We will examine members of America's Chattering Classes in two meeting places: television political talk shows and radio call-in programs.

## VISIBLE AND INVISIBLE PUNDITS: TALK SHOWS ON TV

The principal progenitor of political talk shows, on television or on radio, is "Meet the Press." It dates back to the era when network radio reigned over electronic journalism. As TV supplanted radio, "Meet the Press" made a successful transition to television in that medium's early days. It was scarcely a centerpiece of network programming on either radio or TV; executives scheduled the public affairs show in time slots that were unlikely to attract large audiences—time slots the noted radio and TV journalist Edward R. Murrow was later to liken to the "Sunday Ghetto." "Meet the Press" was an NBC stalwart for years; it continues to appear on Sunday mornings on that network. The format consists of an important public official, candidate, diplomat, or other dignitary responding to questions posed by a panel of journalists. Appearing regularly on the panel during the show's early days were its cocreators, Lawrence Spivak and Martha Roundtree (who finally left the program to be host of her own short-lived talk show, "Press Conference"). During the formative years of "Meet the Press," "print" journalists for the wire services or newspapers shunned appearances on the panel. They regarded the program as electronic entertainment, not true journalism. That perception, however, changed. Both print and electronic journalists discovered that "Meet the Press" had a respectable audience of opinion leaders. Appearances on the program brought publicity to reporters, and, when the show moved to TV, instant public recognition in fashionable circles. Moreover, in the give-and-take between politicians and reporters, there was always the possibility of breaking a major story.

"Meet the Press" not only remains on network television but, as any regular TV viewer knows, it has been joined by a plethora of look-alikes, competitors, and alternatives with different formats and styles. All such talk shows incorporate chatter among and about pundits who are visible to audiences on TV screens. In addition, many talk TV shows add viewer call-ins to the format, thus expanding chatter to invisible, unseen pundits. Here we shall explore three general talk TV formats: those emphasizing casual chatter, confrontational chatter, and carnival chatter.

### The Casual Chatter of a Coffee Klatch

Watching TV on a daily basis frequently suggests that the medium, the coffee cup, and the pundit were made for one another. On network, cable, and local television, from predawn until after midnight, appear little knots of people around a table, sitting on a sofa or sprawling in armchairs, sipping coffee and pontificating about a variety of matters from bass fishing to famine in Africa/and from likely Superbowl contenders to probable presidential nominees. Laid-back, casual chatter is the order of the day. In fact, so casual is the chatter in many instances that although coffee has replaced tea, a viewer might be reminded while watching CNN's Larry King resting his chin in his hand, leaning on his elbow on a table between himself and a talk show guest, of Alice observing the March Hare and Hatter using a sleeping Dormouse between them as a cushion: "Very uncomfortable for the Dormouse; only as it's asleep, I suppose it doesn't mind" (Carroll, 1960, p. 93).

In many respects, "Meet the Press" set the standard for casual punditry on TV talk shows in the 1950s. The panel of journalists, who were assembled at the behest of host Lawrence Spivak, interrogated a noted guest in a quiet, dispassionate, almost deferential manner. Rarely did guests give direct answers. More often, the guest's responses circled or begged the question. Such evasion upset reporters on the panel, but seldom did they express open frustration or hound the guest into a response. Once, however, even the mild-mannered, if somewhat acerbic, moderator of "Meet the Press" almost could not contain himself. In a half-hour program in 1960, Senator Lyndon Baines Johnson was the guest. Not once during the program did Johnson answer a question directly. Spivak held his tongue, admitting afterwards that he barely could keep from blurting out following the show, "Now that we're off the air, will you tell us if your name is Lyndon Johnson?" (Rivers, 1965, p. 167).

Reporters today are far more aggressive in their questions and follow-ups, yet on many TV talk shows the general conversational chatter survives along the lines of the panel/interview format of NBC's "Meet the Press." With slight variations, that style and format mark CBS's "Face the Nation" and CNN's "Newsmaker Saturday" and "Newsmaker Sunday": weekend competitors to the venerable NBC offering. Different in many respects yet still well within the confines of casual chatter in spite of efforts to be otherwise is another such competitor: ABC's "This Week with David Brinkley." The "Brinkley" show is both an interview program in the tradition of "Meet the Press" and a roundtable discussion which became a popular talk show format in the 1980s. Approximately two-thirds of the hour-long "Brinkley" program consists of an interview with a guest, frequently a government official, on one or a limited set of topics. Regulars Brinkley, ABC's Sam Donaldson, and columnist George Will ask the questions. Although panelists at times press the guest for responses if they are not forthcoming (Donaldson especially does so), the overall tenor of the interview is scarcely a striking departure from the decorum of "Meet the Press."

The genteel veneer, however, comes off once the guest departs. Most of the remaining portion of the show consists of what Brinkley has labeled an "uninhibited, free-for-all" discussion (Hirsch, 1991, p. 41). That discussion occurs among Brinkley, Donaldson, Will, and an invited panelist: Cokie Roberts, correspondent and pundit of National Public Radio; Hodding Carter, formerly with the presidential administration of Jimmy Carter; Tom Wicker of the *New York Times*; Ellen Goodman of the *Boston Globe*; or another noted journalist. Brinkley and the invited panelist have a presence, but the spotlight is frequently a debate between Donaldson and Will. The former is aggressive, hot, and visceral; the latter is restrained, cool, and cerebral. Although the exchange does not appear contrived or rehearsed, it is superficial, formulaic, and—over time—predictable. Hence, the edge and bite of the "debate" wears off, while the conversational chatter of the punditry prevails.

Where "This Week with David Brinkley" most notably departs the tradition established by "Meet the Press" is the open flaunting of the once sacred practice of reporters keeping their opinions to themselves. The roundtable segment, of course, encourages journalists to be pundits first and reporters second. In the buildup to the Gulf War in January 1991, for example, the "Brinkley" panelists became a mini-Congress of the United States. On January 12 the U.S. Congress had passed a resolution authorizing the president to use force against Iraq. On the "Brinkley" program that was broadcast subsequent to the congressional action, the host asked George Will, Sam Donaldson, and Cokie Roberts how each would have voted on the resolution authorizing force. Will and Donaldson voted for the resolution and Roberts against, while Brinkley added his support for the resolution. Although President George Bush thanked Congress for backing his policy toward Iraq, there was no report that he felt equally relieved by the pundit ballot. Robert Pierpoint, a retired CBS correspondent and a veteran of many radio and TV talk shows, felt moved to question such punditry: "I am also troubled by those reporters who allowed themselves to be quoted on their personal opinions about the war. Let's leave that sort of *indulgence* to the columnists and stick to tough questions and hard analysis" (emphasis added; 1991, p. 9).

In addition to the Sunday coffee klatch formats of ABC, CBS, NBC, and CNN's TV interview/discussion shows, restrained conversational chatter is the style of various programs scheduled throughout the week as well. The formats vary. As part of its nightly newscast on PBS, for example, "The MacNeil/Lehrer Newshour" incorporates interviews with specialists in selected policy areas related to the evening's "top news stories." Either Robert MacNeil or James Lehrer conducts interviews with a panel of specialists: frequently these are pundits who regularly appear on a variety of other talk shows such as David Gergen of *U.S. and World Report* or Norman Ornstein and William Schneider of the American Enterprise Institute. Rarely are the question–answer or discussion segments heated or the chatter anything but amiable. Casual chatter also abounds on PBS's Friday night regular, "Washington Week in Review" (WWR). Moderator Paul Duke joins four correspondents representing prestigious members of the nation's press corps for what program promotions label a "frank," "candid," and "heated" discussion of the week's top stories. In fact, as demonstrated elsewhere (Nimmo and Combs, 1990, pp. 158–161), a set, ritualistic formula simultaneously provides a sense that the panelists are above the rough-and-tumble of the news yet permits them to share their opinions and reach a general consensus that falls far short of either a frank exchange or an in-depth discussion of topics.

Without question the venue where casual, conversational chatter and punditry most abounds is the Cable Satellite Public Affairs Network (C-SPAN). Throughout the week and on the weekends, depending on whether Congress is in session, C-SPAN devotes a substantial block of airtime to TV talk in the form of interviews, roundtables, discussions, and viewer call-ins. Along with CNN, C-SPAN prides itself on having popularized the TV call-in format. Among other cable outlets that have followed the C-SPAN lead in programming call-in shows is CNBC (Consumer News and Business Channel). CNBC has become a haven for a variety of talk and call-in shows (for example, "Talk Live") whose hosts achieved popularity on other networks—for example: Dick Cavett, John McLaughlin, and Morton Downey, Jr. So popular has the talk format become that there were plans to launch an entire cable network in 1991 (tentatively called American Talk TV) devoted to twelve hours of live talk shows daily and boasting an audience of two to four million households.

Many TV critics (see Chapter Six) prophesy that the C-SPAN call-in format will be increasingly adopted by over-the-air commercial networks as well as by cable TV. In its weekly newsletter, *C-SPAN Update*, of April 14, 1991 (Barton, 1991, pp. 1–2), the network proudly headlined a reprint of an article published on March 12 by Rick Du Brow, media critic of the *Los Angeles Times*. The headline read, "Cable's Call-in Format Adopted By 'Big Three' Networks." Du Brow's article described the impact of the "new practices that have been developed effectively by C-SPAN and CNN." Du Brow went on to point out that those practices had been adopted by CBS's "America Tonight." C-SPAN, wrote Du Brow, which is a "pioneer in direct viewer talkbacks to its guests— government officials, journalists, and the like—may be relatively tiny in size, but its impact on television has been gigantic." *Update* expanded Du Brow's claims, noting on behalf of C-SPAN that it was the "first to regularly schedule daily viewer call-ins, starting back in 1980. Now the network airs four call-in programs each day" (pp. 1–2).

One such regularly featured call-in show is the network's "Journalists' Roundtable," a weekly review of major news events. The program consists of a host and a panel of journalists. In many respects the formula derives from "Washington Week in Review," with two exceptions. First, "Journalists' Roundtable" adds a call-in portion that WWR does not have. Second, whereas WWR engages primarily in providing viewers with background information to the week's events, the C-SPAN program—largely because of the viewers' calls—is more an exchange of journalists' speculations and guesses regarding causes and consequences of major political happenings (Nimmo and Combs, 1990, pp. 163–164).

As a measure of the quantity of conversational chatter on C-SPAN, consider the fact that during the forty-four-day period from the beginning (January 16) to the end (March 1) of the Gulf War in 1991, C-SPAN provided call-in interviews with more than 140 executive and congressional officials, journalists, media critics, policy analysts, foreign officials, and professional pundits. On Valentine's Day, C-SPAN featured as a guest a call-in talk show host from a rival radio network, Cliff Kincaid of the Newstalk Radio Network, who is also cohost of a program of media criticism (see Chapter Six). The daily format of the C-SPAN call-in shows during the Gulf War remained essentially the same. A moderator-host opened the program with a guest in the studio, normally with both people sitting at a table. The moderator introduced the guest and her/or his qualifications and chatted briefly with the designated "expert." The moderator then announced, "Now it is time to accept your calls," and the call-in portion proceeded. The pacing of each show was deliberate and voices seldom rose. The punditry, whether offered by the guest or by callers, remained polite. Unknown was the Alice in C-SPAN's Wonderland who, offended by a "piece of rudeness" at the tea party, simply "got up in great disgust, and walked off."

## The Confrontational Chatter of Advocacy

Rudeness and offense, however, are the staples of an alternative approach to TV talk. In the 1980s with the diffusion of cable TV into many households, the proliferation of talk shows on cable channels posed a problem. There were so many of them that talk show producers were forced to devise striking formats to set their "chatter programming" apart from competitors. A revolution in style occurred. Controversy took precedence over conversation; confrontation took precedence over contemplation; and combative advocates took precedence over courtly hosts. Granted, the "Meet the Press" brand of punditry did not vanish. However, the watchword of TV punditry shifted. "Let us talk" became "Let's you and him fight!"

The confrontational format had been tried off and on throughout the growth of TV. For example, in 1956 a former actor, quiz show host, and radio announcer for a popular western radio serial entitled "The Lone Ranger" began an interview program called "Night Beat." He was Mike Wallace, who later would obtain celebrity status on CBS's highly rated "60 Minutes." Whereas most TV interview shows of the period were polite, bland exchanges between host and guest, Wallace did something different. He played the role of a prosecuting attorney who shocked his guests with accusations, harassed them for answers, and made them squirm. The guest sat in a chair that was brightly lit from a spotlight above. Wallace was, by contrast, virtually shrouded in darkness; often, only the curling smoke of his cigarette was visible rising in the air. Wallace was aggressive, pugnacious, and insulting, earning for him such titles as "Mike Malice" and "the Grand Inquisitor" (Gates, 1978, pp. 287–288).

Other attempts at confrontational programming followed. In 1958 David Susskind's "Open End" featured roundtable bickering between guests who were often peculiar and bizarre; the exchanges resembled the Mad Hatter's tea party. In 1964 the "Joseph Pyne Show" elevated controversy and rudeness to a new plane. Pyne, an ex-marine, backed off from no guest or issue, political or nonpolitical. He employed insults and invective for shock value. In a far more erudite, sedate, and restrained way, William F. Buckley's "Firing Line" (recall Chapter Three) contributed to the evolution of confrontational chatter. It began in 1966 and in its early years consisted of host Buckley in a caustic exchange with a guest. Buckley's sharp tongue and subtle invective often left the guest as frustrated as Mike Wallace's badgering, yet the show was far more erudite and less sensationalist in tone.

For the most part, "Night Beat," "Open End," and the "Joseph Pyne Show" focused on guests who were eccentric, weird, or controversial in their own right. "Firing Line" 's guests, too, were out of the ordinary, for they had to be clever persons who were able to hold their own in the verbal sparring match with Buckley. For Wallace, Susskind, Pyne, and Buckley, the guests were means to an end, props in entertainment programming as much as information sources. For Wallace, Pyne, and, occasionally, for Buckley, there was a hint of a game devised by playwright Edward Albee (1962) for his drama, *Who's Afraid of Virginia Woolf*. The play's protagonists, George and Martha, invite an innocent young couple, Nick and Honey to their home. As part of a bizarre evening of rudeness, insults, and degradations heaped on each other, George and Martha play a game they call "Get the Guests" which extends the madness to Nick and Honey. Early confrontational TV relied heavily on guests that could be "gotten" in what was often a contrived game.

In 1969 appeared a political TV talk show that moved strikingly away from the "Meet the Press" format yet did not play "Get the Guest." "Agronsky and Company" (later, "Inside Washington") became the model for what today, with variations, is the convention of confrontation on TV talk shows. "Agronsky" began on a local commercial TV station but was more widely seen on public affairs television, including PBS. It was not an interview show. There were no guests to be gotten and no politicians to probe. Nor were there call-ins. It employed a roundtable format consisting of a panel of four journalists discussing the week's events with the moderation of a host, Martin Agronsky. In that respect it was like "Washington Week in Review." However, there the similarity ends. Panelists did not discuss; they debated. Posturing, disagreement, and dispute marked each program. Many of the journalists/pundits appearing on "Agronsky" honed their skills and moved to more confrontational roles (and lucrative paychecks) on public affairs programs on the commercial networks: for example, columnists James Kilpatrick for "60 Minutes" and George Will for "This Week with David Brinkley."

Although "Agronsky and Company" featured argument for argument's sake, journalists quibbled among themselves with decorum, restraint, and a style that was sedate and civilized. The next innovation in confrontation formats was not only to make argument (not information) *the* show, but to throw civility to the winds. By the mid- to late 1980s, that "advance" was achieved. Among the TV talk shows entering the punditry market on network and cable TV were "The McLaughlin Group," "Crossfire," "Capitol Gang," "Evans and Novak," and "McLaughlin." So loud and tumultuous did the exchanges between TV pundits become on many of these programs that it would certainly not have struck anyone as surprising—as it apparently was not surprising for Alice after having attended the tea party—to look back after watching and see talk show panelists "trying to put the Dormouse into the teapot" (Carroll, 1960, p. 103).

As but one example of the confrontation talk genre let us reflect on the original "McLaughlin Group." (We say "original" only to designate the fact that since its origins in 1982, the panelists, not the format, have changed; columnist Robert Novak left the "Group" to become a regular on "Capitol Gang," a variation on the "Group" theme. Moreover, John McLaughlin now has a second show, "McLaughlin," on CNBC.) The "Group" has all the characteristics of verbal professional mud wrestling. As with professional wrestling, feigned combat is the show; the confrontation is contrived and verbal assaults are personalized. Screaming, shouting, sweeping generalizations are the sum and substance of the show. The show's host, John McLaughlin, is, as Alan Hirsch noted (1990), "a master showman and provocateur, insulting his guests and moving the discussion along at a breathtaking rate" (p. 33). Taking their cue from McLaughlin, each of the four journalists comprising the show's panel interrupts, speaks at a breathless pace, and reaches for the perfect putdown. Frequently that perfection reflects the maturity of six-year-old sibling rivals as illustrated by such remarks as: "You should be ashamed of yourself"; "Oh, come on. That's ridiculous"; "Oh boy, naive"; "That's a silly question"; "That's not a silly question"; "All right. It's a crazy question!"

Confrontational TV talk shows such as the "Group" have raised questions in the minds of journalists. At issue is whether reporters should appear in Mad Hatter and March Hare roles. For instance, the editor of the *Boston Globe*, Thomas Winship (1990), has objected to the "intermingling of reporting, commentary, and posturing." He urged people to "think of the ethical implications of *The McLaughlin Group* spectacle: mainstream journalists playacting in a shouting-match Gong show. Each is paid an estimated $1,000 for their [sic] 30-minute, on-camera act." Moreover, said Winship, it gets worse: "For $35,000 or thereabouts, the National Association of Tire Dealers, or the like, can close out their convention banquet with those same journalists screaming at one another" (p. 60). Such criticism, however, apparently does not dampen public interest in confrontational chatter. "The McLaughlin Group" retains an audience of 3.5 million viewers each week; moreover, in the allegedly politically savvy nation's capital, it is the number one–rated weekend public affairs show (Lieberman, 1991, p. 14). Perhaps decision makers like to watch a dormouse being stuffed into a teapot.

### The Carnival Chatter of Political Sideshows

We would be remiss if we did not consider briefly another form of political chatter on TV talk shows, even though political discussion is not the principal topic in most cases. We speak of the most viewed and watched of TV talk shows, those frequently called "tabloid television" by critics: "Donahue," "Geraldo," "Sally Jesse Raphael," "Joan Rivers," "Oprah Winfrey," "Larry King Live," "The Morton Downey Jr. Show," and other syndicated programs. These are as much the staples of daily TV as soap operas, game shows, and late night comics.

Although prone to chatter about marital infidelity, transvestites, female impersonators, satanic cults, anorexia, or teenage sadism, political issues are not beyond the purview of such programming. For example, during the prelude to the 1991 Gulf War, "Donahue" devoted programs to the potential for armed conflict, even bringing together a panel of Congressmen favoring and opposing the use of force in the crisis. So much has Phil Donahue moved into and out of political topics on "Donahue" that he has moderated forums between political candidates seeking the nominations of both major political parties, making him a virtual coequal with the likes of Dan Rather or Tom Brokaw.

The formats of such talk shows are familiar to everyone: a host with either a pleasing or offensive personality, one or more guests, a studio audience invited to participate in questioning guests (although not on "Larry King Live"), and, in some instances, viewer call-ins. The guests selected to discuss political topics may or may not be politicians or journalists; moreover, the level of interest in and information about politics among members of the studio audience varies considerably. The style of the host also varies: Witness the witty, skeptical Phil Donahue;

the bemused Geraldo Rivera; the curious Larry King; the abrasive Morton Downey, Jr.; the alternatingly outraged and compassionate Sally Jesse Raphael, Oprah Winfrey or John McLaughlin on his "McLaughlin" talk show appearing on CNBC. From their demeanor one might not think of such hosts as journalists, or even believe that they regard themselves as such. They are more like barkers at a carnival seeking to draw a crowd than reporters covering a story.

However, one of the key issues surrounding tabloid television is whether it is journalism. In 1989 at the annual convention of the American Society of Newspaper Editors, several TV talk show hosts gathered with members of the press to discuss the topic, "Who's a Journalist? Talk Show Sensationalism" (Public Affairs Video Archives, 1989). Among the hosts were Phil Donahue; Morton Downey, Jr.; Larry King; and Geraldo Rivera. Such members of the press as Jack Nelson of the *Los Angeles Times*, Geneva Overholser of the Des Moines *Register*, Tom Shales of the *Washington Post* (see Chapter Six), and F. Gilman Spencer of the New York *Daily News* were also present.

Each of the talk show hosts argued that he was, in fact, a journalist, in spite of protests from other panelists, most pointedly Jack Nelson, that none had a serious news-gathering role. Saying "I am not a host, I'm an advocate," Morton Downey, Jr., viewed himself as an advocacy journalist. Geraldo Rivera thought himself like all reporters, explaining, "unfortunately sometimes reporters are voyeurs." Larry King claimed that TV talk shows give viewers the prerogative of choice, just like a newspaper; one may choose to read it or not. The strongest defense of the talk show host as journalist came from Phil Donahue. Granted, he said, "I get paid to draw a crowd. . . . Part of my job is to attract an MTV audience." However, he said, "There is a great deal of information in talk shows," and the carnival format builds new audiences for that information by "sneaking issues like the Persian Gulf in between the male strippers." After all, he concluded, "Journalism is supposed to be messy, just like a democracy" (Who's a Journalist? Talk Show Sensationalism, Public Affairs Video Archives, 1989).

Journalism or not, conversational, confrontational, and carnival chatter abounds on television and offers a vehicle for punditry that virtually anyone can ride who possesses the persistence to get on the air. In that sense virtually everyone is now a pundit. If TV does not make it so, certainly talk radio does.

## "EVERYMAN, DIAL 1-800-PUNDITS": TALK RADIO

Performed frequently in the late fifteenth century in England was a morality play entitled *Everyman* in which the leading character, Everyman, is summoned by Death. Death allows Everyman to take along to the grave anyone willing to travel with him. Everyman implores each of his "friends" to follow, but Beauty will not go, Kindred will not travel, and Worldly Goods turns him down. Only Good Deeds, Everyman learns, can and will travel with him to meet Death: "Everyman, I will go with thee, and be thy guide, in thy most need to be by thy side" (quoted in Burke, 1953, p. iii). Setting aside the sexist language of the fifteenth century, the moral of the tale is clear. Good Deeds will go, guide, and fulfill Everyman's need by being at his side. In the current era it appears that there is something else for Everyone to have at hand: the telephone. Home phones, office phones, pay phones, car phones, and cellular phones (and conceivably the shoe phone of agent Maxwell Smart in the 1960s TV series "Get Smart") are everywhere for everyone. On that fact thrives the burgeoning punditry of talk radio, a new medium for the "chattering classes."

Daily, 80 percent of Americans tune in to one or more of the approximately 10,000 radio stations in the United States. Of that number, 500 stations have some form of news/talk format. That total represents a jump of almost 200 stations moving to the format from 1988 to 1990 (Roberts, 1991). In addition to individual stations, there are also broadcasting networks specializing in talk formats or providing ample hours of talk programming: Newstalk Radio Network, NBC's Talknet, A.M. Talk, the EFM Network, the Sun Network, and the Mutual Broadcasting System (airing the widely broadcast "Larry King Show"). Across the country, talk radio hosts have built regional and national reputations for both their broadcasting skills and their political views. In addition to Larry King, for example, there are nationally syndicated radio "personalities." Among them are the veteran talk show host Tom Snyder, conservative Rush Limbaugh of WABC in New York (syndicated on 350 stations), Michael Jackson of KABC in Los Angeles, and Cliff Kincaid of the Newstalk Radio Network. At the regional/local level are Mike Siegel of KING in Seattle, Roger Hedgecock of KSDO in San Diego, Bob Hardy of KMOX in St. Louis, and David Gold of KLIF in Dallas.

Given the growing pervasiveness of talk radio it is not surprising that its political role has come under scrutiny. The question of precisely how far-reaching that role is has no firm answer. On some issues, talk radio has appeared to be a potent force. The most notable example occurred in 1989. Congress was considering voting its members a 51 percent pay raise. Radio stations with talk formats received a flood of protesting calls, as did congressional offices. Many talk show hosts aided and abetted their callers in the protest. Congress postponed the pay increase, only to follow a year later with a smaller one tied to measures for ethics reform. Although political columnists credited talk radio hosts and audiences with blunting the 1989 pay increase, however, not every student of broadcasting is convinced that talk radio has that much impact. For one thing, the callers consist of only 5 percent of the listening audience. What that 5 percent represent—opinion leaders, populists, chronic know-nothings, conservatives, liberals, or simply lonely people—is not clear. Hence, observed Lawrence Lichty, who is director of the Woodrow Wilson Center's Media Studies Program in Washington, D.C., the audience for the talk format is "small and very limited" and probably always will be (quoted in Roberts, 1991, p. 61).

Regardless of the political impact of talk radio, there is no question that it provides a major forum for chattering punditry—from the host, from guests, and from callers. Formats vary but typically incorporate a brief news segment at the beginning of each hour and at the half-hour. The remainder of the hour, excluding commercial time, consists of a host interacting with callers. Some hosts interview guests, while others do not. Any given host's show normally involves a three-hour block. For stations that program nothing but talk, this provides an ample opportunity to fill the air waves with chatter.

To sample but a few variations in the format, style, and content of punditry on talk radio, we will examine three talk radio programs aired during the period of the 1991 Gulf War. The three were the Newstalk Radio Network's show with host Cliff Kincaid, the same network's "Battleline," and the special call-in coverage provided by National Public Radio (NPR) with host Daniel Shorr. For each of the Newstalk Radio Network programs we constructed and recorded a random week by selecting, for example, a Monday for one week, a Tuesday for another, a Wednesday for another, and so on. Moreover, we randomly selected for each sampled day a single hour of the two- or three-hour time period over which the program aired. Hence, for the six-weeks war, we examined one hour of each program for one randomly constructed week. For the analysis of the NPR special programs we selected at random ten of the two-hour shows from all the programs recorded across the war period, thus producing a total of twenty hours of programming for investigation. (Consult the Bibliography for the dates of specific programs included in this analysis.)

### Greet, and, Perhaps, Get the Guest

Cliff Kincaid, host of a three-hour morning call-in program on the Newstalk Radio Network, is a self-styled conservative. Moreover, as we shall see in Chapter Six, he is a principal media critic and a spokesperson for the media watchdog organization Accuracy in Media. Each hour of his radio talk show is normally broken into segments with a different topic serving as the conversation piece of the segment. Although Kincaid sometimes offers his punditry in the form of a soliloquy followed by listener's calls, his more usual format is to chat via telephone with a guest "expert" or protagonist and then accept calls from his audience. In the sampled week under study, Kincaid averaged five listeners' calls per hour. Kincaid follows a convention of radio talk shows in greeting callers; namely, he identifies them by first name and locale: "John" from Silver Springs, MD; "Mike" from Virginia; "Kim" from North Carolina, "Carlos" from Oklahoma City; and so on.

Given that the period we are examining involved the six weeks of the Gulf War, it is not surprising that Kincaid's guests reflected that topic. Among his guests were a policy officer of the United States Information Agency (USIA), described as an "expert on disinformation"; a legislative assistant to the Senate Foreign Relations Committee; an author of a report detailing Soviet efforts to aid the Iraqis in the war; a former member of the National Security Council who years earlier had *"warned against* support for Saddam Hussein"; and a coordinator for Peace in the Middle East, an antiwar protest group. Kincaid, however, did not dwell exclusively on the war. For example, another of his programs focused on the issues of birth control and gay rights; his guest was a representative from an organization called the AIDS Coalition to Unleash Power (ACT UP).

To typify the flavor of the punditry espoused by all parties on Kincaid's program and to illustrate the host's style, we will consider a few of the topics discussed. One was the recurring question of television's coverage of the war, especially the coverage by CNN and ABC, and how well that coverage served the interests of Iraq's "disinformation campaign." Individual journalists, broadcast networks, and news publications were the targets of criticism from the host, guest, and callers. The most frequent *bête noir* was CNN's Peter Arnett. Arnett remained in Baghdad to report the impact of the war on the Iraqi capital, and his reports were subject to Iraqi censorship. The "chattering class" of Kincaid's show rebuked Arnett's reports for serving Iraq and being destructive of U.S. interests. In several segments Kincaid invited callers to suggest apt nicknames for Arnett, along the lines of those applied to the Nazi broadcasters "Axis Sally" and "Lord Haw Haw" during World War II. Callers proposed "Propaganda Pete," "Baghdad Arnett," and "Peter Armpit," among others.

During the war, Coalition forces bombed an installation claimed by Iraq to be civilian rather than military. Iraq identified it as a plant producing baby milk powder; the United States said it was a biological weapons factory. In the case of the biological weapons/baby milk factory, CNN's Arnett provided a censored, filmed report of the Iraqi claim. For Kincaid, his guest, and the callers, this was proof of Arnett's culpability. Call-in and studio chatter reached a general accord that Arnett was "willingly" going along with "the old lies and disinformation" Hussein "has been putting out for some time."

Kincaid's guest from the USIA was more charitable toward Arnett than either the show's host or the callers. The specialist in disinformation suggested that the correspondent might be under coercion and hence might be filing reports favorable to Iraq that he (Arnett) did not believe to be factual. In any event, the policy officer stated that CNN was certainly "a prime target" and a "victim" of disinformation. Noting that the "baby milk issue" had surfaced in September 1990 when an alleged "Peace Ship" had been prevented from going to Iraq by United Nations sanctions, the guest assured listeners that Hussein had tried to "pull at the world's heart strings" for "months and months." Moreover, according to the USIA officer, the story about the baby milk factory had been planted by the Iraqi News Agency well before Arnett reported it. The officer had verified the factory as a biological warfare site. The story, he concluded, was a "totally set-up operation."

With phone lines open, Kincaid's callers voiced their views on the issue at hand. "Sal" asked if Arnett was an American citizen, why reporters "knock" the United States, and why did Arnett not "get the hell out of there?" "Jay" pointed out that William Shirer left Nazi Germany in order to report freely: "Are we dealing with a different brand of journalism today?" Kincaid responded that journalists are no longer "morale boosters"; Arnett was "so valuable to them" that he might not be allowed to leave. "Jay" concluded that Arnett was a "satellite" and "they don't have one." "John" offered his suggestion: "nuke" Baghdad, Arnett, and Iran as well! (After the Gulf War, Arnett returned to the United States; ironically, in June 1991 the National Association of Radio Talk Show Hosts presented Arnett with its "Freedom of Speech Award").

It is Kincaid's style to greet all guests and callers warmly. Those with whom he agrees on such issues as denouncing Iraq's "notorious lies," the Soviets "playing both sides of the street," or officials of the Carter administration for having "served *him*" (Saddam Hussein), he chats with enthusiastically. However, "Get the Guest" time comes quickly when host and guest disagree. One female guest, a member of ACT UP, had distributed condoms to students outside a Catholic high school on St. Valentine's Day. "What gives you this right?," asked the host. The guest's answer was that since "kids" that age were already having sex, they must be protected against AIDS and other diseases. Since "nobody else" was doing it, her organization did so by distributing the condoms. Kincaid asked whether the guest disagreed with the Catholic teaching that "homosexuality is immoral." She thought it "hypocritical." "Do you hate the Catholic Church?" came the question. "Of course not!" was the reply. Why did "your people" throw condoms at the Cardinal during a service, asked Kincaid. The reply: Members of the church "beat up one of our group."

Kincaid went to the phones. "Steve" accused the guest of being a member of the "immoral minority" promoting sex and AIDS. Again, she responded that young people were already having sex and needed information about the risks. Here, Kincaid made the checkmate move: "Obviously, you are a lesbian!" (An exclamation not a question). The guest said she was. "Steve" weighed in: "Why is it *your* job? Do you promote lesbianism?" The guest responded that her group promoted tolerance. How can you do so, chided Kincaid, when you disrupt Mass? The guest responded that the "Catholic Church has been disrupting people's lives for thousands of years." As the hour wore on in this Wonderland it is well that Alice was not there, for the "rudeness" would have been too much to bear. Here are examples:

*"Tracy"*: "Lady, you have *no* right! God help them [ACT UP] 'cause their ass will be mine!"

*"Jerry"*: "[You're] trying to force your will on others. I represent the majority of the world."

*"Danny"*: "These people have more in mind than sex education. They are trying to recruit our kids."

And a final exchange: "Robert" asked the guest, "What use do *you* have for a condom?" Guest: "I think this question is getting kind of personal." Kincaid summed up his position and what he thought of the by now "gotten" guest: "Male bodies are made to fit in female bodies and vice versa."

Producer/director Oliver Stone's 1989 Hollywood film *Talk Radio* characterized the abrasiveness, torment, and views expressed by talk show hosts and callers alike. It captured well the proposition that the host dominates the format, style, and content of punditry on the medium. Cliff Kincaid is but one of many talk show personalities who demonstrate that a host's warmth or coolness toward guests and callers is uppermost in encouraging or discouraging dispassionate discourse. We turn now to a case of talk radio where not the host but the formula dominates the direction of chatter and the quality of punditry.

### Ritual Outrage

"Battleline" is a three-hour, drive-time, call-in show airing five days a week on the Newstalk Radio Network. It is the contemporary radio version, with modifications, of a format that has appeared before on TV and radio. For example, in 1970 the producers of CBS's "60 Minutes" teamed columnists James Kilpatrick and Nicholas Von Hoffman (who was replaced in 1975 by Shana Alexander) in a segment called "Point/Counterpoint." Each argued a position on a selected topic: Kilpatrick, the conservative, or rightist, position, and Hoffman/Alexander the liberal, or leftist, position, thus adhering to the age-old view that there are "two sides to a story," and *only* two. The segment ended in 1979 but was to have its imitators when cable TV proliferated, CNN's "Evans and Novak" being one. On radio in the early 1980s a five-minute syndicated segment featured U.S. senators Robert Dole and Edward Kennedy in a "face-off" between the conservative and liberal positions, respectively; later, U.S. Senator Alan Simpson took up the conservative position.

"Battleline" employs the point/counterpoint, face-off concept using male cohosts, one "on the right" and one "on the left." The cohosts interview guests, and there are listener call-ins and commentary. What drives the show, however, is the quasi-debate formula. The cohosts spar with one another and align themselves with guests or callers along lines of right versus left. The cohosts take turns introducing one of "the issues that make the news" for consideration during a show's segment. The cohost introducing the issue offers a sharp commentary hinting at his position, and the other cohost responds, usually by interrupting. This introduction takes approximately a minute, and then there is a telephone interview with a guest expert. The guest, however, is but a means to an end; namely, the staged debate—replete with each cohost breaking in, degrading the other cohost or guest, and, as the tempo of the show demands, shouting. As the interview/debate unfolds, the cohosts accept listeners' calls and weave them into the staged warfare. The overall impression is one of punditry as equivalent to urchins arguing at the dinner table using Mom or Pop for support.

Although it is a call-in program, "Battleline" has few callers relative to the number of guests interviewed "on the Newsline." In the randomly constructed sample week under investigation, there were twenty-one guests (an average of five per one-hour show) and ten callers. The nature of the guests, of course, depended on the nature of the issue discussed (although it may well be that issues are selected on the basis of those "experts" who are willing to submit to the interview and/or bashing derived from the debate format). Of twenty issues in the sampled week selected during the period of the Gulf War, only six dealt with the war itself. Occasional issues did not deal with politics; for example, the issue of the appropriateness of sexual relations between lawyers and clients and that of what movie would win the Oscar for best picture of the year. With an average of four issues per hour and with time taken up for news summaries and commercials, little more than ten minutes is available per issue for the opening exchange, the "newsline" interview and ensuing debate, and listeners' calls. Such are the depth and insight of punditry on talk radio.

As a case in point, consider an hour time block aired on February 5, 1991, a Tuesday. There were four "issues that made the news" for that segment. Those were whether English should be made the nation's "official language," whether immigrants to the United States should be tested for AIDS, whether the budget for the National Endowment for the Arts (NEA) should be increased, and whether the nation's air traffic control system should be reformed. There were "newsline" interviews with guests for each issue: a representative from a group called U.S. English, an American Medical Association spokesperson, the executive director of the National Association of Artistic Organizations (NAAO), and the president of a libertarian group, the Reason Foundation. For illustrative purposes, let us look at the chatter over the NEA budget to get the flavor of the punditry on "Battleline." No doubt, the similarities with the "Mad Tea Party" attended by Alice will be apparent.

The self-identified cohost "on the left" (liberal) introduced the issue, pointing out that there was but a "flat" budget recommendation for the NEA. The cohost "on the right" (conservative) expressed surprise that "it gets funding at all." The two traded comments and put-downs before turning to the "newsline" interview. The guest (NAAO executive director) sought to establish legitimacy in the debate by stressing that the NAAO represented 250 artistic organizations. Did not, asked the liberal, the NAAO director think that the rationale for a flat budget recommendation for NEA appeared "political" and "very dangerous?" The executive director responded that the "White House" was simply not willing to take a strong stand for "freedom of expression." This produced an interruptive howl from the conservative; freedom of expression was not at issue, only what "we should spend money on."

In the free-for-all that followed, the conservative claimed that the NEA did not have popular support. The executive director refuted the charge that "Americans don't like the NEA." Not so, said the conservative, for "hardly a single American" was not offended by controversial artist Andres Serrano's "crucifix in a bucket of urine," part of an NEA-funded project, which the conservative erroneously ascribed to Robert Mapplethorpe. The executive director rose to the bait and argued that such art was "experimental"; since the NEA budget never had more than small amounts for experimental art, there was scarcely a danger, The conservative said we should "cut out" the experimental. The liberal said that homoerotic art should be supported. "Alice" of Silver Spring called to say that she did not like photos of a homosexual urinating into a homosexual's mouth. The executive director answered that "If you can't take chances, then [art] is bad." The cohosts, having pulled their watches out of the tea in the manner of the March Hare, ended the party with a commercial break.

Such "debates" are typical of the point/counterpoint formula. Each debate is brief, pointed, exaggerated, and entertaining. Whether each is probing, evidential, and informative is another matter. The outrage that each cohost expresses is more expected than sincere. It conforms to the long talk show tradition that Hirsch (1990) has labeled "contrived nastiness" (1990 p. 58). The highly ritualized "Battleline" formula contains the imperative of couching issues as two-sided, guests as either genuine experts or gullible fools, and callers as vultures waiting for the kill. Such punditry is not priestly, bardic, or sagelike, but gladiatorial.

### Punditry via Panel

If hosts drive the "Get the Guest" format and formulaic, contrived nastiness drives the "debate" format of talk radio, on the surface, the callers drove the panel format of NPR's "call-in programs to answer your questions" during their coverage of the 1991 Gulf War. At least callers posed the questions. Whether each program's panel of experts answered, or even entertained them, was another matter.

There were far more callers to NPR on the average than to either of the other sampled talk radio formats. NPR's panel format averaged six calls per hour. Callers directed their questions to the show's host, correspondent Daniel Shorr (or Linda Wertheimer if Shorr took a day off), or callers questioned a panel consisting of two or three designated "experts": representatives of thinks tanks such as the Brookings Institution or the Washington Institute for Near East Policy; scholars; journalists, both from U.S. newspapers and from the Middle East; military analysts; and diplomats from foreign nations.

NPR devoted two hours per day to such call-ins, with each hour opening with news of the Gulf War, other national and international events, and financial news. The host then introduced the panelists and each spoke briefly before the program shifted directly to calls. Shorr served as both host and panel member, answering callers and commenting on the remarks of other panelists as well as those made by callers. Rare was the caller who heeded Shorr's injunction simply to ask questions or, preferably; a single question. Most questions were prefaced by callers' comments, which were often lengthy. Hence, as much of the punditry espoused on the program derived from the callers as from Shorr or the guest experts.

A few examples demonstrate the tenor of call-in punditry. "Matthew" of Norfolk, VA, argued that military censorship, which was justified by the Pentagon as necessary for protecting the lives of combat soldiers, in fact does nothing more than hide the "bungling" that kills. The caller's wife, a nurse serving in Saudi Arabia, was a member of a detachment that had been assured that "no Scuds [missiles] would ever take off" when they in fact had; moreover, the detachment was denied protective bunkers against attacks. "Matthew" urged journalists to break the military censorship and report as they pleased. "Denise" of Allentown, PA, lamented the criticism leveled against antiwar protestors; they "should not quit," she said and urged them, "Don't be intimidated to war's acceptance." Two callers, "Peter" of New York City, and "David" of Appleton, WI (on different days), provided extended summations of the cause of the conflict, namely, arms sales. "Peter" described a "commercial orgy of arms sales" which led to the crisis, while "David" viewed the war as "product-motivated," a "testing ground for equipment" that could later be placed on the market.

During the Gulf War it was typical of talk radio hosts who identify themselves as conservative to provoke calls from listeners challenging the patriotism of journalists who criticized U.S. censorship policies or war aims. This was not the case on NPR. Many callers were indeed critical of news coverage of the war, but for a very different reason. They thought it either shallow or too much in league with Pentagon aims. "Fred" from Chicago, for instance, reproached war correspondents for doing nothing more than relaying to audiences the numbers of sorties flown, missile sites destroyed, planes shot down, and so on: facts supplied to them by military briefers. It seemed to "Fred" that each branch of the military was in rivalry with the other, a rivalry aided by a press that simply "provides quantities, not substance." (In response, one panelist asked, "How else do you keep score?" while a second attributed the focus on numbers to the fact that the Air Force was in charge.) "Sharon" of Santa Rosa, CA, took her criticism of the media closer to home, namely, against Daniel Shorr. Why, she wanted to know, was it that when callers raised the specter of George Bush having "enticed and entrapped" the Iraqis into invading Kuwait did Shorr always dismiss the possibility? Shorr denied such a dismissal. "Sharon" disagreed. Shorr, she said, was an "apologist" for the U.S. government. Shorr ended the exchange with a droll comment that the government "would be very surprised to hear that."

The popular punditry voiced in callers' chatter on NPR covered an array of topics too numerous and diverse to review here. So also did the callers' questions, when they actually got to asking questions. What stands out, however, in reviewing NPR's talk about the Gulf War is how frequently "expert" panelists either evaded callers' questions or simply expressed ignorance. In many instances the ignorance stemmed from questions that had no immediate answers. For example, "Kirk" from Seattle asked about atrocities in Kuwait and the murder of Kuwaiti hostages by Iraqi troops; what, he wanted to know, could prevent it? Shorr responded that Saddam Hussein was "not home free" if there were atrocities, a second panelist simply said he did not know, and a third responded that in war there are "always a lot of messy things to clear up."

At other times the ignorance came from different panelists possessed with different information. The result was a panel construction of shared confusion. When "Michael" from Detroit called, the answer given his question might have made some listeners wonder how "expert" an "expert is." "Michael" wanted to know why, when TV viewers were privy to an aircraft shooting a missile into a doorway, did the ground seem to stand still even though the airplane was moving? Shorr explained that the camera was on the nose of the airplane; that gave an illusion of no movement of the ground. A second panelist said that the camera was not on the nose but mounted on pods. A third said that the pods adjust to the target which makes it seem that the ground is stationary. To this, the second panelist said (seriously) that it was "technology borrowed from Hollywood" which produced "special effects."

More often, however, callers received from panelists answers to questions that had not been asked. Thus, "Adele" from Philadelphia asked if there was any comparison between the Israeli occupation of Palestinian lands and the Iraqi occupation of Kuwait. One panelist responded that any such "linkage" was "not acceptable" but did not say why. The other panelist, the author of a book about the Middle East, ignored the question, mentioned "a double standard," and then promoted her book— by title and publisher. "Richard" of Austin, NY, had read a book about the Baath party in Iraq and wished to know if the political party was the source of intransigence and tyranny in that nation. One panelist went into great detail about the Baath party but said nothing in response to the questioner; a second brought up the issue of oil rather than Kuwait as piquing U.S. interest, thus again ignoring the question; and a third described the "lackluster" U.S. energy policy, a response that introduced a topic unrelated to the caller's query.

This is not to say that the "call-in program to answer your questions" always evaded questions or had no answers. In many instances, listeners put down the phone with the information they sought. Nonetheless, there was a marked tendency for panelists to use talk radio as a forum to promote their own expertise, views, and, if they represented think tanks, their organizations. Callers' comments and questions drove the NPR panel format, but the panelists themselves demonstrated their own agendas when they were able to seize the chatter away from those callers.

## CONCLUSION: "THEN YOU SHOULDN'T TALK?"

At the outset of this chapter we noted that critics of the Chattering Classes argue that political chatterers are concerned only with the "marginalia of life, far removed from the nitty gritty political realities" and "are people of no real influence whatsoever" (Watkins, 1989, p. 25). It might be too harsh a judgment to say that the chatterers of talk TV and radio are far removed from political realities and without influence. The degree of influence of their priestly, bardic, sagacious, and oracular punditry on policymakers or on viewers and listeners is more a matter of speculation than of confirmed evidence gathered by systematic research. Influence aside, however, we can assert that the content of their chatter—the substance of their punditry—is intertwined with the formats common to the forums where that chatter and punditry take place.

TV talk shows and talk radio are not basically intended to convey knowledge. They are forms of entertainment programming. If, as part of that entertainment, they provide viewers/listeners with chatter about issues and an opportunity to express themselves, then they serve a purpose attributed by Robert Park to news generally. That is, TV/radio chatter yields an "acquaintance with" but not "knowledge about" (Park, 1940, p. 669) the world. Format, formula, and style mark the successful talk show, and not necessarily the quality of the information conveyed. As we noted earlier, Phil Donahue said it well: "I do not apologize for wanting to draw a crowd" and, incidentally, "I believe there is a great deal of information in talk shows" (Who's a Journalist? Talk Show Sensationalism, Public Affairs Video Archives 1989). Information there may be in electronic talk, but when it is there it may be a by-product of the more important concern, namely, drawing a crowd.

The Dormouse turned to Alice and asked, "Did you ever see such a thing as a drawing of muchness?" "Really, now [that] you ask me," said Alice, very much confused, "I don't think—. . . ." Interrupted the Hatter, "Then you shouldn't talk." As we turn away from the punditry of the Chattering Classes to pundits who critique chatter and other forms of punditry (in Chapter Six), we conclude by asking, "If format, formula, and style are the content of talk shows, not informed thought, is it perhaps that talk shows shouldn't talk?"

*Chapter Six*

# The Critical Eye: Mediating the Realities of Mediated Politics

In its televised ads, the *New Yorker* magazine claims itself to be "Perhaps the finest magazine that ever was." Be that as it may, the weekly carries a regular feature of notes and comment that assesses the impact of current events on the community and nation, entitled "The Talk of the Town." In the issue of January 28, 1991, one note featured a "letter from a man we know." What was called the "Gulf War" was but a few days old. The man's letter described how he had learned of the war's beginning via a telephone call from his son who was visiting friends in California. The son said he'd just been watching a CNN news program that included the voices of three reporters in a Baghdad hotel describing the sights and sounds of the bomber attacks and the antiaircraft fire going on around them: "the sights and sounds of war." Consequently, the father too turned on TV to find out what was happening. As they continued the telephone conversation, the man found that "my son sounded scared, and who can blame him? He is twenty years old" ("The Talk of the Town," 1991; p. 21).

Over the days that followed, the man, his son, and countless millions of others across the nation and the globe epitomized Walter Lippmann's 1922 definition of news: "circumstances in all their sprawling complexity, the overt act which signalizes them, the stereotyped bulletin which publishes the signal, and the meaning the reader himself injects, after he has derived that meaning from the experience which directly affects him" (Lippmann, 1922, p. 239). Missile attacks, air strikes, oil slicks, tank battles, and oil well fires signalized the complexities of war; bulletins announced "Scud" raids, "Patriot" missile firings, air "sorties," "collateral damage," and "friendly fire." The father mentioned in the *New*

*Yorker* injected meaning from "more than twenty years of mornings when I awakened with the knowledge of war" during his lifetime of seventy years, while the twenty-year-old son wondered what the Gulf War would do to his life ("The Talk of the Town," 1991; p. 22).

Almost seven decades have passed since Lippmann's definition of news. Now another element has been added. In addition to the wizardry of TV, satellites, and instant news, there is now another step in the mediating process. Events still occur, journalists still select and report some of them, and readers/viewers still select and interpret some of those reports. Now, however, telling readers/viewers what they have read and heard, or should have read and heard, are media critics who pour over the news coverage of events and tell audiences what was good, bad, and indifferent about it. In the process they add interpretations, embellishments, and judgments.

Consider a resident of Dallas, Texas, the day after the Gulf War began on January 16, 1991. The Dallasite may have seen network TV coverage, indeed, perhaps the same CNN coverage viewed by the *New Yorker*'s father and son or coverage by competing networks. Opening the pages of the *Dallas Morning News*, the viewer found an evaluation of TV's opening war coverage. The paper's television critic, Ed Bark (1991), painted a picture of "16 extraordinary hours" when CNN's correspondents in Baghdad "were the world's only firsthand link to the U.S. bombing." Bark described the correspondents "peering from their hotel room windows," "crawling on the floor," and "filing live telephone reports of unprecedented immediacy." When CNN correspondents were no longer permitted by Iraqi authorities to file live reports, wrote Bark, "Even without the vivid reports from Baghdad, CNN continued to set the standard for coverage. . . . The once-ridiculed all-news network established on June 1, 1980, scored a number of exclusives" (p. 1AA).

Whether Bark's portrayal of CNN's coverage or of its correspondents' activities is accurate or overdrawn is beside the point, as is Bark's implicit criterion of judging a news organization's merits by the number of its exclusives. We single out Bark not for being right or wrong but for being typical of a growing number of pundits both inside and outside the news media who critique news coverage on a regular basis. These critics stand between news reports of firsthand realities and the citizen who reads, hears, or views those reports. The contributions to punditry—primarily priestly or bardic—of these mediators of news that has already mediated realities are our concern in this chapter.

## ROLES AND TYPES OF MEDIA CRITICS

Bardic Mark Twain had little regard for critics. He called the "trade of the critic . . . the most degraded of all trades" and said it was without "real value—certainly no large value" (1817, p. 274). In his study of how public figures, including political celebrities, are manufactured through "hype" (i.e., promotional means), Steven Aronson (1983) claimed a more exalted status for critics. Aronson drew a distinction between true criticism and mere reviewing. The latter, he wrote, imparts "information on a fairly simple-minded level: what happens and what it is like to read this book, or see this film or play." Criticism, by contrast, "is an inspection of the work in relation to larger issues" (p. 211). Robert Root's (1987) account of the rhetoric of popular culture is more generous to reviewing, essentially treating it as preliminary to criticism. Reviewing involves a description of the contents of a given work, an evaluation substantiated with illustrations and examples, and an implicit or explicit recommendation for people to either explore or ignore the work. Reviews may go beyond "these basic elements to add the element of interpretation" (p. 64). This brings the review to the realm of criticism: "more analytical, more involved, more expansive than reviewing[, it] . . . links itself more closely to the critic's understanding of the art form or his understanding of the world that art represents and also relates to" (p. 64). Root went on to conclude, "As a rhetorical act, criticism attempts to persuade the reader of the validity of the reviewer's opinion; it advocates a specific position on art or ideas" (p. 71).

Our focus on political punditry of necessity directs us toward anyone, whether labeled reviewer or critic, who performs the critical task characterized by Aronson and Root. The word *critic* is derived from the Latin *criticus*, meaning "decisive"; the Greek *kritikos*, "to discern"; and from the Greek *"kritos,"* to separate or choose. All pundits, of course, think they discern political nuances and decisively choose between them. The pundit who is a critic of political media, however, goes beyond that. Anthony Downs (1957) has argued that rational citizens weigh the costs of being politically informed. Those costs are so high, given the surfeit of media and information available, that rational choice would dictate not being informed at all, or alternatively, endeavoring to cut the costs of information gathering. One way to cut the costs is to delegate the task of gathering, assimilating, and weighing information to someone else. Obviously, wrote Downs, whoever performs that task—such as the political pundit—"has a potentially enormous influence upon decisions" that the citizen makes (p. 211). The role of the pundit as media critic, however, is not as a gatherer of information about politics per se but as an analyst of how the news media cover politics. The critic's descriptions, evaluations, substantiations, and interpretations provide citizens with recommendations regarding which news sources to choose as political information gatherers. In this role, critics potentially have an even more "enormous influence over decisions" (to repeat Downs) as filters of the politics that citizens read, hear, and view. In a sense, critics separate who gets to speak to citizens about politics and who does not (Foucault, 1981).

There are a variety of types of political media critics, and they employ different vehicles to air their decisive discernments and choices. Like popular film critics Roger Ebert and Gene Siskel, a few have a star status brighter than many of the actors or actresses they critique. Others achieve modest reputations working in local venues or among specifically targeted audiences. For a useful scheme that classifies different types of critics, we turn to H. L. Mencken (1965), a journalist who won considerable notoriety during the first half of this century as a literary, social, and political critic—and as a critic of critics. Mencken discerned several types of critics and singled out four for specific comment, based on what it is that critics think they do.

Wrote Mencken, "One group argues, partly by direct statement and partly by attacking all other groups, that the one defensible purpose of the critic is to encourage the virtuous and oppose the sinful—in brief, to police" on behalf of "the moral order of the world." They perform a "constabulary function." A second group has "nothing to do with morality whatsoever. . . . [T]heir concern is solely with beauty"; although not artists themselves, they pretend to be by defining the canons of artistic sophistication. A third holds that a work of art, and we can include works of news as popular art, is a "psychological document—that if it doesn't help men to know themselves it is nothing." Finally, the fourth group "reduces the thing to an exact science" (pp. 170–171). As critics, then, we have the constable, the artist, the psychologist, and the scientist. Let us examine each of these types of political media critics separately with special reference to critics of television news coverage of politics and the punditry involved in interpreting it.

## IS THE POLITICAL PICTURE MORAL? THE CRITIC AS CONSTABLE

There is no shortage of organizations that have surfaced in the last two decades devoted to the full-time observation, recording, analysis, and critique of news media coverage of politics. These critics characterize themselves in different ways: as media watchdogs, monitors, analysts, combatants, and adversaries. Whatever label they use, all, to refer to Mencken, police the press on behalf of a moral order that is allegedly violated by political news coverage. As moral guardians, however, they are not priestly: They are jeremiads, bards prone to deliver elaborate and prolonged lamentations or tales of woe. In their constabulary capacity, they ferret out alleged media bias in the name of accurate, balanced reporting.

However, one critic's bias is another's accuracy, and vice versa. Media constables agree that the major TV, newspaper, and newsmagazine organizations are biased in their political coverage. They also agree that such bias can be placed on a right–left continuum. Where they differ is on whether the media lackeys serve the liberal cause or the conservative conviction.

### The News Is Tilted toward the Right

To suggest the flavor of such constabulary criticism, we offer a sampling of the increasingly populated universe of media police. We do so not to argue that the news media are or are not "liberal" or "conservative" but to illustrate the typical commentary that addresses that assumption. Consider first media critics who focus on the overly conservative content of the news. Fairness and Accuracy in Reporting (FAIR) describes itself as a national media watch organization. Along with other self-styled watch organizations, FAIR is concerned with how the media cover all aspects and phases of politics. Indicative of FAIR's approach is a critical assessment of how journalists covered the 1988 Democratic National Convention. FAIR critics placed media terminology under a microscope. They charged in a news release, for instance, that the "media's use of the pejorative term 'special interests' is biased" (FAIR, 1988, p. 1). "Special interests," announced FAIR, was a denigrating label applied to backers of Jesse Jackson but not applied to conservative Democrats such as oil and business backers of Democratic vice presidential nominee Lloyd Bentsen. FAIR also criticized news reports that spoke of presidential nominee Michael Dukakis as "coddling" or "caving in" to Jackson but never to the selection of Bentsen as coddling or caving in to "the right wing or the business elite." Finally, FAIR criticized reporters for questioning whether Dukakis was "too liberal" to win the presidency yet failing to question if the Republican nominee was "too conservative" (p1). The mainstream of Americans, said FAIR (citing a New York Times/CBS poll), was actually to the left, and not the right, of Dukakis on key issues.

A second example of a constabulary group that is critical of a conservative posture in the news media is the Institute for Media Analysis, Inc. The institute publishes a monthly magazine of media criticism, Lies of Our Times (the acronym being LOOT). "Our Times," says the magazine, "are the times we live in but also the words of the New York Times, the most cited news medium in the U.S., our paper of record. . . . Our Lies," the editorial statement continues, "are more than literal falsehoods; they encompass subjects that have been ignored, hypocrisies, misleading emphases, and hidden premises—the biases which systematically shape reporting" (LOOT, 1991, p. 2). It takes but a few issues of *LOOT* to illustrate the nature of the monthly "sampling of the universe of media lies and distortions":

- The *New York Times*'s distortion implying that Palestinians in the West Bank were not entitled to free gas masks because, unlike Israelis, they paid no taxes, ergo, "no taxes, no masks"; LOOT argued that Palestinians in the occupied territories paid "enormous taxes to Israel" (Abraham, 1991, p. 3).
- Attacks on academic pluralism for teaching history as inclusive of other than U.S. cultures, namely; distortions contained in the *Washington Post*, *New York Times*, *Wall Street Journal*, and *U.S. News & World Report*; the claims of "media vigilantes" are "sad examples of the thinking that results from the narrow and exclusive education system in the U.S." (Rattley, 1991, p. 4).
- The elite media's (*Newsday*, *Chicago Tribune*, *Wall Street Journal*, etc.) "infatuation" and "endorsement" of the opinions of black conservative thinkers (Thomas Sowell of the Hoover Institute, Walter Williams of George Mason University, Shelby Steele of San Diego State); the "effusive treatment of this clique does not merely hinder progress, it leads to regression" (Boyd, 1991, p. 10).
- The *New York Times*'s "highly laudatory, and remarkably selective and superficial, news reporting and editorial on Margaret Thatcher's exit as Prime Minister of Great Britain" which displayed "class and chauvinistic bias" (Herman, 1991, p. 16).

In their respective critiques of news coverage of the 1991 war in the Persian Gulf, constables of Fairness and Accuracy in Reporting and the Institute for Media Analysis joined forces. In the February 1991 issue of *LOOT*, an associate of FAIR, Stuart Skalka, took major newspapers, including the *Christian Science Monitor*, the *New York Times*, and *Newsday*, to task for creating and imposing stereotypes on Arabs and the world. One such stereotype, "the most insidious of all" is "that Arabs are inherently less rational than other people." The U.S. and Western world, by contrast, loom in news coverage as logical, moral, and rational. Moreover, Skalka found that the newspapers he analyzed treat Arab politics as degenerate. They are seen as "treacherous"; "politics and conspiracy are one and the same," the "typical Arab style" is "a veiled reference," and Arabs have "nationalist visions, *the pursuit of which justified murder*" (Skalka, 1991, p. 9). Simply put, FAIR and *LOOT* view news coverage as canted to the right, frequently in a racist way.

### The News Is Tilted toward the Left

Matching the constabulary criticism that the news media are conservative and establishment-oriented in their political coverage is the indictment that political news is canted toward the left. A variety of watch organizations take that stand. We will examine two of the most vocal: the Media Research Center (MRC) and Accuracy in Media (AIM).

*Media Research Center*

Incorporated in 1987 as a tax-exempt foundation, the MRC is avowedly conservative in its constabulary intent. MRC's promotional literature defines the purpose of the watchdog organization, namely, "to confront and neutralize the liberal media elite" (Media Research Center, n.d., p. 3). "The most critical aspect" of the "program to combat the media is the compilation of empirical, irrefutable evidence necessary to make a genuine case against the media." The promotional booklet continues, "We conservatives have known for many years just how liberal the media is, but simply could not prove it conclusively due to the lack of current research information." Hence, "research is the cornerstone" of the MRC (p. 4). On the surface, the MRC research program is impressive. It includes taping news and public affairs programs of ABC, CBS, CNN, NBC, and PBS; a computerized news retrieval process accessing over two thousand newspapers, magazines, and wire service reports; and the accumulation of "personnel files on the media elite" (p. 5).

Through syndicated columns to newspapers, a "Media Watch" commentary to radio stations; an advertising program, a data distribution service to specialized organizations; conferences; books (see Bozell and Baker, 1990); a bimonthly newsletter monitoring the entertainment industry (*TV etc.*); a biweekly newsletter of *Notable Quotables*, "listing the latest outrageous and humorous quotes reflecting the media's liberal bias" (Media Research Center; January 1989, p. 3); and other means, the MRC promises to inform citizens of the news media's liberal transgressions.

The avowed "flagship enterprise" of MRC's diverse dissemination system, however, is its monthly newsletter, *MediaWatch*. Printed in a format of eight pages in blue type on an off-blue or cream face, the newsletter bears a logo of the letters MW superimposed on a TV screen. Semiregular newsletter items include study reports confirming liberal media bias in selected cases and reviews or analyses of media coverage. A regular feature, "Revolving Door," reports and tallies the movements of journalists and/or officials in and out of news jobs or public office. The running tally suggests that "liberals/Democrats" move between press and government jobs more often than do "conservatives/ Republicans."

Three specific *MediaWatch* features indicate how the MRC performs the role of constabulary critic. "Newsbites," runs as a single column on the front page and on one or more following pages. Several topical pieces (each rarely more than three paragraphs in length) comprise the feature.

Typical newsbites from Volumes 3 and 4 (1989–1990) of *MediaWatch* (*MW*) included:

- Quotes from NBC and CBS nightly news telecasts demonstrating that both networks heaped blame on Ronald Reagan for the plight of the homeless.
- Comment on a report by CBS correspondent Leslie Stahl that President George Bush's advisers were critical of chief of staff John Sununu for botching the attempt of John Tower to receive confirmation as secretary of defense: *MW* reminded readers that Stahl's source for the report was Jody Powell, former president Jimmy Carter's press secretary.
- Criticism of ABC news for contributing to the rehabilitation of Jimmy Carter by naming him "Person of the Week" in a May 12, 1989, "World News Tonight" segment.
- A charge that CBS's Connie Chung, in presenting two alternatives to abortion, criticized "pro-lifers both times: first for impeding progress; then for being unrealistic" (September 1989, p. 8).
- A report stating that "CBS stonewalls" in failing to comment on a September 27, 1989, *New York Post* story that the network had aired faked footage in covering the Afghan war in 1985.
- A note that the TV networks air reports on stories that confirm the "greenhouse effect" of atmospheric deterioration but ignore studies that challenge it.
- "Bryant Grumbles," highlighting the liberal persuasion of NBC "Today" host Bryant Gumble.

In 1989 alone, MRC constables ferreted out and reported well over one hundred such examples of alleged liberal bias.

Joining "Newsbites" as a front-page feature in each issue is a more lengthy feature documenting the liberal tilt of the media. Among the stories typifying those on the front page of *MediaWatch* in 1989: a former *Wall Street Journal* and *Los Angeles Times* reporter's admission of being a Marxist; media biases, especially by CNN, in reporting the Supreme Court's ruling in a key case on the legality of anti-abortion laws; four separate pieces highlighting the dormant efforts of the news media, especially nightly TV networks news, on behalf of increased federal income taxes and federal spending; a feature headlined "Peter Jennings and Mike Wallace Agree They're . . . REPORTERS FIRST, AMERICANS SECOND"; a charge that PBS provides a platform through special programming for the liberal views of Bill Moyers and others but excludes any conservative voices; and the renouncing by CBS and *USA Today* of the 1980s as being little more than a Reagan decade of "greed, sleaze, and decline" (December 1989, p. 1).

A final regular feature of *MediaWatch* that is illustrative of the MRC's constabulary role as critic is the monthly "Janet Cooke Award." Named for "*The Washington Post* reporter who won the Pulitzer Prize for a story about an eight-year-old heroin addict which was later proven completely false," the feature (varying from one to two inside pages) reports "the most outrageously distorted news story of the month" (*MediaWatch*, February, 1989, p. 4). Typical are awards to CBS, CNN, and NBC for stories of "homeless hype" (October 1989, pp. 4–5); ABC for reporting on day care for children; Ted Turner's thirty-minute documentary "Abortion: For Survival"; *Time* magazine for calling for the firing of Republican National Chair Lee Atwater; and ABC's "World News Tonight" for continuous critical coverage of British Prime Minister Margaret Thatcher.

The recipients and *cause célèbre* for the awards, of course, may vary, but by singling out on a monthly basis the "most outrageously distorted" of media accounts, the MRC illustrates a principle of Roland Barthes (1973), a student of societal myths. One way in which myths are fashioned, argued Barthes, is by converting the outrageous to the routine. As a guardian of political values, MRC constructs and reinforces the myth of liberal media bias by using the Janet Cooke Award to document the belief that outrageous reporting is so routine that *MediaWatch*'s "most distorted" examples prove all reporting to be outrageous.

## Accuracy in Media

Of the pack of watchdogs on guard for media bias, AIM (Accuracy in Media) is virtually the Rin Tin Tin of canine constables. Founded in 1969, AIM has a tax-exempt status which makes its annual fee attractive to potential members. Its National Advisory Board includes retired admirals and generals, corporate presidents and chief executive officers (CEOs), retired university presidents, and such notables as a Noble Laureate in physics (Eugene Wigner), physicist Edward Teller, and actor Charlton Heston. A promotional leaflet identifies AIM as "Your Watchdog of the News Media" and lists four key activities: to (1) investigate complaints of serious media misdeeds; (2) take proven cases to the top officials of media organizations, asking for corrections; (3) publicize the most serious cases and mobilize public pressure to bring about remedial action; and (4) work for adoption by the media of higher standards of reporting, editing and a responsible approach to news. Like the MRC, Accuracy in Media has a host of channels for distributing its message: a twice-a-month newsletter, a weekly newspaper column, five-day-a-week radio commentary, paid advertisements, speakers, conferences, videotapes, films, and a program for publishing books and articles. AIM members are even eligible to apply for an Accuracy in Media Gold MasterCard.

The AIM watchdog barks most frequently and regularly through the *AIM Report*. Reed Irvine, AIM's president, edits the newsletter, writes columns, comments on his "Media Monitor" radio show, and appears on countless radio and TV talk programs. In format and style, the *AIM*

*Report* differs markedly from the MRC's *MediaWatch*. The black-on-white (black in two shades) typeface lends a toned-down, serious, almost ponderous quality to the newsletter that is a marked contrast to the *MediaWatch* use of two shades of blue on a cream-colored parchment. The only color in the *AIM Report* is the title in red block letters beside the logo of a three-ringed (red center, white circle, red outer circle) target akin to that of a dart board. Although the content of the *AIM Report* is certainly critical, primarily of reporting canted to the left, when contrasted with *MediaWatch* the language is less hyperbolic—no "Bryant Grumbles," Janet Cooke Awards, revolving doors, or newsbites. The single regular feature of the *AIM Report* is a one- to two-page insert written by Irvine, "Notes from the Editor's Cuff." It serves much the same purpose as "Newsbites" in *MediaWatch* but has the tone of personal, priestly, inside-the-media explanations for media culpability: a refined, cause-and-effect analysis. AIM's attire, in short, is the conservatism of a dark, pin-striped three-piece suit; MRC's is the conservatism of a subdued sports jacket, contrasting sweater vest, and jaunty tie. AIM is priestly, MRC more bardic.

The bulk of each *AIM Report* consists of an in-depth probing of a single case of media inaccuracy or a series of apparently related such cases. Nightly network TV news programs and anchors are frequent AIM targets. During 1989 the *Aim Report* featured stories, for example, chastising ABC, CBS, and NBC for failing to report a judicial judgment against "the leftist Christic Institute" whose attacks on anticommunists AIM regarded as "leftist McCarthyism" (March-A, 1989, p. 1). AIM also took critical note of ABC anchor Peter Jennings's tribute to I. F. Stone upon the liberal journalist's death (July). Moreover, ABC, CBS, and NBC took heat for "shallow" coverage of the execution by Cuba's Fidel Castro of one of his nation's top military commanders (July).

CBS's "60 Minutes," ABC's "20/20," and CNN's owner Ted Turner are also favorite AIM targets. Former anchors are also in AIM's sights. In May 1989, an *AIM Report* asked, "Has Walter Cronkite Been Bought?" AIM answered that he had. The proof was in an "arrogant abuse of his power to block the showing" of a film, narrated by Cronkite, that revealed, according to a press release, "why most of our fears of chemicals in the environment are unfounded and that the recent Alar pesticide/apple scare was nothing less than a hoax." Consumer advocates who were apprised of the film's contents, suggested AIM, brought pressure on Cronkite to prevent its showing (May-A 1989, p. 1).

Although the nightly network TV newscasts receive ample criticism, AIM's targets are spread more broadly. In 1989–90 AIM drew a bead on PBS numerous times, for example: in February 1989, for documentaries undermining U.S. capacities for covert action and intelligence gathering; in August 1989, for documentaries that "inundate the public with anti-technology, business-bashing reports that blame corporations and 'the government' for any discomforts in a modern society (Accuracy in Media: August 1989, p. 1); in November 1989, for canted reporting in its "Frontline" series; and in December 1990, for a "perversion" of the Korean War in the PBS documentary, "Korea: The Unknown War."

AIM's constabulary role consists of more than detecting and exposing liberal media bias. The organization invites *AIM Report* readers to join in the hunt as vigilantes by contacting individuals who are influential enough to correct canted reporting. Whatever the topic at hand, AIM includes with its newsletter a postcard addressed to a responsible official; the back of the card contains a typed appeal and need only be signed and stamped by the citizen enlisting in the crusade to correct media abuses. For example, while calling the PBS series "Secret Intelligence" one-sided, unfair, and an inaccurate attack on U.S. intelligence services, AIM provided a postcard addressed to Democrat of South Carolina Ernest Hollings of the Senate Committee on Commerce, Science, and Transportation. "Isn't it time your committee took a close look at the misuse of our taxpayer dollars by PBS?" asked the preprinted postcard.

### Bias Is in the Eye of the Beholder

To illustrate the striking contrast between constabulary critics of the left and right regarding news media bias, we turn to responses to the Cable News Network (CNN) coverage of the Gulf War immediately following the outbreak of hostilities on January 16, 1991. In the early days of the war, CNN provided round-the-clock coverage, and indeed, had the first live reports of air strikes on Baghdad by U.S. and Coalition forces. As we noted early in this chapter, many media critics such as Ed Bark of the *Dallas Morning News* heaped lavish praise on CNN's efforts. However, constabulary critics of the left and right thought otherwise.

Writing of CNN's coverage in *Lies of Our Times* (February 1991), Phyllis Bennis stressed the selectivity of war coverage. "We were not really seeing most of it," she noted, "for all the techno-wizardry, made possible by portable satellite transmitters, a lot of news simply did not get through." In fact, she continued, while CNN brought the "moment-to-moment terror" of Iraqi missile attacks on Israel, it left out "any visceral, image-created sense of the far greater devastation of Iraq, which was subjected to relentless bombing." Such "intense, human-drama coverage of the Tel Aviv bombings, when Baghdad remained unseen, contributed even further to Americans' lack of understanding or interest in the human dimension of the air war against Iraq." Moreover, the fact that Palestinians in the West Bank and Gaza Strip, who possessed no gas masks, were in harm's way during missile firings at Israel received scant mention in the telecasts. Bennis concluded, "CNN is not really televising the war—but the danger is that too many people believe it is" (pp. 4–5).

In AIM's nationally syndicated radio commentary, "Media Monitor" (February 8, 1991), Reed Irvine and Cliff Kincaid—the latter, as noted in Chapter Five, a radio talk show host—made CNN's war coverage a target for quite different reasons. They voiced dissatisfaction with CNN's Peter Arnett's reports from Baghdad. As we noted in Chapter Five, Arnett, after being taken on a tour of bombed areas of Baghdad by Iraqi officials, provided a live (and censored) report which was aired by CNN of an air strike on what the Iraqis called an "infant formula milk plant." Irvine and Kincaid described the report in detail and then pointed out that CNN made no reference to the fact that U.S. military officials had denounced it as false, claiming that the plant actually produced biological weapons. It was "heavily guarded, surrounded by a high security fence, and camouflaged," said Kincaid.

Irvine was critical both of CNN and of another favorite target of AIM, the *Washington Post*. Said Irvine, "Peter Arnett has been praised extravagantly by his friends in the media as a great reporter who's doing an outstanding job in covering the war from Baghdad." By way of example, Irvine cited a column in the *Post* that "even praised Arnett's false reporting about the bombing of the biological warfare weapons plant." Irvine was especially critical of the *Post* column for dismissing the "outrage at the White House" that was provoked by Arnett's report. Said the column, "Washington *claims* [the *Post*'s emphasis, according to Irvine] it was a biological warfare plant." The column went on, "Arnett's careful choice of words left judgment on truth to others." Irvine thought otherwise: "Well, as we have noted, Arnett's choice of words gave not the slightest hint that the claim that the plant was making baby formula was a phony. Arnett was helping Iraq. He was certainly not helping the United States or the American soldiers in the Gulf."

In a review of three separate book-length studies produced by three constabulary organizations, David Shaw, media writer for the *Los Angeles Times*, pointed to a problem raised by the media watchdogs. Coauthor of one of the books was L. Brent Bozell III, chairman of the Media Research Center. Coauthor of another was Reed Irvine, president of Accuracy in Media. Both Bozell's and Irvine's books critiqued the media for serving liberal interests. The third book, written by Martin A. Lee and Norman Solomon, critiqued the media as serving the conservative establishment. Shaw's summation after reading the three works applies as well to the divergent views of constabulary critics regarding CNN's coverage of the war in the Persian Gulf. Wrote Shaw, it "is a bit like listening to two people's accounts of a football game in which each rooted for the opposite side" (1991, p. 56).

## IS THE POLITICAL PICTURE ART? THE CRITIC
## AS ARTIST

On the surface, being a "media" or "TV" critic for a major newspaper or magazine is a daunting task. A drama critic writes solely about stage productions. A film critic comments on movies. A music critic evaluates music. Even a political analyst concentrates only on politics, wide-ranging though that activity is. By contrast, a media critic must review, analyze, and evaluate not only the medium (usually television) but the content of that medium, whether situation comedy, miniseries, documentary, soap opera, spectacle, or live coverage of a presidential press conference, election returns, national convention, terrorist act, or even war. H. L. Mencken mused that to expect a media critic to know so much about so many things was unthinkable.

Media critics, it seems, must be journalists of renaissance proportions. However, few critics even make such a claim. Most come to their critical tasks after years as a general assignment reporter, beat reporter, sports writer, or some other role largely unrelated to artistic criticism or politics. Interviews with media critics of leading metropolitan dailies (see Bibliography) suggest typical backgrounds. One, for example, does not even think of being known as "strictly a critic; I'm a reporter, I mean I cover the industry." That means one covers "everything, the gamut; I cover entertainment, I cover news programming, executive shake-up at the nets, anything that's the hard news side of the business." This critic estimated that 20 percent of the job involves criticism of political media, in primary elections, national conventions, and presidential debates. Another critic who was interviewed is a political media specialist, a former "TV kid and political junkie" who was asked to write a column on media issues in general and TV in particular. A third critic began as a sports reporter. When asked to replace the departing TV critic, the reporter did so. Saying that reviewing TV's "coverage of politics [is] like anything else," the critic noted that "politics is not my beat; I'm not political; I don't know much about politics." Not knowing about politics, however, is apparently no problem to some critics: "I cover entertainment and politics exactly the same. I cover politics on TV as entertainment."

Given their lack of both political and broadcasting backgrounds, it is not surprising that both politicians and TV journalists are often as critical of media critics as media critics are of political and news performances. A notable target of scorn from politicians, journalists, and media watchdogs alike is Tom Shales of the *Washington Post*, a Pulitzer Prize winner. Shales was one of the first TV critics to dare to analyze political television just as he would normally probe entertainment TV. Whether a presidential news conference or "Family Feud," both are grist for his mill (except that Shales prefers the spontaneous quality of the game show in marked contrast to the formula-driven, canned quality of a politician's news conference). Reed Irvine of Accuracy in Media regularly refers to Shales as "Tom Shalesgate" in *AIM Reports*, a label pinned on the critic for using his journalistic position to secure privileged access to selected TV network notables. Detractors say that Shales's credentials as high priest of media criticism mar his judgment. He is so close to members of the media elite—for example, CBS's Dan Rather—that it biases his critical acumen: Tom Brokaw of NBC and Peter Jennings of ABC can do no right, and Rather can do no wrong (Flander, 1988). In defense, Shales points to his columns which are caustic comments on the celebrated political journalists at all networks.

In any case, although scorned, Shales is also widely respected and influential. Richard Sklar, a film critic of considerable note, described Shales as "hands down the most interesting television critic I know of who writes for daily newspapers" (1980, p. 150). Shales illustrates precisely what H. L. Mencken meant in referring to critics who are not artists themselves but try to be so through their criticism. Shales is neither a politician nor a broadcast journalist, yet his critiques of political TV yield him celebrity status. To those who dislike him, however, Shales is the celebrity defined by novelist Thomas Thompson (1982): "The prefix *cele* (or, more accurately, *coele*) means 'cavity.' The suffix *brit-y* probably comes from *brat*, defined as a 'spoiled child.' . . . Is 'celebrity' therefore 'a trap for poorly behaved children'?" (p. 79).

Illustrative of leading media critics' judgments which are couched as political and/or TV artistry were their initial responses in 1991 to television news coverage of the Gulf War. Here are a few critical verdicts:

- Walter Goodman, *New York Times*: "As usual with TV it's the pictures that are important. The shots of Scuds falling in Israel was a natural for TV."
- Matt Roush, *USA Today*: "I think we're still knocking out the kinks of live TV in a war theater."
- John Carman, *San Francisco Chronicle*: "We're seeing a lot of information that would have been eliminated from a finished broadcast and a lot of that information is incorrect."
- Phil Klouer, the *Atlanta Journal*: "This is a war. We are going to see wounded Americans. We are at some point going to see dead Americans. It's TV's job to show that to the American people so that we can truly see what's going on."
- Barry Garron, *Kansas City Star*: "a buckshot of facts" (Holmberg and Roach, 1991, p. 25).

We have already seen that one TV critic, Ed Bark of the *Dallas Morning News*, rendered his artistic verdict that CNN "set the standard for television news" during the early days of the Gulf War. Many leading critics agreed: for example, Marvin Kitman of *Newsday*: "CNN has no equal" (Holmberg and Roach, 1991, p. 25). A few critics were more cautious. One was Bob Greene of the *Chicago Tribune* (1991). Greene called the praise for CNN "well deserved." He hoped, however, that the network would not "start believing it is as important as everyone says it is." The "Big Three" networks (ABC, CBS, and NBC) long ago began to cover politics not as unfolding news but as spectacle. Indeed, the Big Three became part of the spectacle: "As often as not the big-name correspondents might as well have been touring diplomats." By contrast, CNN, in Greene's artistic eye, covered news as news without frills and with no self-importance: "At the Big Three networks, the anchors might have been the stars [read that as *celebrity* with Thompson's definition], but at CNN news was the star." The artist-critic in Greene was not optimistic about CNN's future. He worried with an "uneasy feeling" each time a pundit-journalist, such as Bill Moyers or Walter Cronkite, or a world leader appeared in the CNN anchor booth calling anchor Bernard Shaw "Bernie." For "every minute they're on CNN's air, some no-name CNN crew somewhere—the kind of crew that has made CNN what it is—is cooling its heels and being told that there's no time available for its report" (p. 5J).

In sum, as Mencken pointed out, the critic as artist rather than as constable "has nothing to do with morality whatsoever," but instead the critical concern is "solely with beauty" (Greene, 1991, p. 5J) Aside from Tom Shales, whose contacts with Washington's high and mighty cloak him in the robes of a priestly pundit, the critic as artist is in the bardic tradition of punditry. The bardic critic judges political media not from the viewpoint of elitist preferences but from that of the average reader, listener, or viewer. Bob Greene's "uneasy feeling" expressed his concern for the future of beauty at CNN, a journalistic beauty that will be blemished if too much of network time shifts to the celebrated, famous, and uppity, for example, the priestly Bill Moyers. Moyers is himself a political media critic but is not of the ilk of a Bark, a Greene, or even a Shales.

## IS THE POLITICAL PICTURE FULFILLING? THE CRITIC AS CULTURAL PSYCHOLOGIST

In H. L. Mencken's typology there is the critic that views a work of art as "a psychological document" that is "nothing" if it "doesn't help men to know themselves." In the forefront of media critics who fall into the category of cultural psychologist is Bill Moyers. Moyers is a jack-of-all-trades. As a young man he considered a career in the ministry. In high school, however, he became editor of the school paper's sports page. That turned him toward a journalism major in college. A meeting with Senator Lyndon Johnson introduced him to the world of politics. Intrigued by religion, politics, and writing, Moyers at first chose religion. He attended a theological seminary, graduated, and served as a thirty-five-dollar-a-week pastor in a small town church. However, politics beckoned and he became an aide to Senator—soon to be Vice President and then President—Lyndon Johnson. His relationship with Johnson cooled over the years, so Moyers turned again to journalism. He served as publisher of *Newsday*, and then as analyst (à la Eric Sevareid), documentary host, and producer for CBS News; then he moved to, from, and back to the Public Broadcasting System (PBS). At PBS he has been a producer of "ideas TV": documentaries rich in historical context, filled with interviews of persons he considered the "value shapers" of the world, and replete with Moyers's critical commentaries on the cultural relevance of social, political, and economic change (Swartz, 1989, p. 217). Among those documentaries have been the notable "Creativity," "A World of Ideas," "A Walk Through the Twentieth Century," "The Power of Myth," and "The Public Mind."

To illustrate the role of the media critic as a priestly pundit specializing in cultural psychology we turn to Moyers's televised PBS series "The Public Mind" (1989). Bearing the subtitle "Image and Reality in America," the series consisted of four programs covering, in order, the topics of visual imagery in social and political life, opinion polls and market research, the news media, and lying and deception. Each, according to Moyers, "shapes the public mind." As works of art, however, imagery, polling, news, and lying do not help people to "know themselves" (Mencken's phrase); indeed, they mask and conceal the harsh realities facing American culture.

Moyer's method mixes classical psychiatry with priestly intervention. In each TV program, Moyers interviewed a series of value shapers, analysts, experts, and insiders. That is, as priest he talks to and with elites. He permits those interviewed to talk freely, with an occasional nod, smile, or prompt; Moyers is the noncommittal priest-psychiatrist. Moyers bridges these interviews and visual materials with either voice-over or talking head commentaries. In either case Moyers offers a priestly interpretation of the deep, cultural implications of the content of what the person interviewed said. Moyers integrates the overall meaning of the various interviews with a closing commentary to each documentary.

The opening program in "The Public Mind" series, entitled "Consuming Images," ranged over the topic of visual images as popular art, creations that mediate what people see, feel, know, and think about themselves. Moyers kicked off the program and the series by commenting on a cultural psychological note that the consuming of images has transformed the way you and I see and understand the world. . . . In politics, in business, in journalism, the visual media have taken center stage, shaping the public mind with powerful tools of fiction that both please and deceive. Dramatic visual effects, synthetic dreams, counterfeit emotions, preconceived spontaneity—public life is a media show.

If the stakes were not so high, he went on, we could sit back and enjoy the show. However, at stake, in psychological terms, is "our sense of meaning and of language." The stakes are our ideas of history, democracy, and citizenship; even notions of beauty and truth.

As the opening program developed, Moyers stressed that leading the parade in producing the contemporary world's graven images is the advertising commercial. The ad is the "communion wafer of the marketplace." In a marketplace culture driven by visual imagery, the very essence of politics has changed. Once, said Moyers, the idea of "concerned citizen" implied free people thinking and acting for themselves and participating in the civic life of a nation. For Americans today, however, argued Moyers, "representative democracy is nothing but the *representation* of democracy" through the politics not of acting together but of consuming images together. Moyers concluded that in politics and in the marketplace, we-the-citizens' rights are the rights of consumers to pick a product (or candidate) from an endless array of "prefabricated images."

Enhancing the consumption of consuming images is the technology of probing what people want, wish, value, and fear. Polling is the heart of market research. "Pollsters want to know everything," said Moyers, leading off the second program in "The Public Mind" entitled "Leading Questions." Research sells cake mixes, toothpaste, and candidates. Polling makes money, and polling even makes presidents, but does it make a democracy? Moyers thought not. Continuing the metaphor of the marketplace, Moyers devoted the program to "the opinion industry" which rests on a view that it is easier to appeal to "the heart than the mind." Pollsters, said Moyers, want us to tell them how we feel, not how we think, so that those in the opinion industry can make us feel better. Hence, politics today, concluded Moyers in his capacity as cultural psychologist, is not concerned with the state of the nation but with the state of our emotions. The pollsters' message is, all is well if "everybody's feeling good."

The news media are no protection against either the culture of marketplace or market research. Imagery, entertainment, and drama: These constitute the "Illusions of News," the title of the third in the series of "The Public Mind." Illusions of news yield victories for candidates and profit for corporations, "but they keep on crowding out the real thing," observed Moyers. Then, perhaps following the principle that confession is good for the soul (even the psychologist's soul), Moyers concluded:

I've been a player in this game. I've seen it from about every angle of the field—in presidential politics, as a journalist for CBS, and as a newspaper publisher. I've done my share of image making, used my share of sound bites, fought my share of circulation battles, and felt my share of desperation over that picture not quite perfect.

However, despite all this, Moyers remained upbeat. He had also worked with his share of journalists trying to bring readers and viewers a realistic view on which to act. Perhaps there would be such journalists again.

"The Public Mind" series finished with an episode entitled "The Truth about Lies." The program was an exploration of deception and deceit, particularly the self-deceptions by individuals and by the nation in private and in public life. Aside from a brief account of instances when the news media fake and simulate "live" news events, Moyers departed his role as media critic per se and undertook a more far-reaching critique of social and political practices of lying. Central to his critique is a psychological analysis of his former political mentor, Lyndon Johnson, for lying and deception regarding the Vietnam War, practices born in Johnson's "devious and secretive ways." The practices contributed to the president's "wishful thinking," observed Moyers.

The concluding commentary to "The Truth about Lies" summed up the program, the series, and Moyers's view as critic: "What have we learned?" he asked. We learn that nations, "like families," can die from too many lies: too many self-deceptions, marketplace images, marketed emotions, and news media illusions. However, Moyers said, beneath the distortion and deception of life in the United States today there is "hard reality." Unfortunately, the "public mind" is filled with "images of an America where the vending machines are always full, the wounded always recover, and the bills never come due." In that, the public mind lies to itself: "Reality is fearsome, but as we've learned in this series, experience tells us more fearsome yet is evading it."

As critic, then, Bill Moyers views the media in all forms as nothing more than the man behind the curtain in *The Wizard of Oz* (he showed the scene from the movie), deluding and conning the public mind. Moyers is not alone as a media critic clothing himself as cultural psychologist. We could as easily point to Jeff Greenfield: author, syndicated columnist, and ABC News commentator, or TV anchor, commentator, and analyst Linda Ellerbee. Each might assess the impact of the media on political culture differently, and both are more humorous in their style than the ministerial Moyers. However, in Mencken's terms, all such critics treat media content as psychological documents that, in the end, constitute "nothing" if they do not help us to know ourselves.

## IS THE POLITICAL PICTURE REPRESENTATIVE?
## THE CRITIC AS SOCIAL SCIENTIST

The constabulary punditry of media watchdogs rests on doctrinal definitions of accuracy and fairness in political reporting. The artistic punditry of TV critics rests on aesthetic judgments of what is good—not necessarily fair—network performance. Critics as cultural psychologists practice a punditry of long-term consequences of a spectacle-oriented society. A final group of media critics, to use Mencken's term, "reduce" political television to an "exact science." A partial sense of how the critic as social scientist differs from the constable derives from a 1991 *TV Guide* column (Rosenthal, 1991). It pertained to televised news coverage of protests against the Gulf War. The column quoted Jeff Cohen of Fairness and Accuracy in Reporting as saying "the networks have failed to present dissenting or anti-war viewpoints." An AIM spokesman, Joseph Goulden, disagreed: The networks gave "a disproportionate amount of time to the protests." The column called on a third analyst, Robert Lichter, codirector of the Center for Media and Public Affairs. The center counts the number of stories of various types on nightly network TV newscasts. "Although the data are still being analyzed," said *TV Guide* (a scientific caution), Lichter reported that "there were as many news stories on the anti-war movement the first two weeks of this year as there were the first four months of the crisis" (p. 33).

Quantification and caution are the hallmarks of the critic's role as scientist. Although there are others who analyze media content by counting and classifying news stories (for example, Andrew Tyndall, who publishes *The Tyndall Report*), for illustrative purposes we shall look in more detail at the Center for Media and Public Affairs. The chief vehicle for communicating center findings is a periodic newsletter, *Media Monitor*, which has been published since 1987. The newsletter's logo, format, and style strive for an aura of scientific credibility, suggesting membership in the "priesthood of science." The logo at the top of the first page consists of the title "Media Monitor" on the left side of a rectangle approximately seven inches long and one inch high. The upper two-thirds of the rectangle bears the design of a graph: it is squared off like graph paper with a trend line across the rectangle that rises and falls as if charting the peaks and valleys of some phenomenon. The words "Media Monitor" are a portion of the trend line. Below the line the rectangle is not squared off but instead lists the office address and the telephone number of the center.

Early issues contained on the back page a listing of center staff and a note stating that the *"Media Monitor* is a monthly publication of the Center for Media and Public Affairs, a nonpartisan and non-profit research organization." Beginning with Volume 3 (January 1989), the newsletter moved this notice to the front page, announced that the *Monitor* was published ten times a year, and added, "The Center conducts scientific studies of how the media treat social and political issues."

The basic format and style of the newsletter has changed only marginally since the initial issues. Through 1990 each issue possessed a restrained three-color scheme appropriate for a scientific report: black on white, with logo, headings, and selected graphics in a third soft, delicate hue. The front page bore a title pertaining to the major topical area covered by the issue. Here are examples from each of the first four years of *Media Monitor*: "From Irangate to Olliemania: How TV News Covered the Hearings" (August 1987), "Moscow Meets the Media: Comparing Coverage of the Moscow and Washington Summits" (July 1988), "The Budget and the Deficit: Covering the Battle over the Budget" (July/August 1989), and "Crisis in the Gulf: TV News Coverage of the Persian Gulf Crisis: Phase I" (November 1990). Below the topical title readers find a blocked statement summarizing media coverage and the number of stories and/or total air time devoted to the topic over a specified period of time. The front page also lists "Major Findings" and indexes the page of the newsletter discussing each.

In any given year the number and variety of topics contained in *Media Monitor* reflect the topical areas emphasized in the news media, especially network TV news. Each January issue considers "The Year in Review," a compilation of key findings regarding news media content in the preceding twelve months. Moreover, in addition to analyzing strictly news coverage, the *Media Monitor* contains an occasional side feature. For example, the July/August 1989 issue analyzed six months of NBC's "Tonight Show" and "Late Night," cataloging the political subjects of jokes. Readers discovered that of 1,228 jokes, George Bush was the subject of 83, Dan Quayle of 78, John Tower of 58, Ayatollah Khomeini of 49, Jim Wright of 33, Ronald Reagan of 28, and Oliver North of 24. The subjects of the remaining jokes consisted of scores of individuals. In a list titled "Top Ten People Targeted on Late Night TV" based upon the number of jokes told about each subject, being the target of 83 jokes made George Bush Number One on the list; Manuel Noriega came in 14th on the list.

The quantification of jokes suggests how far the center goes in its scientific criticism. It takes bardic humor and transforms it into priestly data. The design of the inside and back pages of the newsletter marks how far the center goes to impress readers with its scientific intent. Interspersed throughout the two-column format (with key findings underlined in the pastel color of the day) are all manner of "scientific" signs: bar diagrams, pie charts, trend lines, histograms, polygons, scales, maps, illustrative drawings, and assorted other graphics. Block quotations from people in the news or by journalists are also scattered across

the newsletter's pages. For example, "This is becoming a television ne-
gotiation: brinksmanship by television," said CBS anchorman Dan
Rather on his newscast of August 8, 1990, in commenting on the Persian
Gulf crisis (*Media Monitor*, November 1990, p. 3). It may not be science,
but the newsletter also promotes the judgments of other media critics.
For instance, a highlighted quote from the September 1989 issue was
from Tom Shales, a comment on TV news coverage of protests in Bei-
jing's Tiananmen Square: "What made the crackdown so startling was
. . . the rosy view of China that had been painted by the media" (p. 2).
  For the most part, the center's analysis consists of counting and classifying the number of news stories pertaining to a given topic area.
Simply monitoring the *Media Monitor* on a regular basis, however, provides readers with no clue as to what constitutes a "story," the precise
definition of each classification scheme, the techniques of classification,
or the reliability of the center coding scheme. A favorite center tool for
evaluating news coverage of political figures—candidates, the president,
world leaders, and so on—magnifies the uncertainty of how scientific
the "scientific studies" of the center actually are. For example, heading
into the 1988 presidential election season, *Media Monitor* reported a content analysis of 379 election stories on the three major TV news networks
that were aired from February 8, 1987, to the close of the year. Without
indicating the basis of the coding, the study reported on how much air
time each network devoted to the upcoming presidential election; how
many stories were about Democrats or Republicans; how many stories
were about campaign issues, the "horse race," candidate profiles, policy
issues, media coverage of campaigns, and campaign strategy; how many
mentions each of ten policy issues received; who the sources of stories
were; and the number of stories about each of fourteen candidates in
the two parties. Such precision would be more laudable if readers knew
on what it was based. One is reminded of the football referee who
casually places the ball down at some point where the play allegedly
stopped and then calls for a precise measurement from the sideline
officials to determine if there has been a first down.
  Finally, to discern the quality of coverage, "we coded all on-air evaluations of each candidate's personal traits, job performance, campaign
behavior, and issue stands, after excluding horse race judgments." Then,
"to provide a single index of good vs. bad press, we subtracted negative
from positive assessments after excluding comments from the candidates' own camps" (*Media Monitor*, January 1988, p. 5). We do not wish
to belabor the point, but precise, specific, and even jargon-spiced as this
explanation appears, in the absence of criteria for how coders differ-
entiated between "positive" and "negative" assessments, or even how
they recognized an "assessment," readers find it difficult to judge the
representativeness, reliability, and validity of such scientific criticism,

just as they find it hard to judge the constabulary "research" of *MediaWatch*, the *AIM Report*, or *Lies Of Our Times*.

Like the constabulary watchdogs, members of the Center for Media and Public Affairs have other outlets for their scientific claims. Two publications of the American Enterprise Institute (see Chapter Four), the now defunct journal *Public Opinion* and the current *The American Enterprise* publish center findings (Lichter and Noyes, 1991). Moreover, codirector Robert Lichter not only makes the pages of *TV Guide* but has served as the source for analyses by TV critics of major dailies; for example, David Shaw of the *Los Angeles Times* (August 15, 1988, pp. 1, 5) and has had columns published on the op-ed sections of metropolitan newspapers (for instance, see the *Dallas Morning News*, September 23, 1990, p. 4J). Center analysts, as do constabulary critics, also appear as "media analysts" on radio and TV panels.

Finally, in conjunction with the American Enterprise Institute, the center published a book-length treatment of its study of media coverage of the 1988 presidential primaries. Aside from being told that "every fact or opinion that appeared" in a story, and not the overall news stories themselves, were the "building blocks" of analysis, and that "only the variables on which . . . coding decisions were in agreement 80 percent of the time" were used in analyses, readers still remain in the dark about the scientific foundation of findings (Lichter, Amundson, and Noyes, 1988, pp. 5–6).

## CONCLUSION: ORDERS OF MEDIATED POLITICS

The fourfold typology of media critics is but an illustration of the variety evident in critical reviews of the political media. Moreover, a given critic may play more than one of these four roles. For example, Ed Bark of the *Dallas Morning News* engages in no advocacy criticism of the watchdog but regularly applies aesthetic standards of the artist in evaluating political media; in the manner of a cultural psychologist, he asks what the media tell us about ourselves, and during the 1988 presidential election he analyzed statistically on a weekly basis the airtime each presidential candidate received in major TV network news coverage from the primaries through the general election.

Philosophers are often intrigued by the orders of reality and speak of "firstness," "secondness," and "thirdness" (see, for example, Peirce, 1958). In politics, firstness consists of the acts of politicians, secondness of the reports and interpretations of those actions by political journalists, and thirdness of the reviews of journalistic pictures by critics of the political media. By its very content, this chapter suggests a "fourthness." That order of the mediation of political reality is made up of reviewing the acts of media critics who tell us what journalistic accounts are biased, artistic, culturally informative, or statistically sound. We invite readers of this chapter to engage in yet a "fifthness" in mediated politics, namely, to examine our account of media critics and then explore the constructions of various critics themselves. The role of media critics in politics is scarcely trivial. Hence, they, too, require monitoring.

# Chapter Seven

# Conclusion: Democracy
# or Punditocracy?

In a popular 1976 movie, *Network*, Howard Beale, a news anchor for a fictional TV network, learns that he is to be fired. The once loyal anchor turns media critic and starts bashing both his network and all of TV on the air. He tells his viewers, with the fever of a crazed man, that television is a powerful instrument but that what they see is not "truth" but only an "illusion." In the manner of a bard with faith in the populace, he urges viewers to revolt. He counsels them to turn off the TV, go to their windows, and shout that they are "mad as hell" and "not going to take this anymore."

Beale's ratings soar. The shout, "I'm mad as hell, and I'm not going to take this anymore," becomes a rallying cry for the politically disenchanted. Instead of being fired he becomes the featured personality on a news show that exploits a populist, sensationalist, entertainment formula. Beale no longer simply reports the news; he pontificates. The network bills him as "The Mad Prophet of the Airwaves." Joining him on the program are other seemingly bizarre "news personalities," including "Sybil the Soothsayer." Although the show is a runaway success, Beale's critical punditry hits too close to home. It threatens the very elites that run the network, the government, the economy, and indeed, the country. In a final blockbusting newscast, Beale falls dead, the victim of an assassin and an elitist plot.

Movie reviewers found *Network* amusing but also outrageous and preposterous. News could never be like that, or can it? From what we have seen in the course of this book, there is an infestation of prophets and soothsayers, priests, bards, sages, and oracles who are mediating politics in the age of show business. They ponder in consultants' offices, bureaucratic settings, and think tanks. They mediate the realities of our already mediated politics of elections and policies. They chatter in casual, confrontational, and carnival settings on TV, and on call-in, debate, and panel talk shows on radio. Moreover, not satisfied with that, they act as critics of the same news coverage and interpretations of politics of which they are themselves the principal celebrities. Is it true, or, as Beale claimed, illusion? Does the hypothetical traveler to the United States whom we met in our Introduction come away from it all informed, enlightened, and empowered, or confused, apathetic, and politically blind/deaf not "mad as hell" but merely bored to distraction? Let us conclude our discussion by considering a few possibilities.

## THE DEATH OR TRIUMPH OF PUNDITRY?

Not everyone regards pundits as being omniscient as they deem themselves, as omnifarious in types or omnipresent in visibility as we have portrayed them, or as omnipotent in politics as a Howard Beale might think. For example, David Shaw (1989), the media critic of the *Los Angeles Times*, has argued that we have witnessed "the death of punditry" (pp. 1–8). Shaw raised a question, namely, "Are all putative opinion makers—editorial writers, op-ed page columnists, arts critics, television and magazine commentators—just a bunch of irrational quacks?" Moreover, and more to the point, "does anyone really "make" opinion' in America today?" (p. 1). Harking back to earlier times, including the glory days of Walter Lippmann, Shaw compared today's political pundits to opinion makers of the past. He observed that "today's syndicated pundits" do not "wield the influence they once did" (p. 4).

Moreover, commentary on TV—Shaw cites Eric Sevareid, John Chancellor, and Bill Moyers as examples—is "intelligent" and "moderate," but the first quality probably limits its appeal and the second, its influence. "The McLaughlin Group," although filled with "histrionics," avoids giving offense or truly opinionated debate. To be sure, TV commentators are everywhere: on the "tube," writing columns, and giving lectures and seminars. "Ubiquitous they may be," remarked Shaw, "but are they influential?" His response: "I think not" (p. 6). Shaw offered as evidence a national survey that found that even a pundit as omnipresent as George Will is scarcely a widely known figure: Only 12 percent of those questioned knew who Will was.

Who, then, are the opinion makers in the United States? For Shaw, there are none, at least not in the sense of telling people what to think. Moreover, when it comes to telling people what to think about, pundits do not do that either. Shaw argues that setting the agenda of what Americans talk and think about is now dominated by lead stories in daily TV news broadcasts, on the front page of the *New York Times*, and on the cover of *Time* and *Newsweek*. "The demise of the opinion maker is not necessarily a devastating loss to the republic," observed Shaw (p. 6); it may simply mean, he concluded, "that many Americans are finally applying their own common sense to the issues of the day, instead of taking their cue from elitist pundits" (p. 8).

Shaw's report of the pundit's death, however, as Mark Twain said after reading a news account of his own demise, may be a bit "premature." Shaw's premise is that the influence of pundits rests on their role in defining, in direct fashion, issues for discussion and the opinions that citizens form on those issues. There may be, however, other indirect consequences of the utterances of priests, bards, sages, and oracles that are more far-reaching and long-lasting than influencing transitory opinions. Let us consider a few.

### Political Punditry as Symbolic Healing

Throughout this book we have linked the roles played by pundits in contemporary society with those of their ancient ancestors: priests, wise men, prophets, Homeric bards, sages, oracles, soothsayers, seers, fortune-tellers, astrologers, and so on. Although pundit, the anglicized version of the ancient Sanskrit word for "learned man," is of relatively recent vintage, in one form or another it seems that punditry has always been with us. One reason for the long-term persistence of punditry lies in a human need that learned individuals fulfill. That need goes beyond offering expertise, information, intelligence, and guidance. It lies in providing what anthropologists call "symbolic healing" (Dow; 1986; Moerman, 1979).

People in all societies suffer illnesses, be they of the body, mind, spirit, or whatever labeling a culture adopts. Therapeutic treatment of illness has various components, most notably the physical and the pharmacological. Frequently combined with physical and/or pharmacological healing is another form of treatment, symbolic healing. Moreover, in some societies neither physical nor pharmacological therapy may exist; all healing may be symbolic. Symbolic healing involves the manipulation of symbols by a healer; such symbols are those that the ill person believes in, holds dear, and regards as having a virtually magical quality. For example, "shamanism and faith healing are types of magical healing, a type of symbolic healing that involves the ritual manipulation of superhuman forces" (Dow, 1986, p. 57).

Entertain the possibility that in any society, when people confront strange, puzzling, and inexplicable events that leave them helpless to understand and hopeless to cope, it is very much as though they are stricken with a malady. Something is out of the ordinary, the stricken person does not know why and is powerless to find out. In a socially, economically, morally, and politically complex world, the likelihood of people being "stricken" by ignorance, confusion, and helplessness in coping with the strange, the unconventional, the untoward, and the perplexing is considerable. They need a medicine man, shaman, or therapist; they require "medicine" or "equipment for living" (Burke, 1967, p. 293). That medicine comes not in the form of pills and potions but as symbols, a bromide of therapeutic punditry prescribed by contemporary priests, bards, sages, and oracles. The medicine may or may not heal (influence opinions) or even make patients feel well enough to move about (express and follow up those opinions). It does, however, convince the patient that "all is being done that can be done" and encourage him or her to "continue on with the prescription and see me again in a week."

Anthropologist James Dow (1986) has contended that symbolic healing is so common historically and across societies that it has a universal structure. That structure has four features; as we shall see, each has its parallel in political punditry. First, "the experiences of healers and healed are generalized with culture-specific symbols in cultural myths" (p. 56). The key here is the cultural myth. Myths, for Dow, are cultural truths that arise out of longterm experience; in other words, a myth is "true" because people have experienced it as such: "These truths may be more salient than scientific truths because they represent solutions to personal human problems" (p. 59). We have seen repeatedly that myth surrounds the pundit's task, chiefly the myth of where special knowledge derives from and how it must be mediated: For the priest, special knowledge lies among political elites to be revealed as "inside dope"; for the bard, wisdom resides in the populace, to be given the bard's comic touch; the sage finds wisdom in the ages and brings lofty learning and experience to its interpretation; and the oracle's special knowledge is of the future and its revelation.

The second aspect of Dow's universal structure of symbolic healing involves a suffering patient coming to a healer who persuades the stricken person that the illness can be defined in terms of the myth. The myth forms a basis for symbolic healing, for "curing is often based on restructuring a disorder modeled in a mythic world"; that is, the patient responds to the therapist's myth: "In the curing process the healer particularizes part of the general cultural mythic world for the patient and interprets the patient's problem in terms of disorders in this particularized segment" (p. 59). For example, recall the case of H. V. Kaltenborn from Chapter One. Kaltenborn looked at the ills of post–World War II America and interpreted them in the context of a long-standing myth of the demonic nature of Communism. This allowed him to take a hard-line stance against the Soviet Union even before U.S. policy recognized a Cold War.

The example of Kaltenborn also touches on the third of Dow's characteristics of the universal structure of symbolic healing. That pertains to the healer's efforts to attach the patient's emotions to symbols that particularize the general myth. The therapist, whether healer or pundit, places human or political illness in a mythic context. However, patients are not simply free to interpret mythic truths as they wish. If they did, they would have no more need for the healer; they could discover their own cure. "However," said Dow "in most magical healing, it is the healer who dramatizes and projects the particularized mythic world" (p. 60). This Kaltenborn did. He dramatized and particularized the mythic world of the Communist Menace, emphasizing that in spite of close relations between the United States and the USSR in World War II, long-standing Communist aims and ambitions had not changed. It was with *Russia* and, more important, the Russian people that the United States had found common cause in the struggle against Nazi Germany; it was not really the Union of Soviet Socialistic Republics (i.e., not the Soviets or the Socialists) that had fought loyally at our side.

Finally, in the universal process of symbolic healing, said Dow, the healer manipulates symbols to help the patient "transact his or her own emotions." As when people transact business; namely, carry on, conduct, and manage exchanges, they must manage their own emotions in symbolic healing. Transactions require media; for example, currency is the medium of business transactions, and mythic symbols are the media of healing transactions.

Once particularized by the healer, the manipulation of a transactional symbol in a particularized mythic world can suggest a change in the way that the patient evaluates personal experiences. To a culturally uninitiated observer or even to one outside the complementary relationship, the manipulation of transactional symbols may seem ridiculous. Nails may be pulled out of the body; "demons" may be cast into darkness; "souls" may be found; sorcerers may be identified and so on. However, if the healer has done the job well, the symbolic healing will be a significant experience for the patient. (Dow, 1986, p. 65)

Kaltenborn did his job well, at least initially. The "demon Communism" was cast into darkness. So too, in a different vein, did Edward R. Murrow: He identified Senator Joseph McCarthy as a sorcerer. Similarly, Mark Twain, Will Rogers, and even the character Mr. Dooley, found and refound the "soul" of the United States in its people. David Shaw, however, suggests that today's pundits do not do their jobs well; they do not heal. However, if their medicine does not heal, might it not sedate?

## Political Punditry as Paternalism

As we have noted often, what sets pundits and healers apart from the rest of "mere mortals" is their claim to special, and even secret, knowledge that we do not possess. That knowledge privileges them to speak, while we, the Alices in Wonderland (i.e., "*We* the People") should not. In offering therapy neither the healers of ancient times nor today's physicians tell their patients everything about the illness that they suffer. In part, they think the information too technical, subtle, and fraught with conditions and qualifications for patients to understand. Alternatively, the healer's diagnosis may be tentative; what mythic worlds should be provoked by the manipulation of which precise symbols may be unclear. Furthermore, there may be another reason, one that philosophers call "epistemic paternalism."

Alvin Goldman (1991) provided an example that helps define epistemic paternalism. He drew it not from the world of medicine but from the realm of law. In jury trials, judges frequently want to protect jurors in their search for the truth in a case. If jurors would likely be misled by a certain type of evidence that might, say, give undue weight to matters that are at best peripheral to guilt or innocence, judges may allow such evidence to be withheld from the jury. Clearly, one can just as easily find medical examples; in other words, a physician may withhold certain aspects of a patient's diagnosis lest it produce needless anxieties over symptoms that may prove misleading or turn out to have no bearing on the illness. "The general idea," wrote Goldman, "is that the indicated rules of evidence are designed to protect jurors from their own 'folly,' just as parents might keep dangerous toys or other articles away from children, or might not expose them to certain facts" (p. 118).

This, then, is epistemic paternalism: withholding information from people for their alleged own good. "I shall think of communication controllers as exercising epistemic paternalism whenever they interpose their own judgment rather than allow the audience to exercise theirs" (p. 119). Goldman provided several examples of epistemic paternalism: school boards selecting curricular materials to protect students from avowedly pernicious ideas, actions of the U.S. Federal Trade Commission to protect consumers from deceptive advertising, and so on. Even TV and radio news engages in epistemic paternalism:

American network newscasts offer a relatively limited variety of interpretations of each news event; nor do they detail the evidence for each of the possible interpretations. This is partly due, no doubt, to severe time constraints. But there is also the deliberate attempt to simplify, to make the news understandable and digestible to a large audience. Certainly this must be included under the rubric of epistemic paternalism. (p. 123)

As we have seen repeatedly throughout this book, if we substitute "pundits" for "newscasts" in Goldman's statement, we have precisely the limited, middle-of-the-road type of commentary served up by formulaic columnists, TV analysts, talk show hosts and guests, and media critics, no matter what their professed and dramatically performed postures "on the right" or "on the left" might suggest otherwise.

What is not clear is the degree that such paternalism reduces the sovereignty of a person in deciding what to believe and in weighing reasons for, and courses of, action. When pundits routinely and ritually interpret politics in simplified, understandable ways—in keeping with the canons of the age of show business—are citizens' epistemic rights served? We have seen that critics such as David Shaw are relatively unconcerned about a reduction in citizens' sovereignty. The "death of punditry," as we quoted Shaw (1989) earlier, permits citizens to apply "their own common sense to the issues of the day, instead of taking their cue from elitist pundits" (p. 8). Other critics are not so optimistic. They argue that pundits have so often interposed their own judgment rather than allowing citizens to do their own thinking that we have become voyeurs of knowledge, a nation that sits and watches other people talk, defers to experts about what is important, and readily accepts the myth that knowledge resides in the special few: a political class "unlike us."

### Political Punditry as Surrogate Citizenship

Christopher Lasch (1990) made a telling point about the relationship between opinion makers and popular opinions in democracy. It is a point we encountered in Chapter One in John Dewey's critique of Walter Lippmann's *Public Opinion*. "What democracy requires is public debate," Lasch said, "not information." Obviously, Lasch was not denying the need for information. He did, however, suggest a prior and more probing question, namely, what do we need information for? The kind of information that democracy needs, he argued, "can be generated only by vigorous popular debate," for "when we get into arguments that focus and fully engage our attention, we become avid seekers of relevant information. Otherwise, we take in information passively—if we take it in at all" (p. 1).

Lasch's words are reminiscent of John Dewey's position in his disagreement with Lippmann's call for a press that would provide "a picture of the world" (Lippmann's term for information) on which the "citizen can act" (1922, p. 358). A press that encouraged debate and argument, thought Lippmann, did little to reveal truth; instead, it merely provoked opinions; and the truth value of opinion is notoriously unreliable. In this view Lippmann was voicing the reformist aims of the Progressive

Era in the early part of this century, aims we encountered in discussing the role of technicians as pundits in Chapter Four. Progressives "liked to contrast the scientific expert with the orator—the latter a useless windbag whose rantings only confused the public mind" (Lasch, 1990, p. 4). As we saw in Chapter One, Dewey thought Lippmann had the cart before the horse. A professional press corps could only provide information on which people could act if, first, journalists asked relevant questions. Those questions, in turn, could only be generated by free, open, and lively debate.

Lasch, and Dewey before him, were suggesting that Lippmann and those who share his view of the press favor epistemic paternalism. That is, to return to Goldman's argument, journalists are communication controllers who "interpose their judgment rather than allow the audience [through debate] to exercise theirs" (Goldman, 1991, p. 119). Such paternalism is out of place in a democracy.

If we insist on argument as the essence of education, we will defend democracy not as the most efficient but as the most educational form of government—one that extends the circle of debate as widely as possible and thus forces all citizens to articulate their views, to put their views at risk, and to cultivate the virtues of eloquence, clarity of thought and expression, and sound judgment. (Lasch, 1990, pp. 7–8)

Given that viewpoint, the role of the press in a democracy is not chiefly as a dispenser of information—it is not a library—but to act as the equivalent of a town meeting. Lasch believes that the press performs poorly in that town meeting role; in that respect he shares the position, as outlined in this chapter, of media critic David Shaw and philosopher Alvin Goldman. It is a judgment reached by other recent observers of press performance as well (Bennett, 1988; Entman, 1989; Rosen, 1991). The press engages in symbolic healing, but the medicine it prescribes is a placebo, not a cure for the ills in public discourse that plague democracy.

The formulaic and ritualistic practice of political punditry that we have described in this book is not an adequate substitute for public debate. Mainstream pundifications; government, think tank, and academic experts hawking subsidized expertise; contrived and rehearsed exchanges; talent hunts by broadcasters in search of analysts who "fit" selected sound bites; or ten-minute cross fires, face-offs, and mini-debates between talk show hosts, guests, and callers—these are scarcely the stuff of vigorous, probing, challenging public discourse. Nor do media critics who ritually bash the news media for being too far left or right, unbalanced in coverage of major events, and lacking in artistic form contribute to improving the journalistic town meeting.

Punditry, and the punditocracy it has spawned in the age of show business, is yet another form of *la technique* (Chapter Four): pundits technically—and certainly for the TV camera, radio microphone, or daily newspaper "quotable quote"—pretend to undertake the tedious, frustrating, time-consuming, and painstaking task of public discussion and debate. Mastery of show business techniques permits them to do so in an entertaining, facile, and healing manner. Moreover, pundits do it efficiently, without all the errors, stops and starts, hesitations, and meanderings that characterize open town hall debate.

The efficiency of *la technique* of punditry, however, has another side. Pundits frequently engage in banal discourse. They lull the critical faculties, pretending to know, show, and tell things that nobody else knows. To listen, heed, and act (or, more likely, sit idly by) is to be lulled into a trap. It is not the trap set by a conspirator, not the trap of the petty tyrant, and not even the trap of the ambitious politician who is wise to the ways of pundits and skilled in exploiting and manipulating their technique. It is, rather, a trap set by hubris: by excessive confidence, arrogance, pretense, and guile. It is the hubris typified in Thomas Thompson's 1982 novel, *Celebrity*, which we alluded to in Chapter Five. In the novel a grizzled newspaper editor asks an ambitious young reporter, "What do you wanna be[?] Good? Or famous?" Without hesitation the reporter says he wants to be both. The editor responds, "That's illegal. It's bigamy. And it's hardly possible" (p. 167). Eventually forced to make the choice, the reporter becomes famous, a "celebrity."

Not all pundits are guilty of hubris, and not all ignore the problems raised by citizens' perceptions that today public discussion and debate is something that "they" (pundits) do and that "we" do not have the special knowledge and performance skills to undertake. Political observers have long worried about the failures of Americans to be actively interested in politics—to vote in higher proportions, to work on behalf of candidates, and to learn, ponder, and discuss public issues. There has been for some time a sense of political disenchantment in the United States, a sense provoked by low voter turnout, citizens expressing little confidence in government, negative campaigns, noncompetitive elections, special interest politics, and declining levels of public services, facilities, and ethics.

In 1991 a think tank, the Kettering Foundation, commissioned a study by the Harwood Group to explore through focus groups the state of the public mind regarding politics and government. The findings provided the grist for numerous op-ed columns and TV commentaries (Leubsdorf; 1991; Mathews and Harwood, 1991). The general conclusion was that Americans see a governmental arrangement dominated by a professional political class: recycled politicians, lobbyists, and others. There is a widespread perception that taking part in politics really does not count anymore, so why bother? Election campaigns, for example, simply stir up old resentments and anger as candidates trot out the same old issues (abortion, crime, drugs, taxes, etc.) that they have used many times before to lull voters into one more ballot of angry protest. Voters "do not see their concerns reflected as current issues are discussed, nor do they find issues termed in ways they understand" (Leubsdorf, 1991, p. 31A).

That issues are not framed in ways that citizens understand may be in part the reflection of another segment of the professional political class that people see governing the United States—namely, the punditocracy. Strikingly, the analysis of focus groups revealed that many citizens suggested a simple corrective, the same urged by Lasch, Dewey, and others: "They want to restore the integrity, vitality and scope of public dialogue." Citizens no longer want to be spectators; they do not endorse surrogate citizenship. Public dialogue "is the natural home for democratic politics; it is the 'home' that people feel forced out of and want back" (Mathews and Harwood, 1991, p. 20). How do they do that?

## IS LAUGHTER THE BEST MEDICINE? PRICKING THE BUBBLE OF THE PUNDIT'S PRIDE

We saw in Chapter Two that Mark Twain was a pioneer of bardic punditry. He exploited humor in criticizing politics and politicians as well as in pricking the pride of his contemporary priestly brethren. In *A Connecticut Yankee in King Arthur's Court*, Twain (1889, pp. 12–14) described the Yankee's first impressions upon arriving at the Round Table of Arthur and his illustrious knights. Scale down the scene and Twain could be describing any radio or televised talk show, public seminar, or any other gathering of pundits, especially how pundits act and what they talk about.

The table was "as large as a circus-ring." Around it sat a "great company of men" (p. 13) (today there are also women pundits). The company were "dressed in such various and splendid colors that it hurt one's eyes to look at them" (p. 13) (today's pundits dress more conservatively, to be sure, but they also trot out their equivalents of attention-getting gimmicks: horned-rimmed and aviator glasses, splashy ties, or rehearsed nastiness). All wore plumed hats, except "whenever one addressed himself directly to the king, he lifted his hat a trifle" (p. 13) (the pundit's ritualistic genuflect to the concept of "We, the People" and the "People's Right to Know"). "Mainly they were drinking—from entire ox horns" (try coffee cups and water glasses). Each man had brought along a couple of dogs to the banquet, much like each regular on "This Week with David Brinkley" or any other talk show brings along a couple of ostentatious and dog-eared arguments that were employed on past shows.

The Yankee noted that each time a morsel or scrap of food would fall from the table or be flung at the dogs, there would be a ferocious dog fight accompanied by "howlings" and "barkings" that "deafened all speech for the time." No matter, "for the dog fight was always a bigger interest anyway" (p. 13) (just as contrived chatter is always a bigger interest to pundits than public debate).

"Mainly the Round Table talk was monologues," observed the Yankee, and as a rule, the speech and behavior of the people were "gracious and courtly," (p. 14). Moreover, the Yankee observed them to be "good and serious listeners when anybody was telling anything—I mean in a dog-fightless interval," (p. 14). It was, thought the Yankee, "hard to associate them with anything cruel or dreadful; and yet, they dealt in tales of blood and suffering with a guileless relish that made me almost forget to shudder" (p.14). For alternating grace/courtliness and dogfighting, substitute bland commentary and verbal wrestling; for tales of blood and suffering, substitute prophesies of gloom and doom. The Yankee might as well have been watching "The McLaughlin Group."

The Yankee was not at Arthur's Court voluntarily. He was a prisoner, and there were approximately twenty other prisoners as well. None uttered "a moan or a groan" or showed "any sign of restlessness or any disposition to complain." Why was this so? The "thought was forced upon me." The "rascals" knew that this was their lot as prisoners, for they, too, had once been knights, trained as animals to duel when there "was no cause of offense whatsoever," and to take prisoners. They knew what to expect—to sit watching others drink, talk, and eat; tell tales of knightly manhood, of blood and suffering, with guileless relish. "They were not expecting any treatment better than this; so their philosophical bearing is not an outcome of mental training, intellectual fortitude, reasoning; it is mere animal training." (p. 14).

It is difficult to claim that American citizens who watch, hear and read pundits confronting one another over issues that citizens themselves find irrelevant (i.e., when there is "no cause of offense whatsoever") are products of "mere animal training." However, they increasingly are conditioned to the pundit's formulas and rituals. That is not to say, however, that they are "not expecting any treatment better than this." Those who call for a return to a public discourse of dialogue and debate rather than pundit monologue and chatter clearly do expect better. To achieve it, perhaps they should assess punditry as Twain's prisoner did his captors. He compared their behavior and talk to a "couple of boys" who meet by chance and say simultaneously, "I can lick you," and "Go to it on the spot." The prisoner had always

imagined until now that that sort of thing belonged to children only. . . . [However,] here were these big boobies sticking to it and taking *pride* in it. . . . Yet, there was something very engaging about these great simple-minded creatures, something attractive and lovable. There did not seem to be brains enough in the entire nursery, so to speak, to bait a fish-hook with; but you didn't seem to mind that, after a little, because you soon saw that brains were not needed *in a society like that*, and indeed would have marred it, hindered it, spoiled its symmetry—perhaps rendered its existence impossible. (emphasis added; p. 15)

We began this book with a hypothetical foreign traveler in the pundit's court seeking to find out "What's happening?" and "Why?" Instead of getting answers, our traveler returned home pondering another question, "Who knows?" We close with another traveler, this one a Yankee in King Arthur's Court. He is a prisoner of "what's happening," but must answer for himself, "who knows why?" We do not claim that there are no brains in the pundit's society that our first traveler encountered, but only that the special knowledge about what is happening that pundits claim to have may not be so special after all. Considering what goes on in the Pundit's Court, however, we add one final question. To paraphrase a great American bard, Groucho Marx, should a citizen want to be a member of any punditocracy, even if it would have members of the populace as members?

# Bibliography

Abraham, N. (1991, January). Taxes, lies and gas masks. *Lies of Our Times*, p. 3.

Accuracy in Media, (1989). Vol 18. (Available from Accuracy in Media, Inc., 1275 K Street N.W., Suite 1150, Washington, DC, 20005).

Adler, J. (1990, May). Michael Kinsley goes to hell. *Esquire*, pp. 100–106.

Ailes, R. (1988, May/June). The power of the tube: *C&E* interview with Roger Ailes. *Campaigns & Elections*, Vol. 9, pp. 25–27.

Ailes, R. (1991, January/February). TV-spot critics: "Boring and biased." *Washington Journalism Review*, Vol. 13, p. 27.

Albee, E. (1962). *Who's afraid of Virginia Woolf?* New York: Atheneum Publishers.

Alterman, E. (1988, August 7). A neocon job: punditocracy has shifted political debate in Orwellian fashion. *Dallas Morning News*, p. 35A.

Althiede, D., and Snow, R. (1979). *Media logic*. Beverly Hills, CA: Sage.

American Association of Political Consultants. *The Politea*. (1990, 1991). Vols. 5, 6. (Available from the American Association of Political Consultants, 1920 L Street, N.W., 6th Floor, Washington, DC, 20036.)

Aronson, S. M. L. (1983). *Hype*. New York: William Morrow.

Associated Press. (1990, November 5). Wire service news account, untitled, no author. [Subject: George Bush campaigning for Republican candidacy.]

Barber, J.D. (Ed.). (1978). *Race for the Presidency*. Englewood Cliffs, NJ: Prentice-Hall.

Barber, J.D. (1980). *The pulse of politics: Electing presidents in the media age*. New York: W. W. Norton.

Barber, J.D. (1985). *Presidential character: Predicting performance in the White House*, 3rd ed. Englewood Cliffs, NJ: Prentice-Hall.

Bark, E. (1990, October 28). Video diplomacy. *Dallas Morning News*, pp 1A, 26A.

Bark, E. (1991, January 18). Iraq silences CNN's live Baghdad. reports. *Dallas Morning News*, pp 1AA, 9AA.

Barry, Dave. (1988, August 15). [*Miami Herald*.] Personal interview by Melinda Talbert.

Barthes, R. (1973). *Mythologies*. London: Paladin.

Barton, M. A. (1991, April 14). Cable's call-in format adopted by "Big Three" networks. *C-SPAN Update*, Vol. 9, pp. 1–2.

Batra, R. (1988). *The great depression of 1990*. New York: Dell Publishing.

Bayley, E. R. (1981). *Joe McCarthy and the press*. New York: Pantheon.

Beiler, D. (1991, December/January). The 1990 campaign scorecard: Candidates weren't the campaigns' only winners and losers. *Campaigns & Elections*, Vol. 11, pp. 26–33.

Bennett, W. L. (1988). *News: The politics of illusion*. New York: Longman.

Bennis, P. (1991, February). The CNN war that wasn't. *Lies of Our Times*, p. 10.

Boorstin, D. (1973). *The image: A guide to pseudo-events in America*. New York: Atheneum.

Born, L. K. (1973). Introduction. *The Education of a Christian Prince*, Ed. D. Erasmus. (pp. 3–53) New York: Octagon Books.

Boyd, H. (1991, January). Black conservatives. *Lies of Our Times*, p. 10.

Bozell, L. B., III, and Baker, B. H. (Eds.). (1990). *And that's the way it isn't*. Alexandria, VA: Media Research Center.

Broder, D. (1989a, January 13). A warning for those in the press. *The Norman Transcript*, p. 6.

Broder, D. (1989b, January/February). On "Insiders." *Washington Journalism Review*, Vol. 2, p. 9.

Broder, D. (1990, February 7). Noonan book makes old political hand look with fresh eyes. *Kansas City Times*, p. A-13.

Burke, E. (1953). *Reflections on the French revolution*. New York: E. P. Dutton & Co.

Burke, K. (1967). *Philosophy of literary form*. Berkeley: University of California Press.

Burke, K. (1968). *Language as symbolic action*. Berkeley: University of California Press.

Burke, K. (1969a). *A grammar of motives*. Berkeley: University of California Press.

Burke, K. (1969b). *A rhetoric of motives*. Berkeley: University of California Press.

Burner, D. and West, T. R. (1988). *Column Right: Conservative journalists in the service of nationalism*. New York: New York University Press.

Burns, T. (1977). *The BBC: Public institution and private world*. London: Macmillan.

Carey, J. (1989). *Communication as culture*. Boston: Unwin Hyman.

Carnegie, D. (1948). *How to win friends and influence people*. New York: Pocket Books.

Carroll, L (1960). *The annotated Alice: Alice's adventures in wonderland and through the looking glass*. New York: Bramhall House.

Cassirer, E. (1955). *The myth of the state*. Garden City, NY: Doubleday.

Center for Media and Public Affairs. (1987–1991). *Media Monitor*, Vols. 1–5. (Available from the Center for Media and Public Affairs, 2101 L Street, NW, Suite 505, Washington, DC, 20037).

Cooper, M., and Solely, L. C. (1990, March). All the right sources. *Mother Jones*, pp. 20–27, 45–48.

Daley, Steve. (1988, August 16). [*Chicago Tribune.*] Personal interview by Melinda Talbert.

Dessauer, C. (1990, April/May). *Washington Post* staffs up with watchdogs. *Campaigns & Elections*, Vol. 11, p. 11.

Dow, J. (1986). Universal aspects of symbolic healing: A theoretical synthesis. *American Anthropologist*, Vol. 88, pp. 56–69.

Downs, A. (1957). *An economic theory of democracy*. New York: Harper & Row.

Dye, T. (1990). *Who's running America? The Bush era*. Englewood Cliffs, NJ: Prentice-Hall.

Eliott, R. C. (1965). The satirist and society. *Comedy: Meaning and form*, Ed. R. Corrigan. (pp. 327–342). San Francisco: Chandler.

Ellul, J. (1964). *The technological society*. New York: Vintage Books.

Ellul, J. (1968). Technique, institutions, and awareness. *American Behavioral Scientist*, Vol. 11, pp. 38–42.

Ellul, J. (1965). *Propaganda*. New York: Vintage Books.

Ellul, J. (1967). *The political illusion*. New York: Vintage Books.

Entman, R. M. (1989). *Democracy without citizens*. New York: Oxford University Press.

Fairness and Accuracy in Reporting. (1988, July 19). News coverage biased against Jackson forces, media group charges. [News release], p. 1.

Fang, I. E. (1977). *Those radio commentators*. Ames, IA: Iowa State University Press.

Fiske, J. (1990). *Introduction to communication studies*. New York: Routledge.

Flander, J. (1988, September). A case of coziness: Tom Shales and CBS news. *Washington Journalism Review*, Vol. 10, pp. 16–19.

Fletcher, W. B. (1991, February). Arts and economy. *Campaign Magazine*, Vol. 5, pp. 10–11.

Foucault, M. (1981). The order of discourse. *Untying the text*, Ed. R. Young. (pp. 51–77). London: Routledge & Kegan Paul.

France, A. (1909). *Penguin island*. Trans. A. W. Evans. New York: Blue Ribbon Books.

Frye, C. N. (1964). *The educated imagination*. Bloomington, IN: University of Indiana Press.

Galbraith, J. K. (1991, March). Owning up to the recession. *Harper's*, pp. 21–25.

Gates, G. P. (1978). *Air time*. New York: Berkeley Publishing.

Goldman, A. I. (1991). Epistemic paternalism: communication control in law and society. *Journal of Philosophy*, Vol. 85, pp. 113–131.

Grauer, N. A. (1984). *Wits and sages*. Baltimore: Johns Hopkins University Press.

Greene, B. (1991, February 17). Here's hoping that success won't spoil Cable News Network. *Dallas Morning News*. p. 5J.

Greider, W. (1987). *Secrets of the temple: How the Federal Reserve runs the country*. New York: Simon and Schuster.

Harris, L. (1973). *The anguish of change*. New York: W. W. Norton.

Hart, J. D. (1950). *The popular book*. Berkeley: University of California Press.

Herman, E. S. (1991, January). Love that Maggie. *Lies of Our Times*, pp. 16–17.

Herr, M. (1990) *Walter Winchell: A novel*. New York: Alfred A. Knopf.

Hirsch, A. (1991). *Talking heads: Political talk shows and their star pundits*. New York: St. Martin's Press.

Hitchens, C. (1987, March). Blabscam: TV's rigged political talk shows. *Harper's*, pp. 75–76.

Holmberg, M., and Roach, J. (1991, February 9). Top TV critics: gulf war is made-for-TV drama. *Time*, pp. 16–17.

Hosley, D. H. (1984). *As good as any: Foreign correspondence on American Radio, 1930–1940*. Westport, CT: Greenwood Press.

Irvine, R., and Kincaid, C. (1991, February 8). "Media monitor." Recorded from the Newstalk Radio Network, KTLK.

Jacoby, R. (1987). *The last intellectuals*. New York: Basic Books.

Jamieson, K. H. (1984). *Packaging the presidency*. New York: Oxford University Press.

Jamieson, K. H. (1988). *Eloquence in an electronic age*. New York: Oxford University Press.

Jamieson, K. H., and Birdsell, D. (1988). *Presidential debates: The challenge of creating an informed electorate*. New York: Oxford University Press.

Jensen, Elizabeth. (1988, August 15). [*New York Daily News*.] Personal interview by Melinda Talbert.

Joyce, E. (1988). *Prime times, bad times*. New York: Doubleday.

Kanter, D. L., and Mirvis, P. H. (1989). *The cynical Americans: Living and working in the age of discontent and disillusion*. San Francisco: Jossey-Bass.

Kelley, S., Jr. (1966). *Professional public relations and political power*. Baltimore: Johns Hopkins University Press.

Kertzer, D. I. (1988). *Ritual, politics, and power*. New Haven: Yale University Press.

Lapham, L. H. (1988). *Money and class in America*. New York: Weidenfeld and Nicolson.

Lapham, L. H. (1990). *Imperial masquerade*. New York: Grove Weidenfeld.

Lasch, C. (1990, Spring). Journalism, publicity and the lost art of argument. *Gannett Center Journal*. Vol. 4, pp. 1–11.

Lessl, T. M. (1989). The priestly voice. *Quarterly Journal of Speech*, Vol. 75, pp. 183–197.

Leubsdorf, C. P. (1991, June 13). Public losing faith in politics. *Dallas Morning News*, p. 31A.

Levin, M. B. (1987). *Talk radio and the American dream*. Lexington, MA: Lexington Books.

Lichter, R. (1990, September 23). TV war: Journalists' words affect public more than pictures do. *Dallas Morning News*, p. 4J.

Lichter, S. R., Amundson, D., and Noyes, R. (1988). *The video campaign*. Washington, DC: American Enterprise Institute for Public Policy Research/Center for Media and Public Affairs.

Lichter, S. R., and Noyes, R. (1991, January/February). In the media spotlight. *The American Enterprise*, pp. 49–53.

Lieberman, D. (1991, May 4). Item 1: John McLaughlin is (a) TV's most powerful pundit or (b) its biggest blowhard. *TV Guide*, pp. 14–16.

Liebling, A. J. (1961). *The press*. New York: Ballantine.

Liebovich, L. (1987, Summer/Autumn). *Journalism History*, Vol 14, pp. 2–3, 46–53.

*Lies Of Our Times* [LOOT] (1991, September). To our readers. New York: Institute for Media Analysis.

Lippmann, W. (1922). *Public opinion*. New York: Macmillan.

Lorando, Mark. (1988, August 16). [*New Orleans Times Picayune.*] Personal interview conducted by Melinda Talbert.

Lothrop, G. R. (1988, April). West of Eden: Pioneer media evangelist Aimee Semple McPherson in Los Angeles. *Journal of the West*, Vol. 27, pp. 50–59.

Machiavelli, N. (1979). *The portable Machiavelli.* Ed. and trans. P. Bondanella and M. Musa. New York: Penguin Books.

Mankiewicz, F. (1989, Spring). From Lippmann to Letterman: The ten most powerful voices. *Gannett Center Journal*, Vol. 3, pp. 81–96.

Margolis, J. (1991, March 17). War shoots professional pundits to stardom—even if they were wrong. *Chicago Tribune*, Sect. 4, p. 4.

Mathews, D., and Harwood, R. C. (1991, June 7). Putting the people back in politics. *Chicago Tribune*, p. 20.

McGinniss, J. (1969). *The selling of the president, 1968.* New York: Trident Press.

McLuhan, M. (1964). *Understanding media.* New York: Signet Books.

Media Research Center. (n.d.). *Media research Center.* Alexandria, VA: Media Research Center.

Media Research Center (1989). Janet Cooke award: Reagan bashing, ABC news. *MediaWatch*, 3, p. 4.

Media Research Center. (1989, 1990). *MediaWatch*, Vols 3, 4. (Available from the Media Research Center, 111 South Columbus Street, Alexandria, VA, 22314.)

Mencken, H. L. (1965). Criticism of criticism of criticism. *H. L. Mencken: The American scene*, Ed. H. Cairns. (pp. 169–176). New York: Vintage Books.

Metz, R. (1975). *CBS: Reflections in a bloodshot eye.* New York: Signet Books.

Moerman, D. E. (1979). Anthropology of symbolic healing. *Current Anthropology*, Vol. 20, pp. 59–61.

Monroe, B. (1990, August). Covering the real campaign: TV spots. *Washington Journalism Review*, Vol. 12, p. 6.

Moyers, B. (1989). "The public mind." Four-part television series, Public Broadcasting System, WNET, Boston.

Naisbitt, J., and Auburdene, P. (1990). *Megatrends 2000: Ten new directions for the 1990s.* New York: Morrow.

National Public Radio. (1991). "Special call-in program." (January 30, February 1, February 4, February 8, February 18, February 20, February 22, February 25, February 27, and March 1.)

Newstalk Radio Network. (1991). "Battleline." (January 1, February 5, February 13, February 20, and February 26.)

Newstalk Radio Network (1991). "The Cliff Kincaid Show" (January 29, February 8, February 14, February 18, and February 27.)

Nimmo, D. (1970). *The political persuaders.* Englewood Cliffs, NJ: Prentice-Hall.

Nimmo, D. and Combs, James E. (1990). *Mediated political realities.* New York: Longman.

Oreskes, M. (1990, October). Should the press keep the consultants clean? *Campaign Magazine*. Vol. 4, pp. 1, 21.

Park, R. E. (1940, March). News as a form of knowledge. *American Journal of Sociology*, Vol. 45, pp. 669–686.

Peirce, C. S. (1958). *Values in a universe of chance.* Ed. P. Weiner. New York: Doubleday Anchor.

Phillips, K. (1969). *The emerging Republican majority.* New York: Arlington House.

Phillips, K. (1975). *Mediacracy.* New York: Doubleday.

Phillips, K. (1982). *Post-conservative America: People, politics and ideology in a time of crisis.* New York: Random House.

Phillips, K. (1990). *The politics of rich and poor: Wealth and the American electorate in the Reagan aftermath.* New York: Random House.

Piantadosi, R. (1982, September). Art Buchwald. *Washington Journalism Review,* Vol. 4, pp. 27–34.

Pierpoint, R. (1991, May). Too much flag-waving. [Letter to the editor]. *Washington Journalism Review,* Vol. 13, p. 9.

Plowden, W. (1987). Think tank. *The Blackwell encyclopedia of political institutions,* Ed. V. Bogdanor. (p. 611). New York: Basil Blackwell.

Porter, B. (1990, September). Has success spoiled NPR?: Becoming a part of the establishment can have its drawbacks. *Washington Journalism Review.* Vol. 12, pp. 26–32.

Postman, N. (1986). *Amusing ourselves to death.* New York: Penguin Books.

Public Affairs Video Archives. (1989, April 12). "Who's a Journalist? Talk Show Sensationalism." Educational and Research Archives of C-SPAN programming. West Lafayette, IN: Purdue University.

Radday, E. (1991, April 3). In defense of those TV war experts. *Chicago Tribune,* Sect. 1, p. 17.

Randolph, E. (1989, February 15). Writing heads. *Chicago Tribune,* "Tempo" Sect., p. 2.

Rattley, S. (1991, January). White bread history. *Lies of Our Times,* p. 4.

Reese, M. (1987, July/August). *C&E* interview: Matt Reese. *Campaigns & Elections,* Vol. 8, pp. 18–23.

Reeves, R. (1991, March 13). Holding pundits accountable. *Dallas Morning News,* p. 29A.

Regan, D. (1988). *For the record.* New York: St. Martin's Press.

Rivers, W. L. (1965). *The opinion makers.* Boston: Beacon Press.

Roberts, J. C. (1991, May/June). The power of talk radio. *The American Enterprise,* Vol. 2, pp. 57–61.

Rollins, P. C. (1988). Will Rogers and the relevance of nostalgia: Steamboat 'round the bend. *American History/American Film,* Eds. J. E. O'Connor and Martin A. Jackson. (pp. 77–96). New York: Ungar Publishing.

Root, R. L., Jr. (1987). *The rhetorics of popular culture.* New York: Greenwood Press.

Rosen, J. (1991, March/April). TV as alibi. *Tikkun,* Vol. 6, pp. 52–54, 87.

Rosenbloom, D. L. (1973). *The election men: Professional campaign managers and American democracy.* New York: Quadrangle Books.

Rosenthal, H. M. (1991, February 2). There's a new air war on TV: Hawks versus doves. *TV Guide,* p. 33.

Rosteck, T. (1989). Irony, argument, and reportage in television documentary: *See It Now* versus Senator McCarthy. *Quarterly Journal of Speech,* Vol. 75, pp. 277–298.

Rowan, M. (1991, February 2). My message to the fish. *Campaigns & elections*. Vol. 11, p. 19.

Royko, M. (1991, September). My old man was a sucker. *Reader's Digest*, pp. 185–186.

Runkel, D. R. (Ed.). (1989). *Campaign for president: The managers look at '88*. Dover, MA: Auburn House.

Sabato, L. J. (1981). *The rise of political consultants*. New York: Basic Books.

Safire, W. (1978). *Safire's political dictionary*. New York: Ballantine Books.

Safire, W. (1990, May 27). On language: Pundit-bashing. *New York Times Magazine*, pp. 10, 12.

Said, E. (1981). *Covering Islam*. New York: Pantheon.

Sarkar, P. R. (1967). *Human society, part 2*. Washington, DC: Proutist.

Schaaf, B. C. (1977). *Mr. Dooley's Chicago*. Garden City, NY: Doubleday/Anchor Press.

Seboek, T. and Eco, U. (1983). (Eds). *The sign of three*. Bloomington, IN: University of Indiana Press.

Shapiro, W. (1990, February 12). Prolific purveyor of punditry. *Time*, Vol. 35, pp. 62–64.

Shaw, D. (1988, August 15). Television: Candidates' "mine field." *Los Angeles Times*, pp. 1, 6.

Shaw, D. (1989, Spring). The death of punditry. *Gannett Center Journal*, Vol. 3, pp. 1–8.

Shaw, D. (1991, January/February). Of isms and prisms [review of *Unreliable sources: A guide to detecting bias in news media*, by M. A. Lee and N. Solomon; *And that's the way it isn't: A reference guide to media bias*, by L. B. Bozell III and B. H. Baker; and *Profiles of deception: How the news media are deceiving the American people*, by R. Irvine and C. Kincaid]. *Columbia Journalism Review*, Vol. 30, pp. 55–57.

Sherrod, B. (1990, July 6). "Experts" tend to drive some of us batty. *Dallas Morning News*, p. 1C.

Siegenthaler, K. (1990, May 1). Top of the world. *Chicago Tribune*, "Tempo" Sect., p. 2.

Skalka, S. (1991, February). Stereotyping Arabs by media "experts." *Lies of Our Times*, p. 9.

Sklar, R. (1980). *Prime-time America: Life on and behind the television screen*. New York: Oxford University Press.

Smith, J. A. (1991). *The idea brokers: Think tanks and the rise of the new policy elite*. New York: Free Press.

Sperber, A. M. (1986). *Murrow: His life and times*. New York: Freundlich Books.

Steel, R. (1980). *Walter Lippmann and the American century*. Boston: Little, Brown.

Steele, J. (1990a, January 3). Why do television academic experts so often seem predictable and trivial? *The Chronicle of Higher Education*, p. B2.

Steele, J. (1990b, September). Sound bite seeks expert. *Washington Journalism Review*, Vol. 12, pp. 28–29.

Stephenson, W. (1967). *The play theory of mass communication*. Chicago: University of Chicago Press.

Swartz, M. (1989, November). The mythic rise of Billy Don Moyers. *Texas Monthly*, pp. 94–98, 211–217.

Tebbel, J. (1974). *The media in America.* New York: New American Library/Mentor Books.

The talk of the town. (1991, January 28). *The New Yorker,* pp. 21–22.

Theobald, R. (1987). *The rapids of change: Social entrepreneurship in turbulent times.* Indianapolis, IN: Knowledge Systems.

Thompson, T. (1982). *Celebrity.* Garden City, NY: Doubleday.

To our readers. (1991, January). *Lies of Our Times,* p. 2.

Toffler, A. (1990). *Powershift: Knowledge, wealth, and violence at the edge of the 21st century.* New York: Bantam.

Townley, R. (1988, July 11). Let's get rid of those know-it-all pundits. *TV Guide,* pp. 2–5.

Traugott, M. (1988, Fall). Marketing the presidency: Is there a tyranny of media polls? *Gannett Center Journal,* Vol. 2, pp. 57–64.

Trilling, L. (1934). *Techniques and civilization.* New York: Harcourt Brace.

Trilling, L. (1938). *The culture of cities.* New York: Harcourt Brace.

Trilling, L. (1944). *The condition of man.* New York: Harcourt Brace.

Tuchman, B. W. (1984). *The march of folly: From Troy to Vietnam.* New York: Ballantine Books.

Twain, M. [Samuel Clemens]. (1817). *Autobiography.* New York: Harper & Row.

Twain, M. [Samuel Clemens]. (1889). *A Connecticut yankee in King Arthur's court.* New York: Harper & Row.

Veron, E. (1976). (Ed.). *Humor in America: An anthology.* New York: Harcourt Brace Jovanovich.

Waldman, S. (1986, December). The king of quotes: Why the press is addicted to Norman Ornstein. *The Washington Monthly,* Vol. 18, pp. 33–40.

Walker, M. (1990, December 9). [London] *Guardian* article notes cable's contribution to U.S. television. *C-SPAN Update,* Vol. 8, p. 8.

Warren, J. (1990, February 13). D.C. reporters tuned to TV. *Chicago Tribune,* "Tempo" Sect., p. 1, 2.

Warren, J. (1991, February 3). Over their heads. *Chicago Tribune,* "Tempo" Sect., p. 2.

Watkins, A. (1989, December 3). The chattering classes—Who are they? *Manchester Guardian Weekly,* p. 25.

Weaver, R. K. (1989). The changing world of think tanks. *P.S.,* Vol. 22, pp. 563–578.

Weber, M. (1947). *The theory of social and economic organization.* Trans. A. M. Henderson and T. Parsons, ed. T. Parsons. Glencoe, IL: Free Press.

Weiss, H. S., and Weiss, M. J. (1977). *The American Way of Laughter: A Collection of Humor from Benjamin Franklin to Woody Allen.* New York: Bantam.

Will, G. (1988, July 17). [*Washington Post,* ABC News.] Personal interview by Melinda Talbert.

Wilson, E. (1972). *To the Finland station.* New York: Farrar, Straus & Giroux.

Winship, T. (1990, November). Gagging the media stars. *Washington Journalism Review,* Vol 12, p. 60.

# Index

## ABOUT THE AUTHORS

DAN NIMMO is Professor of Communication at the University of Oklahoma. He has authored or coauthored more than 25 books. Among the most recent are *Mediated Political Realities* (1990), with James E. Combs, *New Directions in Political Communication* (1990), and *Cordial Concurrence* (Praeger, 1991).

JAMES E. COMBS is Professor of Political Science at Valparaiso University, where he has taught since 1972. He has authored or coauthored ten books and numerous scholarly articles. His most recent book is *American Political Movies* (1990).